W9-BNH-346

Critical essays on
Robert Frost

Critical Essays on Robert Frost

Critical Essays on Robert Frost

Philip L. Gerber

G.K. Hall & Co.
An Imprint of Simon & Schuster Macmillan
New York

Prentice Hall International
London • Mexico City • New Delhi • Singapore • Sydney • Toronto

Copyright © 1982 by Philip L. Gerber
All rights reserved

Published by Twayne Publishers
An Imprint of Simon & Schuster Macmillan
1633 Broadway
New York, NY 10019

10 9 8 7 6

Library of Congress Cataloging in Publication Data

Gerber, Philip L.
    Critical essays on Robert Frost.

    (Critical essays on American literature)
    Includes bibliographical references and index.
    1. Frost, Robert, 1874–1963—Criticism and inter-
pretation—Addresses, essays, lectures. I. Title.
II. Series
PS3511.R94Z658   811'.52   82-898
ISBN 0-8161-8442-9   AACR2

CRITICAL ESSAYS ON AMERICAN LITERATURE

This series seeks to publish the most important reprinted criticism on writers and topics in American literature along with, in various volumes, original essays, interviews, bibliographies, letters, manuscript sections, and other material brought to public attention for the first time. Philip L. Gerber's volume is a comprehensive gathering of the most important criticism on Robert Frost, one of America's most widely read and admired writers. It contains reviews and essays covering Frost's life and works from *A Boy's Will* to his final poems. In addition to reprinting selections by such writers and critics as Ezra Pound, Amy Lowell, Carl Van Doren, Malcolm Cowley, Bernard DeVoto, Randall Jarrell, and James M. Cox, the volume offers an extensive introduction by Professor Gerber and an original essay, "The Indispensable Robert Frost," by Donald J. Greiner. We are confident that this collection will make a permanent and significant contribution to American literary study.

JAMES NAGEL, GENERAL EDITOR

Northeastern University

To the scholars, librarians, and colleagues who aided this work.

CONTENTS

INTRODUCTION

It is entirely appropriate that American criticism of Robert Frost should begin with the review of *A Boy's Will* sent from London to Chicago in 1913 by Ezra Pound, whom Frost recognized as being "the great original"[1] of the modern poetry movement. The story has often been told of Frost, near the brink of despondency to think of nearing age forty without having made his mark as a poet, leaving his homeland for greener pastures abroad, finding there a publisher willing to print not one book but two, and then returning to America, with Pound's aid a flourishing reputation underway. The weight of the nineteenth-century tradition from which Frost had sprung and then broken away was still too powerful in 1912 to permit an easy emergence of new verse. But even as Robert Frost sailed for England with his family, Harriet Monroe was preparing to launch her new magazine, *Poetry*, which would open the floodgates for a renaissance. During the two decades since the deaths of the last of the "household poets"—Longfellow, Holmes, Whittier and company—no new American poet of stature had been acclaimed. Stephen Crane had died too early in his career and Edwin Arlington Robinson continued to struggle forward alone and unappreciated. Then, with little prior fanfare, appeared the first issue of *Poetry*, a thousand copies bought, read, and passed from hand to hand in one of the genuinely dramatic literary debuts of modern times. It happened literally overnight; and as it occurred to magazine editors that a revolution was underway, that the American populace might actually read and spontaneously discuss the work of new poets, the stranglehold on periodicals held by writers of trite, sentimental, and imitative verse was broken. New voices, many of them long pent up, rose clamoring to be heard.

Following *Poetry's* lead, the editors of general-circulation magazines opened their pages to the new poetry, even to the anathema of *vers libre*, and their cue was rapidly picked up by the major book publishers. Where previously there had been almost no new poets of consequence, suddenly the nation was awash with verse. Besides Ezra Pound, whose name was known to everyone who aspired to poetry, there were now a galaxy: the brothers Benét, Joyce Kilmer, Edna St. Vincent Millay, George Sterling,

1

Hilda Doolittle (H.D.), Vachel Lindsay, Carl Sandburg, Edgar Lee Masters, Wallace Stevens, William Carlos Williams, and Robinson Jeffers, to be joined before long by names such as T. S. Eliot, Marianne Moore, Hart Crane, and the arch-experimentalist E. E. Cummings. Louis Untermeyer, who would become the fast friend of Robert Frost and who acted in dual roles as participator in the revival and as observer of the phenomenon, supplied an accurate summary of the excitement that followed the year 1912:

> By 1917 the "new" poetry was ranked as "America's first national art"; its success was sweeping, its sales unprecedented. People who never before had read verse, turned to it and found they could not only read but relish it. They discovered that for the enjoyment of poetry it was not necessary to have at their elbows a dictionary of rare words and classical references; they no longer were required to be acquainted with Latin legendry and the minor love-affairs of the major Greek divinities. Life was their glossary, not literature. The new product spoke to them in their own language.[2]

To be sure, the nation was in for an embarrassment of riches, no small portion of it to be contributed by Robert Frost.

In England Frost had come together with two of his countrymen, both of whom played significant roles in establishing his fame. Ezra Pound had recognized (and at once relayed to Harriet Monroe) the "vurry Amurrkin" qualities of Frost and his verse. In his capacity as foreign correspondent for *Poetry*, he reviewed both *A Boy's Will* and *North of Boston* as they appeared, thereby lodging the name of Robert Frost with the crucial audience in America even before the poet returned to his native soil. Amy Lowell, although known in Boston as the wealthy heiress of a famous family, was a frustrated poet until the birth of *Poetry* loosed her bonds. Amy sent a gift of money to Harriet Monroe to aid the magazine and then, hearing that Ezra Pound led a new school of poets called Imagists—of whose number she felt herself to belong by nature—she sailed for London to beard the lion in his den. While there she came upon a copy of Frost's *North of Boston*, newly published. Its depiction of the New England she understood so well impressed her deeply and she determined to alert America to the existence of the book and its author.

Robert Frost's return to America early in 1915 coincided with the publication of Amy's laudatory review in *The New Republic*. She remained a steady friend, although Frost did not always think so, and she continued to champion his poetry until her death in 1925. Her description of the British literary situation in 1914 provides a valid summary of Frost's uncanny ability to resist the blandishments of the famous and the influential, including, incidentally, herself and Pound, both of whom would have wished to corral him as a protégé:

London was full of poets, and what is better, the beliefs, and protests, and hates of poets. They made a lively buzzing which meant that the art was in a vigorous condition. . . . here, there, and everywhere, if you happened to be a poet, was talk of forms and directions, technique and substance, the thousand and one things which, if taken in small doses, do so much to keep the poet's craft sound and sane. . . . To anyone less firmly set on his own artistic feet than Mr. Frost, the situation was intoxicating, but it is characteristic of the man that he lost neither his head nor his originality. He changed no whit in poetry, speech, or appearance. He talked and listened, and went home and did the same thing right over again only better. . . . He went his own way, grew his vegetables, and wrote "North of Boston."[3]

Amy Lowell's remarks are but one indication that from the very beginning Frost the man became as much an object of curiosity as Frost the poet. Throughout the early years of his public career, the poems and the personality became inextricably intertwined. In the first rush of enthusiasm for his work there occurred an obvious effort to define Frost as person and as poet. He was perceived, above all, as an American at a time when America needed the reassuring presence of native heroes. Further, he was seen as a genial creature, an idealist, and an optimist, all qualities which Americans revered and desired for themselves as well as for their nation. In the wake of a rich but increasingly ugly industrialism, here was a true son of the soil who awakened a desperate nostalgia for an age vanishing into the past rapidly enough for the majority of Americans to regret its passing. Frost reminded his readers of a better and greener America, a land less complicated, certainly less exploited than that in which most of them lived. Overseas the world was in upheaval. The Great War of 1914–18 raged fiercely, obliterating any lingering dreams of pastoral Eden, and the conflict threatened to engulf America as well. To all of this turmoil Frost responded with a quiet authority which assured that the eternal verities might remain undisturbed no matter how the surface of life might roil.

Within such a context, the reservations expressed by Amy Lowell in her review of *North of Boston* were distinctly unwelcome. Who wished to hear that Robert Frost used a grim and sardonic irony in dealing with the "twisted and tortured lives" of rural New Englanders? Better attuned to the times were William Morton Payne who in *The Dial* expressed his total admiration for the "simple phrasing and patient sincerity" of Frost's poems, comparing his achievement to that of A. E. Housman's popular success *A Shropshire Lad*[4]; and Sylvester Baxter, who depicted Frost upon his return to America as being ready to go back to farming the "beloved soil" of his New Hampshire.[5] Baxter did much to set in motion the myth of Robert Frost as a paragon without blemish. The earliest notices of Frost's work, published by British critics during his 1913 debut, had been mixed in their evaluations. But the American criticism published during the opening years of Frost's prominence was dominated by that glad sense of discovery in which the words, *new, American,* and *New England*—either alone or as combined by Baxter in his title "New England's New Poet"—became something of overnight clichés, easy handles for reviewers to attach to their notices. The years between 1913 and 1920 were devoted primarily to introducing Robert Frost to his reading public and to establishing his as a major voice in American poetry. In three volumes rapidly published, *North of Boston* (1915), *A Boy's Will* (1915) and *Mountain Interval* (1916), Frost's work was placed before readers and simultaneously boomed by friendly reviewers in a campaign which Frost himself often directed from the wings. Upon his return to America from London, Frost had expressed his own private fears that he might lack staying power. But *Mountain Interval,* even though it did not meet the level of quality established by *North of Boston,* did prove that the poet was no flash-in-the-pan. He had not lost his magic, and upon occasion he could surpass the best of his earlier efforts. This knowledge, coupled with lavish praise on the critical front, served to bolster the poet's belief in himself and to renew the inner confidence which had sustained him while undertaking his English venture in 1912.

The first serious evaluation of Frost to appear in book format was that offered by Amy Lowell. Her *Tendencies in Modern American Poetry* (1917) recognized the modern movement as an accomplished fact and identified six poets as being worthy of individual attention: E. A. Robinson, Edgar Lee Masters, Carl Sandburg, H. D., John Gould Fletcher, and Frost. Among these six, the relative importance of Robert Frost was signified by his being discussed in a separate chapter. The others, the exception being Robinson, were considered in groups. The Lowell evaluation of Frost's verse, which enlarged upon the remarks made in her review of *North of Boston,* is now thought by some to be wrong-headed, and surely it is marred by biographical errors (many of these traceable to Frost's withholding the data she had requested from him). But Amy Lowell's chapter on Frost and his work is notable in accepting him as an established figure. Beyond that, Lowell insists that Frost is a major American poet whose verse is deserving of the most serious consideration.

In writing of Frost's tragic sense (which she felt to be obsessive) and the quality of disillusionment which touched so much of his work, Miss Lowell dwelt upon topics which would not be handled easily by other commentators for decades to come. Hers was the first important criticism to imply that the emerging Frost myth—the happy, cheer-bearing farmer—might be one-sided. To her the poet seemed to betray a weakness of breadth by limiting his subject matter to the tiny canvas of New England. In this judgment she was not entirely correct, of course, as Frost's later achievements would establish, and yet her apprehensions were justified in the context of the three books which Frost had so far published. Readers of a later day might disagree with her suggestion that

Frost in 1917 may have touched the limits of his growth, but they will be hard pressed to deny the incisive understanding which leads Miss Lowell to declare that *North of Boston* is "a very sad book . . . [which] in spite of its author's sympathetic touch . . . reveals a disease that is eating into the vitals of our New England life, at least in its rural communities."[6] Lowell's remains the first effort at a balanced evaluation of Frost's strengths and flaws, in all a generous tribute from a fellow poet.

In 1919 Louis Untermeyer, always a booster of Frost, gave his friend the lead chapter in his *New Era in American Poetry*, the first volume to be designed as a comprehensive survey of the modern verse movement. By this date an outpouring of Frost articles and interviews had brought the poet to the attention of a wide audience which included the readers of prominent newspapers in Boston and Philadelphia. Untermeyer singled out the dramatic poems from *North of Boston* as the most powerful and authentic to have come out of America. In Frost more than in any other poet of the day he found the modern expression of the "poetic feeling for ordinary life" which had been Walt Whitman's legacy to his countrymen. But even in what is essentially a paean to a new-found idol, Untermeyer remains sufficiently discerning to hint at something deeper, more complex and paradoxical, restive beneath the calm surfaces of these poems.

The 1920s proved to be boom years for Robert Frost. His service as Poet-in-Residence/Fellow in Creative Arts at the University of Michigan from 1921 to 1923 and his subsequent Professorship at Amherst were but two of the prominent academic posts which enhanced his prestige and widened his visibility. Reading tours took him to far parts of the nation, enlarging his already considerable audience through the display of his winning personality in public recitations and lectures. He possessed great charm and he learned best how to use it; as his biographer, Lawrance Thompson has put it: "his platform name dramatized his ideal image of how he wanted to be viewed."[7] Following Frost's Pulitzer Prize for *New Hampshire* in 1923, no doubt existed that any serious study of American poetry must consider his achievement.

Critics now built upon the foundation which had been established prior to 1920. While little that was truly new was introduced into the study of Frost, the myth of the poet as a genial farmer-philosopher grew ever more pervasive. A minor strain of criticism recalled Amy Lowell's judgment regarding the dark side of Frost's poetry, but these reservations were overwhelmed by more sanguine views. The majority of critics, preferring to emphasize the happy Frost personality, harkened back to Sylvester Baxter's description of him as one of the most endearing men in the world. Percy H. Boynton, who had no way of knowing in 1924 the extent to which the poet had labored to establish himself in the literary world, saw Frost as a man determined to live relaxed and unhurried, one who almost always preferred to work with his hands than to write. It was a fine distinction, perhaps, but one which suggested that Frost's rustic persona was succeeding only too well. For Carl Van Doren the word *Yankee* became the key to Frost's character and writing alike. All the best Yankee traits were his: he was properly individualistic, and his attitude was utilitarian, as befitted a "rustic" of the Yankee stamp. Without question, Van Doren spoke for many. Elizabeth Shepley Sergeant, who later would write a fine biography of Frost (*The Trial by Existence*, 1962), imagined him in 1927 as the *genius loci* of New England, a genial and somewhat puckish creature who, if one were lucky, might surprise a watcher by poking his head roguishly up from behind any New Hampshire blueberry bush or mountain boulder.

Acceptance on the widest possible literary landscape was crucial to Frost's expanding fame, and no small part in achieving that recognition was played by the anthologies which spread the message of the new verse from coast to coast. The influence of two extremely popular collections should be cited: Harriet Monroe's *The New Poetry* (1917) and Louis Untermeyer's *Modern American Poetry* (1919). From her influential editorial post in Chicago, Miss Monroe was in a better position than anyone else in America to comprehend the full extent of the ferment in verse across the continent. Some of the new poets—Carl Sandburg and Vachel Lindsay were the chief examples—had been her personal discoveries, and dozens of the others had appeared at one time or another in the pages of *Poetry*. In the first edition of her comprehensive anthology, edited in collaboration with Alice Corbin Henderson, Robert Frost was represented by seven poems. Even today that edition provides a reader with a quite respectable sampling of verse from the early modern movement in America, and very few later anthologies have managed to equal the breadth and depth of the major revision of 1923, in which Frost's group of poems was increased to sixteen. Untermeyer in the modest five-page preface to his slender first edition of *Modern American Poetry* paid a balanced tribute to the current pacesetters. He restricted his praise of Frost—by now a close and good friend—to a pair of sentences: "Notice, for instance, in the direct but fully-flavored blank verse of Robert Frost, how the words are so chosen and arranged that the speaker is almost heard on the printed page. Observe how, beneath these native sounds, we hear the accents of his people walking the New England farms and hillsides."[8] In 1919 four poems served to represent Frost's output to date: "Mending Wall," "The Tuft of Flowers," "Birches," and "The Road Not Taken," all of which remain standard anthology pieces today. *Modern American Poetry* underwent rapid and continuous revision. By 1921 it had burgeoned from 165 pages to nearly 400. Its new preface occupied thirty-one pages, two of them devoted solely to Robert Frost, whose representation doubled to eight poems although he had not published another book of verse in the interim. In the revision of 1925, a volume whose weighty 600 pages testified to the impressive establishment of the new poetry, Frost improved his position still further; in six years his representation in the book had nearly quadrupled. The certification of Frost's poetic stature by both the Monroe-Henderson and the Untermeyer anthologies reached tens of thousands of readers both in and out of classrooms. The books became the poetic bibles of uncounted study groups which sprang up in cities and hamlets across America. By the time the decade ended in the Wall Street Crash of 1929, Robert Frost had become the most appreciated poet in the nation, and his career was about to culminate in his *Collected Poems*, for which he would be awarded a second Pulitzer Prize.

The financial debacle of 1929 stimulated a resurgence of politics as a legitimate hallmark in judging writers and their works. The 1920s had fostered a spirit of individualism and experimentation in which Frost had prospered, but it was inevitable now that, given new and radically different times, Frost would suffer in company with others who had written without heed of political considerations. After 1930 more than one literary career came to grief either temporarily or permanently under the pressures placed upon the lyric strain by the Marxist critics, for whom activism and a strong social thesis were not only valid criteria but often became the sole determinants of worth in literature. The conscious effort to topple Robert Frost from his pedestal began in timely fashion with reviews of *Collected Poems*. Granville Hicks, a major Marxist spokesman, attacked Frost first in the pages of *New Republic* and later in his revisionist literary study *The Great Tradition* (1933), doing his utmost to establish the total irrelevance of Frost's poems to those for whom communism seemed the only logical solution for a battered capitalist society apparently on the brink of economic and political collapse. Having elected to emphasize rather than to soften his identification with New Hampshire and, further, to concentrate upon special aspects which ignored such phenomena as modern factory towns and state politics, Robert Frost was more vulnerable than some others to criticism from the political left. His work was now perceived by the politically-oriented only within the narrow limits permitted by their ideologies, and he was criticized severely, called not only unrepresentative of American life but fully as "moribund" as the vanished way of life which his poems were accused of espousing. Critical derogation of Frost accelerated noticeably following his Pulitzer Prize for *A Further Range* (1936), in which for the first time Frost published verse which made overt his conservative stance. Typically the charges against him appeared in journals such as *New Republic, Nation, New Masses,* and *Partisan Review,* whose literary pages were dominated by critics with a perceptible leftist tilt. Such commentators were prone to suggest that Frost's political sense equalled that of Calvin Coolidge ("The business of America is Business"), while Frost's poetry was lumped with the doggerel verses of Edgar A. Guest, the popular newspaper rhymer. But even Frost's staunchest admirers took small pleasure from the poet's venture into the current political scene with its clash of ideologies. The case against Frost was capped by a two-part essay by Malcolm Cowley in *New Republic* (1944), which questioned whether the poet could properly be called a complete or even a suitable representative of the New England tradition, particularly when the history of liberal thought inherent in that tradition was considered.

It might be anticipated that unrestrained jabbing at Robert Frost would call forth an equally vigorous defense from his supporters, and there were many. The most notable essay in the rebuttal arrived in the form of an infuriated piece written by Bernard DeVoto for *Saturday Review of Literature*, aimed at establishing Frost not only as a major voice but as a great American poet.[9] Also, Henry Holt and Company published a volume devoted to praise of Frost, *Recognition of Robert Frost*, as a salute to the poet on the twenty-fifth anniversary of the appearance of *A Boy's Will*. This retrospective collection of reviews and essays offered a sampler of opinion published in America, England, and the Continent over the preceding quarter century. Works by a formidable array of critics, beginning with the early estimates by Amy Lowell, Ezra Pound, and William Dean Howells, were gathered. *Recognition* was in no sense an effort to present a "balanced" verdict on Robert Frost. Conspicuously absent from the book were any of the recent and hostile remarks printed by Frost's detractors such as Horace Gregory and Granville Hicks. Such a lapse might be anticipated in a celebratory volume which was issued as adulation; Frost himself referred to it candidly (but in private) as Holt's "book advertising me." Against Frost's hunger for praise must be placed his own speculation that in a volume as supposedly comprehensive as *Recognition*, perhaps his publisher "should have gone the rest of the way and included a fair proportion of the out-and-out hostile in my criticism."[10] Something of the complexity of the man emerges when it is learned that Frost himself played a major role in bringing *Recognition* into being, not only reserving approval of works to be included but himself drawing up both the plan and its preliminary table of contents. He also suggested the title for the book.[11] All this aside, however, *Recognition* succeeds admirably in its purpose. It remains a valuable introduction to favorable criticism on the poet and his work. The most far-reaching effect of the critical fray between 1930 and 1940 was to establish the principle that important and variant schools of thought concerning Robert Frost might legitimately co-exist. This was a salutary development. To proceed further upon the older basis of unquestioning admiration which had characterized the Frost reception through 1929, teetering forever on the brink of sentimentality, was unhealthy for Frost's reputation long-term. At issue now was the relative permanence of Frost's role in literary history.

Having survived the turmoil of the 1930s with his readership undiminished, Robert Frost saw his public reputation widen and grow ever more secure, while his honors, including a fourth Pulitzer Prize for *A*

Witness Tree (1942), accumulated further. In 1942 Lawrance Thompson, who had already agreed to become Frost's biographer, published his *Fire and Ice*, the first scholarly attempt to place Frost and his poetry solidly within the long tradition of English-language verse, both in theory and form. Finding metaphor in its many guises to be the key to Frost's creative principle, Thompson examined rigorously its use in Frost's dramatic narratives, lyrics, and satires, and he made an admirable attempt to define the poet's philosophy of art and life. The negative strain, though muted, continued. Louise Bogan had little positive to say about Frost in her *Achievement in American Poetry 1900–1950*, and Harold H. Watts and Yvor Winters in major articles carried the argument further.[12] Both critics concluded that Frost, however interestingly he may have explored the universal experiences of human beings, had failed to deal pertinently with the man-society relationship. Later, Roy Harvey Pearce in *Kenyon Review* elaborated upon the proposition that Frost's chief flaw resided in his renunciation of the modern in favor of an older, simpler, and more cheerful way of life.[13] The damaging charge that Frost at heart was a poet of nostalgia would necessarily receive serious consideration as the passage of time made obvious the poet's reluctance—or his inability—to delve directly and deeply into issues central to his own time and place.

Offsetting these reservations, which always represented a minority view, a multitude of major essays appeared during the latter years of Frost's career, thoughtful and scholarly works by writers whose judgments could be based upon all but Frost's final efforts. The common purposes of these later critics were: (1) to enlarge the reader's understanding of individual poems; (2) to distinguish among the important thematic strands running throughout Frost's total work; (3) to analyze Frost's use of literary devices and symbols; (4) to clarify Frost's relationship to other writers in the Anglo-American tradition; and (5) to evaluate Frost's craftsmanship in verse. A good many, although far from all, of these writers are represented in James M. Cox's *Robert Frost: A Collection of Critical Essays* (1960), which aims to present the cream of critical thinking regarding Frost up to that time. In making his selections, Cox has taken pains to represent all dominant strains of criticism, balancing detractors against enthusiasts. Given the responsible nature of the critics who are represented and the importance of the lines of thought they pursue, the Cox collection remains of permanent worth to Frost students.

As Robert Frost's career neared its close, friends of long standing began to publish evaluations based upon their personal acquaintance with the poet. Chief among these was Reginald L. Cook, in whose *Dimensions of Robert Frost* (1958) the poet's work is linked at every point with his personality. Far from apologizing for his subjectivity, Cook allows it to stand as a central virtue of his discussion. Thus, Cook's Frost is a man shaped by the Victorian age in which he was raised, and the "high, purposeful optimism" of that time dominates the ethics of the personality whom Cook knew and visited with over a span of thirty years. The farmer-poet image that multitudes of Frost's readers bore so fondly in their minds is found here writ large, an amiable fellow whose sterling qualities include friendliness, cheer, cordiality, warmth, courage, and independence, and whose passion for truth is matched by his sense of humor: all good things and all to be found abundantly throughout the verses of *Complete Poems* as well. In much the same vein are the memoirs of Frost's friend Sidney Cox. In 1929 Cox had offered a brief and tentative portrait, *Robert Frost: Original "Ordinary Man,"* a rather idealized portrait which served to strengthen the current myth of Frost as a paragon in both the personal and artistic spheres; a Frost, Donald Greiner suggests, who stood "just this side of sainthood."[14] Cox's worshipful attitude informs his later expansion of that memoir, *A Swinger of Birches* (1957), in which numerous anecdotes are added as well as direct quotations taken down during his association with Frost.

A pair of book-length appraisals which first appeared in 1960 sum up two major strands of Frost criticism. The first is George W. Nitchie's *Human Values in the Poetry of Robert Frost,* which concentrates upon Frost's central theme, the man-nature relationship. Nitchie argues that Frost, probably deliberately, avoids deep probing of this complex topic, and that he restricts himself instead to the simpler, easier task of describing human reactions to natural phenomena. The prospect that the world around us may be discovered to possess some final and illuminating "meaning" is avoided by Frost in favor of treating nature as an incomprehensible force, and this stance, for Nitchie, reveals a serious weakness. John F. Lynen's *The Pastoral Art of Robert Frost* offers a rather different interpretation of Frost's use of nature. Lynen sees Frost, not as a rustic, certainly, nor as the practicing farmer who inhabits the surface of the poetry, but rather as a sophisticated artist who consciously adopts the pastoral mode and who uses rural New England symbolically, making of it a metaphor through which the problems confronting man may be approached, albeit obliquely. In perceiving a virtue where others had seen a flaw, Lynen explains that Frost, despite appearances, really is less concerned with surfaces than with attitudes, points of view. This always-concealed motive explains for Lynen why a reader is continually impelled to believe that there is "something else" in a Frost poem, more than meets the eye. Frost, concludes Lynen, is not an escapist at all, but a genuinely modern artist fully immersed in his own time.

The death of Robert Frost in 1963 inaugurated a new era in Frost criticism, particularly in the realm of biographical revelations. *The Letters of Robert Frost to Louis Untermeyer* (1963) contains 220 letters written by the poet to the anthologist during a friendship which began in 1915 and never flagged. For the first time the public was treated to a cumulative self-portrait of Robert Frost, one which often was quite startlingly different from the mythical author which readers had imagined.

In his poems Frost had never given full rein to his pervasive sense of humor, but his letters at once revealed him to be an inveterate punster. Of greater importance is the unexpected—and often shocking—sardonic edge which sharpens so much of the humor; Frost openly delights in relating any embarrassment or mischief which may have befallen what he called his "contemptuaries." Indeed, the sinister aspect of the Frost personality so often exceeds its links with the innocently humorous that many a reader nurtured on the image of Frost as generous neighbor came away from the letters with shaken faith. A more comprehensive collection appeared in *Selected Letters of Robert Frost* (1964), edited by Lawrance Thompson. These 556 items of correspondence served to confirm the darker portrait inherent in the Untermeyer letters, but their scope, obviously, was considerably broader. The Thompson collection remains the standard edition. A more limited volume is Margaret Bartlett Anderson's *Robert Frost and John Bartlett* (1963), which reproduces some sixty letters written between 1912 and 1949, most of them personal in nature, to a man who had been Frost's student at Pinkerton Academy from 1907 to 1910 and who remained a lifelong admirer and booster of Frost's poetry. Another 182 letters, including 133 by Frost himself, are gathered in *Family Letters of Robert and Elinor Frost* (1972), edited by Arnold Grade. Here a reader encounters yet another dimension, a considerably more intimate Frost, without axe to grind or career to promote, a husband and father as much as a poet.

By all odds the most valuable document to appear since Frost's death has been Lawrance Thompson's massive life, published in three volumes.[15] The new work superseded earlier and necessarily incomplete attempts at biography by Gorham Munson, Elizabeth Shepley Sergeant, and Jean Gould, and corrected their numerous errors of fact and interpretation (often the result of Frost's own ambiguity or direct obfuscation). As his first biographer Frost had hand-picked a young professor at Ohio State University, Robert S. Newdick, with whom he had established an easy rapport in 1934. But Newdick died quite unexpectedly of appendicitis in 1939, and within three weeks Frost selected his successor, agreeing to work closely with him provided that no biography was published during his lifetime. Thompson was awarded the immense advantage of associating intimately with Frost for a period of twenty-four years, was given first-hand accounts of events in Frost's life, and heard the poet's own interpretations of those events. In addition, by observing Frost's attitudes as they emerged from word and action, Thompson became aware of the man's numerous prejudices, unexpressed in the poems and scarcely revealed by the bare facts of biography. The most important lesson which emerged from this association, says Thompson, was a caveat made explicit by Frost himself: the poet was not invariably to be trusted to reveal the complete truth about himself. Much of what resulted from Thompson's considerable spade work in search of truth appears in the highly readable footnotes to the biography, so that the complexity of the man Frost is conveyed to the reader effectively and with profit. Thompson's first volume appeared in 1966; the second, published in 1970, was awarded the Pulitzer Prize for biography and made explicit the less savory portrait of Frost which had been suggested by the published volumes of letters. When Thompson became aware of his own terminal illness in 1972 he took on the services of a graduate student, R. H. Winnick, as an aide. These two, working together for the better part of the next year, managed to assemble a draft for the final volume of the biography. Following Thompson's death in April 1973 Winnick completed the work, published in 1977.

After Frost died it became known that Robert Newdick's preliminary efforts toward a biography were extant, his papers having been preserved for three decades by his widow. In 1976 *Newdick's Season of Frost* appeared, edited by William A. Sutton. Thirteen "mini-chapters" represented Newdick's aborted attempt at a script. Appended to these narratives, which carried the Frost story through publication of *A Boy's Will*, were numerous examples of Newdick's research findings as well as a substantial narrative record of the Frost-Newdick association contributed by Sutton. Of greatest interest to the general reader, perhaps, are the letters of reminiscence regarding Frost which Newdick was able to obtain from many who had known him in the early days and Newdick's own detailed observations for which he anticipated a use when it should come time for him to describe the poet and his demeanor in mid-career.

A spate of valuable memoirs has appeared, the first being *Robert Frost Speaks* (1964) by Daniel Smythe, a volume which centers upon Smythe's notes dictated to himself immediately following a lengthy sequence of meetings with Frost. Its great virtue is the presentation of events, thoughts, and opinions unavailable elsewhere. Unfortunately, it is flawed by the author's reliance upon memory and a willingness to present as direct quotations materials which apparently represent Smythe's own paraphrases of Frost's speech. But the volume furnishes an extended look at the private Robert Frost and never shies from the man's shortcomings, a view which was all but closed to public scrutiny at the time the book was published. A more extensive memoir, one approaching biography in its scope, is Louis Mertins' *Robert Frost: Life and Talks-Walking* (1965). Like Smythe, Mertins relies upon diary notes, these extending back to 1932. Mertins presents many experiences which he and Frost shared as well as private remarks made by the poet noted during and subsequent to their numerous moments together. Mertins minimizes Frost's character flaws, clearly preferring the more prevalent idolatory tone, and his extensive use of quotation marks in recording Frost's speech remains open, finally, to the same question as Smythe's. A fellow poet and resident of Amherst, Massachusetts, Robert Francis published his reminiscences as: *Frost: A Time to Talk* (1972). Francis offers detailed records of conversations held with Frost during the 1930s and again for a time during the 1950s, being diligent in cautioning his reader that the records of conversations always rely upon his own memory and often consist of paraphrases. Francis emerges as an admirably critical listener, one who will pause to suggest how remarkable it is that Frost should inform him that he had never lifted a finger to further his own career. In his role as creative writer, Francis wonders openly whether Frost is to be trusted entirely when he lavishes upon Francis' poems praise which seems even to their author more effusive than they deserve.

A Time to Talk was followed by a similar volume from Reginald L. Cook and based upon Cook's many conversations with Robert Frost, supplemented by transcriptions of tape recordings in which Frost both reads his poems and comments upon them. Cook tended to assure the authenticity of his *Robert Frost: A Living Voice* (1972) by stressing that he had credited no word or phrase with quotation marks unless he had heard it from the poet's lips. The reader will find Cook's volume to be a gold mine of off-the-cuff remarks upon a variety of Frost poems, as well as being an intriguing commentary upon Puritanism, Marx, Darwin, Freud, Einstein, Emerson, Thoreau, religion and science generally, and upon the hazards of *explication de texte*. Lesley Frost's *New Hampshire's Child* (1969) is a unique, personal account of the life of the Robert Frost family during the years 1905–1909. Her record was preserved because of the special at-home education which the Frost children received while living on the Derry farm prior to their father's emergence into fame. The information carried in the childhood journals which Lesley Frost kept during that residence is supplemented by an introduction in which she expands upon the methods and subject matter employed by her parents.

With Robert Frost's life-work completed, general studies of his poetry have become more frequent. The focus of Reuben A. Brower's *The Poetry of Robert Frost* (1963) is indicated by its subtitle: "Constellations of Intention." Brower declines to write of Frost the man, preferring instead to concentrate upon the poems. In so doing he provides valuable analyses of a variety of titles, particularly in terms of form. His presentations of "After Apple-Picking," "Stopping by Woods on a Snowy Evening," "Design," and "The Death of the Hired Man" are notable examples of his success. Frost's major themes, with emphasis upon nature, are approached in the context of the two poets, Wordsworth and Emerson, whom Brower identifies as being Frost's principal forebears, and his comparisons of Frost's verse with theirs is a stimulating contribution to our understanding of Frost's links with the Romantic tradition. Frank Lentricchia in *Robert Frost: Modern Poetics and the Landscapes of Self* (1975) is adamant in declaring Frost to be "a major poet" over objections to the contrary by George Nitchie, Cleanth Brooks, Malcolm Cowley, Yvor Winters and others. Lentricchia identifies Frost as a man ever aware of the "struggle between the fiction-making imagination and the anti-fictive of the given environment, social and natural."[16] That the human being is forever stranded upon an inhospitable globe, separated from his environment no matter how ardently he desires unity with it and regardless of his efforts to achieve that happy resolution, is identified as being the central fact of existence in Frost's scheme of life. In this context Lentricchia examines Frost's symbolic use of brook, house, and woods with the intention of rescuing him from an overly-narrow classification as the Poet of New England. Richard Poirier mounts a formidable defense of Frost as "a poet of genius" in *Robert Frost: The Work of Knowing* (1977). Poirier declares that Frost's stature must be determined by considering his work within his self-established limits, including his deliberate withdrawal from the elitist literary modernism of Eliot and Joyce as well as from participation in the political left. Poirier grants that Frost's major deficiency was his inability to see as deeply into social systems as he saw into nature. But this failure is not perceived as being of true importance, nor is it sufficient basis for denying Frost the labels "major" and/or "great." Poirier's reading of the poems is always fascinating and usually provocative; for instance, he finds "Directive" (thought by many to be Frost's masterwork) to be stagy, contrived, and undaring. John C. Kemp's *Robert Frost and New England* (1979) is a specialized study with a compelling argument regarding the myth of Frost as New England farmer-poet. That myth, attractive as it might be, is untrue to Frost's temperament and experience. It is Kemp's judgment that Frost, finding himself overly committed to the rustic persona he had donned, was unwilling or unable later to break out of the mold; it proved detrimental to his later work.

Among miscellaneous works of Frost criticism, noteworthy additions have been made by the three volumes of *Centennial Essays*[17] published under the editorship of Jac L. Tharpe and offering discussion by dozens of recent Frost scholars upon a far-ranging variety of issues. Linda W. Wagner's *Robert Frost: The Critical Reception* (1977) collects important periodical and newspaper reviews of all of Frost's books of verse, a valuable reference guide. In the area of bibliography, three works stand out: Peter Van Egmond's *The Critical Reception of Robert Frost* (1974); Frank and Melissa Christensen Lentricchia's *Robert Frost: A Bibliography, 1913–1974* (1976); and Donald J. Greiner's *Robert Frost: The Poet and His Critics* (1974). Greiner's book may be the single most important volume for one interested in Frost scholarship. In six major essays, Greiner identifies and also evaluates on a comparison basis the most important books and essays that have been published concerning Frost. While the opinions expressed are, of course, Greiner's, most readers will find him to be eminently fair and extremely perceptive in his appraisals.

Collections of essays on Frost continue to appear with some regularity, the most recent being *Studies in the Poetry* (1979), edited by Kathryn Gibbs Harris and consisting of fifteen essays arranged according to *Form*,

Attitude, Problems, and *Background.* Without doubt there will be more collections, as well as continued work toward a standard bibliography. It might be hoped that further editions of letters will appear. And those who knew Frost either for brief or extended periods, or who were associated with him in special circumstances, will continue to record their remembrances in print.

Notes

1. Arnold Grade, ed., *Family Letters of Robert and Elinor Frost* (Albany: State University of New York Press, 1972), p. 161.

2. Louis Untermeyer, ed., *Modern American Poetry* (New York: Harcourt, Brace and Company, Inc., 1921), p. xxxi.

3. Amy Lowell, *Tendencies in Modern American Poetry* (New York: Macmillan, pp. 97–103.

4. William Morton Payne, untitled review, *The Dial,* 55 (Sept. 16, 1913), p. 212.

5. Sylvester Baxter, "New England's New Poet," *American Review of Reviews* (April, 1915), p. 434.

6. Amy Lowell, *Tendencies,* p. 105.

7. Lawrance Thompson, *Robert Frost: The Years of Triumph, 1915–1938* (New York: Holt, Rinehart and Winston, 1970), p. xviii.

8. Louis Untermeyer, ed., *Modern American Poetry* (New York: Harcourt, Brace and Howe, Inc., 1919), p. ix.

9. Bernard DeVoto, "The Critics and Robert Frost," *The Saturday Review of Literature,* 17 (Jan. 1, 1938), pp. 3–4, 14–16.

10. Lawrance Thompson, ed., *Selected Letters of Robert Frost* (New York: Holt, Rinehart and Winston, 1964), p. 460.

11. William A. Sutton, ed., *Newdick's Season of Frost* (Albany: State University of New York Press, 1976), pp. 131–38, 418–20.

12. Harold H. Watts, "Robert Frost and the Interrupted Dialogue," *American Literature,* 27 (March, 1955), pp. 69–87; Also, Yvor Winters, "Robert Frost: or, The Spiritual Drifter as Poet," *Sewanee Review,* 56 (Autumn, 1948), pp. 564–96.

13. Roy Harvey Pearce, "Frost's Momentary Stay," *Kenyon Review,* 23 (Spring, 1961), pp. 258–73.

14. Donald J. Greiner, *Robert Frost: The Poet and His Critics* (Chicago: American Library Association, 1974), p. 46.

15. The titles are: *Robert Frost: The Early Years, 1874–1915* (New York: Holt, Rinehart and Winston, 1966); *Robert Frost: The Years of Triumph, 1915–1938* (New York: Holt, Rinehart and Winston, 1970); *Robert Frost: The Later Years, 1938–1963* (New York: Holt, Rinehart and Winston, 1976).

16. Frank Lentricchia, *Robert Frost: Modern Poetics and the Landscape of Self* (Durham, N.C.: Duke University Press, 1975), p. xii.

17. Jac L. Tharpe, ed., *Frost Centennial Essays* (Jackson, Miss.: University Press of Mississippi, 1974); *Frost Centennial Essays II* (Jackson, Miss.: University Press of Mississippi, 1976); *Frost Centennial Essays III* (Jackson, Miss.: University Press of Mississippi, 1978).

A Boy's Will

Ezra Pound*

There is another personality in the realm of verse another American, found, as usual, on this side of the water, by an English publisher long known as a lover of good letters. David Nutt publishes at his own expense *A Boy's Will*, by Robert Frost, the latter having been long scorned by the "great American editors." It is the old story.

Mr. Frost's book is a little raw, and has in it a number of infelicities; underneath them it has the tang of the New Hampshire woods, and it has just this utter sincerity. It is not post-Miltonic or post-Swinburnian or post-Kiplonian. This man has the good sense to speak naturally and to paint the thing, the thing as he sees it. And to do this is a very different matter from gunning about for the circumplectious polysyllable.

It is almost on this account that it is a difficult book to quote from.

> She's glad her simple worsted gray
> Is silver now with clinging mist—

does not catch your attention. The lady is praising the autumn rain, and he ends the poem, letting her talk.

> Not yesterday I learned to know
>   The love of bare November days,
> Before the coming of the snow;
>   But it were vain to tell her so,
> And they are better for her praise.

Or again:

> There was never a sound beside the wood but one,
> And that was my long scythe whispering to the ground.
> . . . .
> My long scythe whispered and left the hay to make.

I remember that I was once canoeing and thirsty and I put in to a shanty for water and found a man there who had no water and gave me cold coffee instead. And he didn't understand it, he was from a minor city

*From *Poetry*, May 1913. Copyright 1913 by The Modern Poetry Association. Reprinted by permission of the Editor of *Poetry* and the estate of Ezra Pound.

and he "just set there watchin' the river" and didn't "seem to want to go back," and he didn't much care for anything else. And so I presumed he entered into Anunda. And I remember Joseph Campbell telling me of meeting a man on a desolate waste of bogs, and he said to him, "It's rather dull here;" and the man said, "Faith, ye can sit on a middan and dream stars."

And that is the essence of folk poetry with distinction between America and Ireland. And Frost's book reminded me of these things.

There is perhaps as much of Frost's personal tone in the following little catch, which is short enough to quote, as in anything else. It is to his wife, written when his grandfather and his uncle had disinherited him of a comfortable fortune and left him in poverty because he was a useless poet instead of a money-getter.

IN NEGLECT

They leave us so to the way we took,
As two in whom they were proved mistaken,
That we sit sometimes in a wayside nook,
With mischievous, vagrant, seraphic look,
And *try* if we cannot feel forsaken.

There are graver things, but they suffer too much by making excerpts. One reads the book for the "tone," which is homely, by intent, and pleasing, never doubting that it comes direct from his own life, and that no two lives are the same.

He has now and then such a swift and bold expression as

The whimper of hawks beside the sun.

He has now and then a beautiful simile, well used, but he is for the most part as simple as the lines I have quoted in opening or as in the poem of mowing. He is without sham and without affectation.

Modern Georgics

Ezra Pound*

It is a sinister thing that so American, I might even say so parochial, a talent as that of Robert Frost should have to be exported before it can find due encouragement and recognition.

Even Emerson had sufficient elasticity of mind to find something in the "yawp." One doesn't need to like a book or a poem or a picture in order to recognize artistic vigor. But the typical American editor of the last twenty years has resolutely shut his mind against serious American writing. I do not exaggerate, I quote exactly, when I say that these gentlemen deliberately write to authors that such and such a matter is "too unfamiliar to our readers."

There was once an American editor who would even print me, so I showed him Frost's *Death of the Hired Man*. He wouldn't have it; he had printed a weak pseudo-Masefieldian poem about a hired man two months before, one written in a stilted pseudo-literary language, with all sorts of floridities and worn-out ornaments.

Mr. Frost is an honest writer, writing from himself, from his own knowledge and emotion; not simply picking up the manner which magazines are accepting at the moment, and applying it to topics in vogue. He is quite consciously and definitely putting New England rural life into verse. He is not using themes that anybody could have cribbed out of Ovid.

There are only two passions in art; there are only love and hate—with endless modifications. Frost has been honestly fond of the New England people, I dare say with spells of irritation. He has given their life honestly and seriously. He has never turned aside to make fun of it. He has taken their tragedy as tragedy, their stubbornness as stubbornness. I know more of farm life than I did before I had read his poems. That means I know more of "Life."

Mr. Frost has dared to write, and for the most part with success, in the natural speech of New England; in natural spoken speech, which is

*Review of *North of Boston*. From *Poetry* (December 1914). Copyright 1914 by The Modern Poetry Association. Reprinted by permission of the Editor of *Poetry* and the estate of Ezra Pound.

very different from the "natural" speech of the newspapers, and of many professors. His poetry is a bit slow, but you aren't held up every five minutes by the feeling that you are listening to a fool; so perhaps you read it just as easily and quickly as you might read the verse of some of the sillier and more "vivacious" writers.

A sane man knows that a prose short story can't be much better than the short stories of De Maupassant or of "Steve" Crane. Frost's work is interesting, incidentally, because there has been during the last few years an effort to proceed from the prose short story to the short story in verse. Francis Jammes has done a successful novel in verse, in a third of the space a prose novel would have taken—*Existences* in *La Triomphe de la Vie*. Vildrac and D. H. Lawrence have employed verse successfully for short stories. Masefield is not part of this movement. He has avoided all the difficulties of the immeasurably difficult art of good prose by using a slap-dash, flabby verse which has been accepted in New Zealand. Jammes, Vildrac and Lawrence have lived up to the exigencies of prose and have gained by brevity. This counts with serious artists.

Very well, then, Mr. Frost holds up a mirror to nature, not an oleograph. It is natural and proper that I should have to come abroad to get printed, or that "H. D."—with her clear-cut derivations and her revivifications of Greece—should have to come abroad; or that Fletcher— with his *tic* and his discords and his contrariety and extended knowledge of everything—should have to come abroad. One need not censure the country; it is easier for us to emigrate than for America to change her civilization fast enough to please us. But why, IF there are serious people in America, desiring literature of America, literature accepting present conditions, rendering American life with sober fidelity—why, in heaven's name, is this book of New England eclogues given us under a foreign imprint?

Professors to the contrary notwithstanding, no one expects Jane Austen to be as interesting as Stendhal. A book about a dull, stupid, hemmed-in sort of life, by a person who has lived it, will never be as interesting as the work of some author who has comprehended many men's manners and seen many grades and conditions of existence. But Mr. Frost's people are distinctly real. Their speech is real; he has known them. I don't want much to meet them, but I know that they exist, and what is more, that they exist as he has portrayed them.

Mr. Frost has humor, but he is not its victim. *The Code* has a pervasive humor, the humor of things as they are, not that of an author trying to be funny, or trying to "bring out" the ludicrous phase of some incident or character because he dares not rely on sheer presentation. There is nothing more nauseating to the developed mind than that sort of local buffoonery which the advertisements call "racy"—the village wit presenting some village joke which is worn out everywhere else. It is a great comfort to find someone who tries to give life, the life of the rural district, as a whole, evenly, and not merely as a hook to hang jokes on. The easiest thing to see about a man is an eccentric or worn-out garment, and one is godforsakenly tired of the post-Bret-Hartian, post-Mark-Twainian humorist.

Mr. Frost's work is not "accomplished," but it is the work of a man who will make neither concessions nor pretences. He will perform no money-tricks. His stuff sticks in your head—not his words, nor his phrases, nor his cadences, but his subject matter. You do not confuse one of his poems with another in your memory. His book is a contribution to American literature, the sort of sound work that will develop into very interesting literature if persevered in.

I don't know that one is called upon to judge between the poems in *North of Boston*. *The Death of the Hired Man* is perhaps the best, or *The Housekeeper*, though here the construction is a bit straggly. There are moments in *Mending Wall*. *The Black Cottage* is very clearly stated.

North of Boston

Amy Lowell*

Some six months ago there appeared in London a modest little green-covered book, entitled "North of Boston." It was by an American living in England, so its publication on the other side of the Atlantic came about quite naturally, and was no reflection on the perspicacity of our publishers at home. To those of us who admire Mr. Frost's book it is no small pleasure to take up this new edition, bearing an American imprint, and feel that the stigma of non-comprehension so often put upon us by expatriated Americans can never be justified in this case.

Indeed, Mr. Frost is only expatriated in a physical sense. Living in England he is, nevertheless, saturated with New England. For not only is his work New England in subject, it is so in technique. No hint of European forms has crept into it. It is certainly the most American volume of poetry which has appeared for some time. I use the word American in the way it is constantly employed by contemporary reviewers, to mean work of a color so local as to be almost photographic. Mr. Frost's book is American in the sense that Whittier is American, and not at all in that subtler sense in which Poe ranks as the greatest American poet.

The thing which makes Mr. Frost's work remarkable is the fact that he has chosen to write it as verse. We have been flooded for twenty years with New England stories in prose. The finest and most discerning are the little masterpieces of Alice Brown. She too is a poet in her descriptions, she too has caught the desolation and "dourness" of lonely New England farms, but unlike Mr. Frost she has a rare sense of humor, and that, too, is of New England, although no hint of it appears in "North of Boston." And just because of the lack of it, just because its place is taken by an irony, sardonic and grim, Mr. Frost's book reveals a disease which is eating into the vitals of our New England life, at least in its rural communities.

What is there in the hard, vigorous climate of these states which plants the seeds of degeneration? Is the violence and ugliness of their religious belief the cause of these twisted and tortured lives? Have the sane, full-blooded men all been drafted away to the cities, or the West,

*From The New Republic, February 20, 1915, pp. 81–82. Copyright 1915 by The New Republic.

leaving behind only feeble remainders of a once fine stock? The question again demands an answer after the reading of Mr. Frost's book.

Other countries can rear a sturdy peasantry on the soil, a peasantry which maintains itself for generations, heavy and slow perhaps, but strong and self-replenishing; and this for a length of time beside which our New England civilization is as nothing. We are often told that the telephone has done much to decrease insanity in the farming districts, and doubtless it is true. New England winters are long and isolating. But what about Russian winters, Polish, Swedish, Norwegian? After all, the telephone is a very modern invention, and these countries have been rearing a sturdy peasantry for hundreds of years. It is said that the country people of these nations are less highly organized, less well educated, than are New Englanders, and so better able to stand the loneliness of long winters. But this does not explain the great numbers of people, sprung from old New England stock, but not themselves living in remote country places, who go insane.

It is a question for the psychiatrist to answer, and it would be interesting to ask it with "North of Boston" as a text-book to go by. Mr. Frost has reproduced both people and scenery with a vividness which is extraordinary. Here are the huge hills, undraped by any sympathetic legend, felt as things hard and unyielding, almost sinister, not exactly feared, but regarded as in some sort influences nevertheless. Here are great stretches of blueberry pasture lying in the sun; and again, autumn orchards cracking with fruit which it is almost too much trouble to gather. Heavy thunderstorms drench the lonely roads and spatter on the walls of farm-houses rotting in abandonment; and the modern New England town, with narrow frame houses, visited by drummers alone, is painted in all its ugliness. For Mr. Frost's is not the kindly New England of Whittier, nor the humorous and sensible one of Lowell; it is a latter-day New England, where a civilization is decaying to give place to another and very different one.

Mr. Frost does not deal with the changed population, with the Canadians and Finns who are taking up the deserted farms. His people are left-overs of the old stock, morbid, pursued by phantoms, slowly sinking to insanity. In "The Black Cottage" we have the pathos of the abandoned house, after the death of the stern, narrow woman who had lived in it. In "A Servant to Servants" we have a woman already insane once and drifting there again, with the consciousness that her drab, monotonous life is bringing it upon her. "Home Burial" gives the morbidness of death in these remote places; a woman unable to take up her life again when her only child had died. The charming idyll, "After Apple-picking," is dusted over with something uncanny, and "The Fear" is a horrible revelation of those undercurrents which go on as much in the country as in the city, and with remorse eating away whatever satisfaction the following of desire might have brought. That is also the theme of "The Housekeeper," while "The Generations of Men" shows that foolish pride in a useless race which is so strange a characteristic of these people. It is all here—the book is the epitome of a decaying New England.

And how deftly it is done! Take this picture:

> We chanced in passing by that afternoon
> To catch it in a sort of mental picture
> Among tar-banded ancient cherry trees,
> Set well back from the road in rank lodged grass,
> The little cottage we were speaking of.
> A front with just a door between two windows,
> Fresh painted by the shower a velvet black.

Or this, of blueberries:

> It must be on charcoal they fatten their fruit.
> I taste in them sometimes the flavor of soot.
> And after all really they're ebony skinned:
> The blue's but a mist from the breath of the wind,
> A tarnish that goes at a touch of the hand,
> And less than the tan with which pickers are tanned.

"The Fear" begins with these lines, and we get not only the picture, but the accompanying noises;

> A lantern light from deeper in the barn
> Shone on a man and woman in the door
> And threw their lurching shadows on a house
> Near by, all dark in every glossy window.
> A horse's hoof pawed once the hollow floor,
> And the back of the gig they stood beside
> Moved in a little.

The creak and shift of the wheels is quite plain, although it is not mentioned.

I have said that Mr. Frost's work is almost photographic. The qualification was unnecessary, it is photographic. The pictures, the characters, are reproduced directly from life, they are burnt into his mind as though it were a sensitive plate. He gives out what has been put in unchanged by any personal mental process. His imagination is bounded by what he has seen, he is confined within the limits of his experience (or at least what might have been his experience) and bent all one way like the wind-blown trees of New England hillsides.

In America we are always a little late in following artistic leads. "Les Soirées de Médun," and all Zola's long influence, are passing away in Europe. In England, even such a would-be realist as Masefield lights his stories with bursts of a very rare imagination. No such bursts flame over Mr. Frost's work. He tells you what he has seen *exactly* as he has seen it. And in the word *exactly* lies the half of his talent. The other half is a great and beautiful simplicity of phrase, the inheritance of a race brought up on the English Bible. Mr. Frost's work is not in the least objective. He is not writing of people whom he has met in summer vacations, who strike him as interesting, and whose life he thinks worthy of perpetuation. Mr. Frost writes as a man under the spell of a fixed idea. He is as racial as his own puppets. One of the great interests of the book is the uncompromising New Englander it reveals. That he could have written half so valuable a book had such not been the case I very much doubt. Art is rooted in the soil, and only the very greatest men can be both cosmopolitan and great. Mr. Frost is as New England as Burns is Scotch, Synge Irish, or Mistral Provençal.

And Mr. Frost has chosen his medium with an unerring sense of fitness. As there is no rare and vivid imaginative force playing over his subjects, so there is no exotic music pulsing through his verse. He has not been seduced into subtleties of expression which would be painfully out of place. His words are simple, straightforward, direct, manly, and there is an elemental quality in all he does which would surely be lost if he chose to pursue niceties of phrase. He writes in classic metres in a way to set the teeth of all the poets of the older schools on edge; and he writes in classic metres, and uses inversions and *clichés* whenever he pleases, those devices so abhorred by the newest generation. He goes his own way, regardless of anyone else's rules, and the result is a book of unusual power and sincerity.

The poems are written for the most part in blank verse, blank verse which does not hesitate to leave out a syllable or put one in, whenever it feels like it. To the classicist such liberties would be unendurable. But the method has its advantages. It suggests the hardness and roughness of New England granite. It is halting and maimed, like the life it portrays, unyielding in substance, and broken in effect.

Mr. Frost has done that remarkable thing, caught a fleeting epoch and stamped it into print. He might have done it as well in prose, but I do not think so, and if the book is not great poetry, it is nevertheless a remarkable achievement.

New England's New Poet

A poet star of exceptional magnitude has risen from New England. Yet it was in old England that it emerged from a misty horizon, there to be recognized for what it was. The book which has brought to its author this measure of fame bears the title, as felicitous as significant, "North of Boston."

The poet is Robert Frost, born in San Francisco of a New England father and a Scotch mother, March 26, 1875. The elder Frost was then a newspaper editor in the Pacific metropolis and was prominent in local politics. He went thither from Lawrence in Massachusetts; he died when the boy was eleven years old and the family returned to their old home.

A POET-PSYCHOLOGIST

His secondary schooling over, Robert Frost went to Dartmouth College for a while. Not finding what he felt he wanted, he turned to Harvard, there to be no better satisfied. This breaking away from educational opportunity made the impression among family connections of ne'er-do-well inclinations, correspondingly impairing material prospects that otherwise would have been bright for him. But his was one of the natures that must grow in their own way if they are not to break. His studies away from academic bounds appear to have given him as much as he had gathered within. Altogether, he managed to assimilate what he needed. His bent was towards psychology, and its fruit is discernible in his poetry.

Marriage, farming in northern New Hampshire, and then school-teaching; in these may be summarized the activities which in the main marked his life up to the great departure which proved the crucial point in his career and definitely determined his future. He had qualified in his special study to a degree that led to his appointment to the teaching staff at Derry Academy, in the charming old New Hampshire town of that

*From *The American Review of Reviews*, April 1915, pp. 432–34. Copyright 1915 by *The American Review of Reviews*.

name. And there he taught psychology with such acceptance that doubtless professorial honors might eventually have become his had he been so inclined.

His urge to poetic expression in verse had been steadily gaining upon him ever since adolescence had turned his thoughts to life's deeper meanings. Fugitive poems ocasionally appeared in the magazines, now and then to be treasured in the scrapbooks where so many poets, young and true, find abiding places in human hearts. Doubtless not a few will recall from shadowy nooks of memory the name of Robert Frost as one remotely familiar. But editors' ears are too often unattuned to new notes, preferring the resinging of old songs. One of Frost's youthful lyrics, called "Reluctance," however, so impressed a certain eminent publisher of choice books with its lofty appeal that only just now, in preparing the index for a monumental series which for about a quarter of a century he has been issuing, he chose for its motto two significant stanzas from it. And it now gratifies him to recall that in correspondence with the youth,—whom he counselled to seek wider fields than his own limited range could offer,—he early recognized the rare quality of his genius. Again at Derry there was a friendly minister who predicted to one of the academy trustees, a newspaper editor of high station in New England, a great future for the young poet. The editor, confessing to little taste for the poetic, was highly gratified to learn, only the other day, that it was "that boy" who as a poet was now coming to his own.

A SOJOURNER IN OLD ENGLAND

It may have been the friendly publisher's counsel, subliminally lingering, which, about three years ago, impelled Robert Frost to resign his comfortable teaching-berth at Derry, "pull up stakes,"—and go somewhere. But it was only two weeks before sailing that he and his wife decided upon England.

It seems now as if he must have been irresistibly impelled thither, obedient to Destiny's silent call. For some months Frost and his family,— which included four children,—lived quietly in a village not far from London. Then came his first book, a small collection of poems called "A Boy's Will," issued by Henley's publisher. For Robert Frost a boy's will had truly been the wind's will: blowing where it listeth. These poems made an intimate record of the gradual unfolding of a personality,— perhaps too intimate, the author is inclined to hold. The book brought quick recognition as the work of a rare nature, and Frost was promptly drawn out from his rural retirement to be heartily welcomed in those choice circles of London's best intellectual life where caste distinctions count for nothing and the sole test is merit. Nowhere is recognition more genuine; in few places does it count so fully as a measure of worth.

LONDON'S RESPONSE TO A YANKEE BARD

Early last year "North of Boston" was brought out by the same publisher. Here the author came fully to his own. The book brought instant acclaim, and without reserve Frost was honored as a poet of high distinction. Perhaps if Walt Whitman himself had chosen England for his advent and had there dawned unheralded upon the world the effect would hardly have been more electrical. Judgment as to the poet's quality was singularly unanimous. The reviews and the great weeklies gave the book exceptional space; the London *Nation*, for instance, devoted three columns to it. Frost was eagerly sought on every side; foremost poets welcomed him as their peer and took him to their hearts.

Frost liked England immensely and has won a host of dear friends there. Beaconsfield, the village where he lived, was also the home of the two young poets, Lascelles Abercrombie and Wilfred Gibson, and he was with them almost daily. But he was of New England in every fiber, and through the dull English winters, bone-chilling, the ground greasy with mud, he felt the most intense longing for the home country, its sparkling and tonic air, the sturdy New Hampshire landscape. He felt desperately homesick, and out of this mood "North of Boston" was conceived and wrought. One almost marvels that such a book, so vividly true to New England scenes and character, could have been created across the water. As with a Monet canvas, one feels that the artist must have produced it in the presence of his subjects. But it was this intense home-longing which visualized his themes. A few of these poems had been written in New England, but for much the greater part the work was done in old England.

Meanwhile the home-public had been singularly slow in responding to the British acclaim of the new poet. There were two causes for this: first, there had been no simultaneous American editions of either work. Indeed "A Boy's Will" is still practically unknown on this side. Second, the war broke out soon after, and little attention was given to anything else beyond the Atlantic. A few echoes from England were now and then heard. One of the poems, "The Code," had first appeared in the Chicago magazine, *Poetry*. And last summer the Boston *Transcript's* accomplished and appreciative "Listener" had found in the London *Nation's* review material for a charming article. A few copies of "North of Boston" found their way across the ocean and into public libraries and private collections. This public was very limited in number, but its interest was deep, and the inquiry, "Who is Robert Frost?" grew insistent,—waxing in volume with the recent appearance of an American edition, promptly exhausted. This article will doubtless furnish the first answer to the question.

THE RETURN TO AMERICA

With the war, and the national upheaval, further stay in England became painful, notwithstanding the many good friends there. So one day late in February Robert Frost and his family were happy to touch American soil again. It seemed a good omen to find at a news-stand, the first thing after landing in New York, a copy of a weekly paper with his "Death of the Hired Man" conspicuously reproduced. The American edition of "North of Boston" had appeared a few days before.

The poet is now in Bethlehem, New Hampshire, about to return to farming on his beloved soil. Early in March, stopping over in Lawrence, the home of his youth, he ran in to Boston intending to spend only a few hours in town. But so many people,—leading people in New England letters,—wanted to see him at dinner, luncheon, and otherwise that, although wholly unprepared for such attentions, having with him only the clothes he wore, he found it impossible to get away inside of four days. Frost's recognition in Boston is gratifyingly cordial and bears out the London estimate of his work. Intellectual Boston naturally feels a high satisfaction that, with all the wide development of poetic talent in other sections of the country, New England is still holding her own. Such men as Edwin Arlington Robinson and Robert Frost will maintain the lofty traditions of her Golden Age when Emerson, Longfellow, Lowell, Thoreau, Holmes, Whittier, and the others were active. One eminent woman author, herself ranking with the best interpreters of New England character, says: "Robert Frost's work is the greatest that has ever come out of New England,—and Mary Wilkins is next." Another author says: "In Frost we have another Masefield,—not a man like Masefield, but one of equally compelling power in his interpretations of life and nature."

THE POET'S PERSONALITY

Frost has a winsome personality, unassuming but not shy; a figure of average height, well built; a finely modeled head, mobile features and sensitive, dark brown hair of youthful abundance, the expressive blue eyes, tinged with a lightness as of summer mist at dawn, suggesting a dash of Celtic blood.

It is interesting to trace the derivations of a new poet. There is a suggestion of Wordsworth in Frost's method; a shade of Whitman in his native flavor and closeness to the home soil, though not the least resemblance in construction; something of Maeterlinck in his sense of lurking mystery, creeping and pervasive; a Hawthorne-like faculty of endowing our familiar New England world, even in its keen every-day reality, with that glamor of romance which Colonel Higginson so felicitously called "penumbra," tracing it back to Arthur Austin; and almost a blood relationship with Edwin Arlington Robinson,—both in the vagueness (so unlike obscurity) which in its blendings with realistic textures confers values and qualities of tone that often lead to exquisite gradations in sensitive shadings; and again in a humor that at times becomes grimly sardonic,—though with Frost as often touched with most delicate charm. To all this Frost has brought an individual quality of compelling force and a sweeping range of dramatic expression. The work is so essentially dramatic, underlaid and interwoven with keen psychological perceptions, as to lead some who most heartily like it to deny that "North of Boston" is poetry at all. But that is merely a matter of definition,—as when some powerful drama work of unconventional construction is declared to be "not a play." It may have been the last lines of Frost's exquisite picture of "The Woodpile":

> "far from a useful fireplace
> To warm the frozen swamp as best it could
> With the slow smokeless burning of decay,"

which inspired some genuine poet to say of "North of Boston" in the London *Times* that "poetry burns up out of it as when a faint wind breathes upon smouldering embers."

Robert Frost, New American Poet

William Stanley Braithwaite*

To appreciate Mr. Frost's poetry perfectly one has got to regard carefully the two backgrounds from which it is projected; fully under the influence of his art these two backgrounds merge into one, though each has its special distinction. There is the background of his material, the environment and character which belong to a special community; and there is the background of art in which the fidelity of speech is artistically brought into literature. This latter is a practice that brings up large and important questions of language and meaning in relation to life on the one hand and to literature on the other.

Mr. Frost has been through the longest period of experimentation in mastering the technique of his art of any other American poet. What he finally arrived at in poetic expression he finds as the highest accomplishment in the greatest English poets and asserts that the American poets who have shown unquestionable genius, especially a man like Edwin Arlington Robinson, have in a large measure the same quality of speech which is at once both artistic and the literal tone of human talk. But no poet in either England or America, except this newly arrived New England poet, has consciously developed and practiced this essential and vital quality of poetry which he characterizes as sound-posturing.

The poet was in his twentieth year when he realized that the speech of books and the speech of life were far more fundamentally different than was supposed. His models up to this period, as with all youthful poets and writers, had been literary models. But he found quite by accident that real artistic speech was only to be copied from life. On his New Hampshire farm he discovered this in the character of a man with whom he used to drive along the country roads. Having discovered this speech he set about copying it in poetry, getting the principles down by rigorous observation and reproduction through the long years which intervened to the publication of his books.

He also discovered that where English poetry was greatest it was by virtue of this same method in the poet, and, as I shall show, in his talk

*From the *Boston Evening Transcript*, May 8, 1915. Copyright 1915 by the *Boston Evening Transcript*.

with me he illustrated it in Shakespeare, Shelley, Wordsworth, and Emerson. That these poets did not formulate the principles by which they obtained these subtle artistic effects, but accomplished it wholly unconscious of its exact importance, he also suggested. But with a deliberate recognition of it as a poetic value in the poets to come, he sees an entirely new development in the art of verse.

The invitation which brought Mr. Frost to Boston to read the Phi Beta Kappa poem on Wednesday at Tufts College gave me the opportunity to get from the poet his views on the principles of sound-posturing in verse and some reflections on contemporary poets and poetry in England and America.

Before returning home, it will be interesting to note, the publication of Mr. Frost's books in England awakened a critical sympathy and acceptance, among English writers, of his ideas. His work won over, by its sheer poetic achievement, critics and poets, who had not realized before the possibilities of reproducing the exact tone of meaning in human speech in literary form. Where the poet's work is not fully appreciated in this country is where this principle is not understood. The substance of New England farm life of which his poetry is made has attracted immense interest, but in some quarters the appreciation of this substance is a little modified because the reader has only partially grasped the significance of the form. So it was this I wished the poet to explain in my very first question.

"First," he said, "let me find a name for this principle which will convey to the mind what I mean by this effect which I try to put into my poetry. And secondly, do not let your readers be deceived that this is anything new. Before I give you the details in proof of its importance, in fact of its essential place in the writing of the highest poetry, let me quote these lines from Emerson's 'Monadnoc,' where, in almost a particular manner, he sets forth unmistakably what I mean:

> Now in sordid weeds they sleep,
> In dulness now their secret keep;
> Yet, will you learn our ancient speech,
> These the masters who can teach.
> Fourscore or a hundred words
> All their vocal muse affords;
> But they turn them in a fashion
> Past clerks' or statesmen's art or passion.
> I can spare the college bell,
> And the learned lecture, well;
> Spare the clergy and libraries,
> Institutes and dictionaries,
> For that hearty English root
> Thrives here, unvalued, underfoot.
> Rude poets of the tavern hearth,

Squandering your unquoted mirth,
Which keeps the ground and never soars,
While Jake retorts and Reuben roars;
Scoff of yeoman strong and stark,
Goes like bullet to its mark;
While the solid curse and jeer
Never balk the waiting ear.

"Understand these lines perfectly and you will understand what I mean when I call this principle 'sound-posturing' or, more literally, getting the sound of sense.

"What we do get in life and miss so often in literature is the sentence sounds that underlie the words. Words in themselves do not convey meaning, and to [. . . prove] this, which may seem entirely unreasonable to any one who does not understand the psychology of sound, let us take the example of two people who are talking on the other side of a closed door, whose voices can be heard but whose words cannot be distinguished. Even though the words do not carry, the sound of them does, and the listener can catch the meaning of the conversation. This is because every meaning has a particular sound-posture; or, to put it in another way, the sense of every meaning has a particular sound which each individual is instinctively familiar with and without at all being conscious of the exact words that are being used is able to understand the thought, idea, or emotion that is being conveyed.

"What I am most interested in emphasizing in the application of this belief to art is the sentence of sound, because to me a sentence is not interesting merely in conveying a meaning of words. It must do something more; it must convey a meaning by sound."

"But," I queried, "do you not come into conflict with metrical sounds to which the laws of poetry conform in creating rhythm?"

"No," the poet replied, "because you must understand this sound of which I speak has principally to do with tone. It is what Mr. Bridges, the Poet Laureate, characterized as speech-rhythm. Meter has to do with beat, and sound-posture has a definite relation as an alternate tone between the beats. The two are one in creation but separate in analysis.

"If we go back far enough we will discover that the sound of sense existed before words, that something in the voice or vocal gesture made primitive man convey a meaning to his fellow before the race developed a more elaborate and concrete symbol of communication in language. I have even read that our American Indians possessed, besides a picture-language, a means of communication (though it was not said how far it was developed) by the sound of sense. And what is this but calling up with the imagination, and recognizing, the images of sound?

"When Wordsworth said, 'Write with your eye on the object,' or (in another sense) it was important to visualize, he really meant something more. That something carries out what I mean by writing with your ear to the voice.

"This is what Wordsworth did himself in all his best poetry, proving that there can be no creative imagination unless there is a summoning up of experience, fresh from life, which has not hitherto been evoked. The power, however, to do this does not last very long in the life of a poet. After ten years Wordsworth had very nearly exhausted his, giving us only flashes of it now and then. As language only really exists in the mouths of men, here again Wordsworth was right in trying to reproduce in his poetry not only the words—and in their limited range, too, actually used in common speech—but their sound.

"To carry this idea a little further it does not seem possible to me that a man can read on the printed page what he has never heard. Nobody today knows how to read Homer and Virgil perfectly, because the people who spoke Homer's Greek and Virgil's Latin are as dead as the sound of their language.

"On the other hand, to further emphasize the impossibility of words rather than sound conveying the sense of meaning, take the matter of translation. Really to understand and catch all that is embodied in a foreign masterpiece it must be read in the original, because while the words may be brought over, the tone cannot be.

"In the matter of poetry," the poet continued, "there is a subtle differentiation between sound and the sound of sense, which ought to be perfectly understood before I can make clear my position.

"For a second let me turn aside and say that the beginning of literary form is in some turn given to the sentence in folk speech. Art is the amplification and sophistication of the proverbial turns of speech.

"All folk speech is musical. In primitive conditions man has not at his aid reactions by which he can quickly and easily convey his ideas and emotions. Consequently, he has to think more deeply to call up the image for the communication of his meaning. It was the actuality he sought; and thinking more deeply, not in the speculative sense of science or scholarship, he carried out Carlyle's assertion that if you 'think deep enough you think musically.'

"Poetry has seized on this sound of speech and carried it to artificial and meaningless lengths. We have it exemplified in Sidney Lanier's musical notation of verse, where all the tones of the human voice in natural speech are entirely eliminated, leaving the sound of sense without root in experience."

A New American Poet

Edward Garnett*

A short time ago I found on a London bookstall an odd number of *The Poetry Review*, with examples of and comments on 'Modern American Poets,'—examples which whetted my curiosity. But the few quotations given appeared to me literary bric-à-brac, the fruit of light *liaisons* between American dilettantism and European models. Such poetry, aesthetic or sentimental,—reflections of vagrant influences, lyrical embroideries in the latest designs, with little imaginative insight into life or nature,—abounds in every generation. If sufficiently bizarre its pretensions are cried up in small Bohemian coteries; if sufficiently orthodox in tone and form, it may impress itself on that public which reads poetry as it looks idly at pictures, with sentimental appetite or from a vague respect for 'culture.' Next I turned to some American magazines at hand, and was brought to a pause by discovering some interesting verse by modern American poets, especially by women whose sincerity in the expression of inner life of love compared well with the ambitious flights of some of their rivals. I learned indeed from a magazine article that the 'New Poetry' was in process of being hatched out by the younger school; and, no doubt, further researches would have yielded a harvest, had not a literary friend chanced to place in my hands a slim green volume, *North of Boston*, by Robert Frost. I read it, and reread it. It seemed to me that this poet was destined to take a permanent place in American literature. I asked myself why this book was issued by an English and not by an American publisher. And to this question I have found no answer. I may add here, in parenthesis, that I know nothing of Mr. Robert Frost save the three or four particulars I gleaned from the English friend who sent me *North of Boston*.

In an illuminating paper on recent American fiction which I hope by and by, with the editor's permission, to discuss along with Mr. Owen Wister's smashing onslaught in the *Atlantic Monthly*, Mr. W. D. Howells remarks, 'By test of the native touch we should not find genuine some of the American writers whom Mr. Garnett accounts so.' No doubt Mr.

*From the *Atlantic Monthly*, August 1915. Copyright 1915 by the *Atlantic Monthlu*. Reprinted by permission of the estate of Edward Garnett.

Howells's stricture is just, and certain American novelists—whom he does not however particularize—have been too affected in spirit by European models. Indeed Frank Norris's early work, *Vandover and the Brute*, is quite continental in tone; and it is arguable that his study of the French Naturalists may have shown beneficial results later, in the breadth of scheme and clarity of *The Pit*.

This point of 'the native touch' raises difficult questions, for the ferment of foreign influence has often marked the point of departure and rise of powerful native writers, such as Pushkin in Russia and Fenimore Cooper in America. Again, if we consider the fiction of Poe and Herman Melville, would it not be difficult to assess their genuineness by any standard or measure of 'native touch?' But I take it that Mr. Howells would ban as 'not genuine' only those writers whose originality in vision, tone, and style has been patently marred or nullified by their surrender to exotic influences.

So complex may be the interlacing strains that blend in a writer's literary ancestry and determine his style, that the question first to ask seems to me whether a given author is a fresh creative force, an original voice in literature. Such an authentic original force to me speaks from *North of Boston*. Surely a genuine New England voice, whatever be its literary debt to old-world English ancestry. Originality, the point is there,—for we may note that originality of tone and vision is always the stumbling-block to the common taste when the latter is invited to readjust its accepted standards.

On opening *North of Boston* we see the first lines to be stamped with the magic of *style*, of a style that obeys its own laws of grace and beauty and inner harmony.

> Something there is that doesn't love a wall,
> That sends the frozen-ground-swell under it,
> And spills the upper boulders in the sun;
> And makes gaps even two can pass abreast.
> The work of hunters is another thing:
> I have come after them and made repair
> Where they have left not one stone on stone,
> But they would have the rabbit out of hiding.
> To please the yelping dogs. . . .

Note the clarity of the images, the firm outline. How delicately the unobtrusive opening suggests the countryman's contemplative pleasure in his fields and woods. It seems so very quiet, the modern reader may complain, forgetting Wordsworth; and indeed, had Wordsworth written these lines, I think they must have stood in every English anthology. And when we turn the page, the second poem, 'The Death of the Hired Man,' proves that this American poet has arrived, not indeed to challenge the English poet's possession of his territory, but to show how untrodden, how limitless are the stretching adjacent lands. 'The Death of the Hired Man'

is a dramatic dialogue between husband and wife, a dialogue characterized by an exquisite precision of psychological insight. I note that two college professors have lately been taking Mr. Ruckstuhl to task for a new
definition of poetry. Let us fly all such debates, following Goethe, who,
condemning the 'aesthete who labors to express the nature of poetry and
of poets,' exclaimed, 'What do we want with so much definition? A lively
feeling of situations and an aptitude to describe them makes the poet.'
This definition, though it does not cover the whole ground, is apropos to
our purpose.

Mr. Frost possesses a keen feeling for situation. And his fine, sure
touch in clarifying our obscure instincts and clashing impulses, and in
crystallizing them in sharp, precise images,—for that we cannot be too
grateful. Observe the tense, simple dramatic action, foreshadowing conflict, in the opening lines of 'The Death of the Hired Man':

> Mary sat musing on the lamp-flame at the table
> Waiting for Warren. When she heard his step,
> She ran on tip-toe down the darkened passage
> To meet him in the doorway with the news
> And put him on his guard. 'Silas is back.'
> She pushed him outward with her through the door
> And shut it after her. 'Be kind,' she said.

'It's we who must be good to him now,' she urges. I wish I had space
to quote the debate so simple in its homely force, so comprehending in its
spiritual veracity; but I must restrict myself to these arresting lines and to
the hushed, tragic close:— . . .

Yes, this is poetry, but of what order? the people may question, to
whom for some reason poetry connotes the fervor of lyrical passion, the
glow of romantic color, or the play of picturesque fancy. But it is precisely
its quiet passion and spiritual tenderness that betray this to be poetry of a
rare order, 'the poetry of a true real natural vision of life,' which, as
Goethe declared, 'demands descriptive power of the highest degree,
rendering a poet's pictures so lifelike that they become actualities to every
reader.' One may indeed anticipate that the 'honorable minority' will ap-
praise highly the spiritual beauty of the lines above quoted.

But what of his unconventional *genre* pictures, such as 'A Hundred
Collars'? Is it necessary to carry the war against the enemy's cardboard
fortresses of convention by using Goethe's further declaration:—

'At bottom no subject is unpoetical, if only the poet knows how to
treat it aright.' The dictum is explicit: 'A true, real, natural vision of
life . . . high descriptive power . . . pictures of life-like actuality . . . a
lively feeling of situation'—if a poet possess these qualifications he may
treat any theme or situation he pleases. Indeed, the more prosaic appears
the vesture of everyday life, the greater is the poet's triumph in seizing
and representing the enduring human interest of its familiar features. In
the characteristic fact, form, or feature the poet no less than the artist will

discover essential lines and aspects of beauty. Nothing is barred to him, if he only have *vision*. Even the most eccentric divagations in human conduct can be exhibited in their true spiritual perspective by the psychologist of insight, as Browning repeatedly demonstrates. One sees no reason why Browning's 'Fra Lippo Lippi' with all its roughcast philosophic speculation should be 'poetry' and Mr. Frost's 'A Hundred Collars' should not; and indeed the purist must keep the gate closed on both or on neither. If I desired indeed to know whether a reader could really detect the genuine poet, when he appears amid the crowd of *dilettanti*, I should ask his judgment on a typical uncompromising passage in 'A Hundred Collars,' such as the following:—

> The night clerk led him up three flights of stairs
> And down a narrow passage full of doors,
> At the last one of which he knocked and entered.
>
> 'Lafe, here's a fellow wants to share your room.'
> 'Show him this way. I'm not afraid of him.
> I'm not so drunk I can't take care of myself.'
>
> The night clerk clapped a bedstead on the foot.
> 'This will be yours. Good night,' he said, and went.
>
> The Doctor looked at Lafe and looked away.
> A man? A brute. Naked above the waist,
> He sat there creased and shining in the light,
> Fumbling the buttons in a well-starched shirt.
> 'I'm moving into a size-larger shirt.
> I've felt mean lately; mean's no name for it.
> I've found just what the matter was to-night:
> I've been a-choking like a nursery tree
> When it outgrows the wire band of its name-tag.
> I blamed it on the hot spell we've been having.
> 'Twas nothing but my foolish hanging back,
> Not liking to own up I'd grown a size.
> Number eighteen this is. What size do you wear?'
> The Doctor caught his throat convulsively.
> 'Oh-ah-fourteen-fourteen.'

The whole colloquy between this tipsy provincial reporter, Lafayette, and the scared doctor, will, at the first blush, seem to be out of court to the ordinary citizen trained from childhood to recognize as 'poetical,' say Bryant's 'Thanatopsis.' The latter is a good example of 'the noble manner,' but the reader who enjoys it does not therefore turn away with a puzzled frown from Holmes's 'The Wonderful One-hoss Shay.'

But is Mr. Frost then a humorist? the reader may inquire, seeing a gleam of light. Humor has its place in his work; that is to say, our author's moods take their rise from his contemplative scrutiny of *character* in men and nature, and he responds equally to a tragic episode or a humorous situation. But, like creators greater in achievement, his humorous perception is inter-woven with many other strands of apprehension, and in his *genre* pictures, sympathy blends with ironical appreciation of grave issues, to endow them with unique temperamental flavor. If one styled 'Mending Wall' and 'A Hundred Collars' idyls of New England life, the reader might remark sarcastically that they do not seem very idyllic; but idyls they are none the less, not in the corrupted sense of pseudo-Arcadian pastorals, but in the original meaning of 'little pictures.' One may contend that 'The Housekeeper' is cast in much the same gossiping style as Theocritus's idyl, 'The Ladies of Syracuse,' with its prattle of provincial ladies over their household affairs and the crush in the Alexandrian streets at the Festival of Adonis. And one may wager that this famous poem shocked the academic taste of the day by its unconventionality, and would not indeed, please modern professors, were it not the work of a Greek poet who lived three hundred years before Christ.

It is not indeed a bad precept for readers who wish to savor the distinctive quality of new original talents to judge them first by the *human interest* of what they present. Were this simple plan followed, a Browning or a Whitman would not be kept waiting so long in the chilling shadow of contemporary disapproval. Regard simply the people in Mr. Frost's dramatic dialogues, their motives and feelings, their intercourse and the clash of their outlooks, and note how these little canvases, painted with quiet, deep understanding of life's incongruous everyday web, begin to glow with subtle color. Observe how the author in 'A Servant to Servants,' picturing the native or local surroundings, makes the *essentials* live and speak in a woman's homely confession of her fear of madness.

But it is best to give an example of Mr. Frost's emotional force, and in quoting a passage from 'Home Burial' I say unhesitatingly that for tragic poignancy this piece stands by itself in American poetry. How dramatic is the action, in this moment of revelation of the tragic rift sundering man and wife!

I have quoted 'Home Burial' partly from the belief that its dramatic intensity will best level any popular barrier to the recognition of its author's creative originality. But one does not expect that even a sensitive taste will respond so readily to the rare flavor of 'The Mountain' as did the American people to Whittier's 'Snowbound,' fifty years back. The imagery of the Quaker poet's idyl, perfectly suited to its purpose of mirroring with faithful sincerity the wintry landscape and the pursuits and character of a New England farmer's family, is marked by no peculiar delicacy or originality of style. Mr. Frost, on the other hand, may disappoint readers who prefer grandeur and breadth of outline or magical depth of coloring to delicate atmospheric imagery.

But the attentive reader will soon discover that Mr. Frost's cunning impressionism produces a subtle cumulative effect, and that by his use of pauses, digressions, and the crafty envisagement of his subject at fresh angles, he secures a pervading feeling of the mass and movement and elusive force of nature. He is a master of his exacting medium, blank verse,—a new master. The reader must pause and pause again before he can judge him, so unobtrusive and quiet are these 'effects,' so subtle the appeal of the whole. One can, indeed, return to his poems again and again without exhausting their quiet imaginative spell. For instance, the reader will note how the feeling of the mountain's mighty bulk and hanging mass, its vast elbowing flanks, its watching domination of the near fields and scattered farmsteads, begins to grow upon him, till he too is possessed by the idea of exploring its high ravines, its fountain springs and granite terraces. One of the surest tests of fine art is whether our imagination harks back to it, fascinated in after contemplation, or whether our interest is suddenly exhausted both in it and the subject. And 'The Mountain' shows that the poet has known how to seize and present the mysterious force and essence of living nature.

In nearly all Mr. Frost's quiet dramatic dialogues, his record of the present passing scene suggests how much has gone before, how much these people have lived through, what a lengthy chain of feelings and motives and circumstances has shaped their actions and mental attitudes. Thus in 'The Housekeeper,' his picture of the stout old woman sitting there in her chair, talking over Estelle, her grown-up daughter, who, weary of her anomalous position in the household, has left John and gone off and married another man, carries with it a rich sensation of the women's sharp criticism of a procrastinating obstinate man. John is too dense in his masculine way to know how much he owes to them. This psychological sketch in its sharp actuality is worthy of Sarah Orne Jewett.

But why put it in poetry and not in prose? The reader may hazard. Well, it comes with greater intensity in rhythm and is more heightened and concentrated in effect thereby. If the reader will examine 'A Servant to Servants,' he will recognize that this narrative of a woman's haunting fear that she has inherited the streak of madness in her family, would lose in distinction and clarity were it told in prose. Yet so extraordinarily close to normal everyday speech is it that I anticipate some academic person may test its metre with a metronome, and declare that the verse is often awkward in its scansion. No doubt. But so also is the blank verse of many a master hard to scan, if the academic footrule be not applied with a nice comprehension of where to give and when to take. In 'A Servant to Servants' the tragic effect of this over-driven woman's unburdening herself of her load of painful memories and gloomy forebodings is to my mind a rare artistic achievement,—one that graves itself on the memory.

And now that we have praised *North of Boston* so freely, shall we not make certain stiff, critical reservations? Doubtless one would do so were one not conscious that Mr. Frost's fellow poets, his deserving rivals, will relieve one of the task. May I say to them here that because I believe Mr. Frost in *North of Boston* has found a way for himself, so I believe their roads lie also open before them. These roads are infinite, and will surely yield, now or to-morrow, vital discoveries. A slight defect of Mr. Frost's subtle realistic method, and one does not wish to slur it over, is that it is sometimes difficult to grasp all the implications and bearings of his situations. His language in 'The Self-seeker' is highly figurative, too figurative perhaps for poetry. Again in 'The Generations of Men,' his method as art seems to be both a little casual and long-winded. In several of his poems, his fineness of psychological truth is perhaps in excess of his poetic beauty,—an inevitable defect of cool, fearless realism. And the corollary criticism no doubt will be heard, that from the intensity with which he makes us realize things we should gain a little more pleasure. But here one may add that there is pleasure and pleasure, and that it seems remarkable that this New England poet, so absorbed by the psychological drama of people's temperaments and conduct, should preserve such pure outlines and clear objectivity of style.

Is his talent a pure product of New England soil? I take it that just as Hawthorne owed a debt to English influence, so Mr. Frost owes one also. But his 'native touch' is declared by the subtle blend of outspokenness and reticence, of brooding conscience and grave humor. Speaking under correction, it appears to me that his creative vision, springing from New England soil, and calmly handing on the best and oldest American tradition, may be a little at variance with the cosmopolitan clamor of New York. It would be quaint indeed if Americans who, according to their magazines, are opening their hospitable bosoms to Mr. Rabindranath Tagore's spiritual poems and dramas of Bengal life, should rest oblivious of their own countryman. To certain citizens Mr. Frost's poems of the life of inconspicuous, humble New England folk may seem unattractively homely in comparison with the Eastern poet's lofty, mystical dramas; but by American critics this view will doubtless be characterized as a manifestation of American provincialism. The critics know that a poet who has no 'message' to deliver to the world, whose work is not only bare of prettiness and sentimentality but is isolated and unaffected by this or that 'movement,' is easily set aside. Nothing is easier, since his appeal is neither to the interests nor caprices of the market. Ours indeed is peculiarly the day when everything pure, shy, and independent in art seems at the mercy of whose who beat the big drum and shout their wares through the megaphone. And knowing this, the critic of conscience will take for his watchword *quality*.

'Mr. Frost is a true poet, but not a *poetical* poet,' remarked a listener to whom I read 'A Servant to Servants,' leaving me wondering whether his verdict inclined the scales definitely to praise or blame. Of poetical poets we have so many! of literary poets so many! of drawing-room poets so many!—of academic and dilettanti poets so many! of imitative poets so many! but of original poets how few!

A Visit in Franconia

Carl Wilmore[*]

This village is forgotten by the whole world. Buried in the snow, with more snow and more snow, nobody comes here. Once a day an old man in a pung drives over with a few bundles, and leaves them, and drives off again in his old pung; and the thermometer is way below zero, just now, too.

So what in the world can mean a jingling sleigh, with two city folks in it, chasing over the snow out to the Notch, over Mt. Lafayette way?

That's surely what the lone straggler thought when the *Post* reporter came up here. He almost asked the same question of himself. Who wouldn't—with twelve-below weather?

"Follow the road to the first bridge, keep to the right, take the second bridge, and about a mile up there is a little house on the right; that's where Robert Frost lives," the old woman in the deserted general store had directed.

So it was Robert Frost the *Post* reporter was after; Robert Frost, the man who wrote *North of Boston*, the volume of the most original American verse in years, which he had to go to England to get published and which has reached goodness only knows how many editions in America since. And here lived Robert Frost, the least-known man in American letters, and one of the most delightful, lackadaisical, lazy, whimsical, promising makers of verse in contemporaneous literature.

More than this, it struck the reporter strangely to realize that in this poor house, buried here in the snows in the out-of-the-way corner of the mountains, lives the man whom England has recognized before his own America, whom France read before we did, and whom they both hail as the one pre-eminent American poet of today—a sort of modern Poe.

Robert Frost: good name—with twelve below.

And so the city folks drove on through the endless drifts and reached the little house. It looked like a three-room affair, with an ell and a shed behind. Nothing stirred, save a bit of smoke from the chimney.

"This can't be the house," the driver said. "A man like Frost wouldn't live here, would he?"

[*]From *The Boston Post*, February 14, 1916. Copyright 1916 by *The Boston Post*.

The reporter also had his doubts. So he piled through the drifts and knocked on the rickety back door—the kitchen door.

Nobody replied. Are they out in the woods? Is everybody gone? Is this a deserted farm? But—the smoke. . . .

The door opened an inch. (People don't throw open doors in twelve-below weather.) A woman peeked out. In an instant the reporter thought: college woman—teacher. Tall, serious face, hair simply brushed back; it was the type.

"Does Mr. Frost live here?" asked the reporter. He had to ask something, though the woman herself had given the answer the moment she appeared.

"Yes, but he's not up."

The reporter made the usual apology for untimely appearance and all the rest of it.

"I'll wake him up and tell him." And the serious-faced woman shut the door and disappeared. The reporter wondered: a farmer and not up at nine in the morning? Mentally he said, "There's a lazy lazy fellow lives here."

Out to the back, then, to join the driver slapping his sides, while the horses stamped and steamed and shook off the ice that hung all over them from nostrils to tails. The roosters and hens, awakened by the commotion in the midst of this deathly morning mountain mid-winter silence, began to crow and cackle. The horses hugged the sun; the blankets made them forget the twelve-below weather.

The house stood on the road, back some rods. Directly in front was Franconia Notch and above, snow-clad and glittering, rose Mt. Lafayette and the others of his companions, with Mt. Washington off in the distance.

The front door opened and a tall man in a brown suit, collar and necktie and all, said apologetically, "Come in; come in." And all hands went in.

It was nice and warm, with the all-night heat of a country home. "Come in and try to get warm," he said.

If ever they get shy of heating apparatus in the nether regions, they can come and get Robert Frost's stove, and the broiling will be better than ever. The stove reached from floor to ceiling. In fact, the room seemed built to suit the stove. It was the heart of the house.

"I don't usually wear a collar as early as this," said the host as he lolled back in a rocker, "but I wore these things last night to a meeting of a Parent-Teachers' Association and threw them beside the bed. So, I just naturally put them on again this morning."

What a lazy man's explanation! The house seemed still lazily half asleep—his writing table was covered with a myriad of letters which, he sheepishly confessed, he had been too lazy to answer—he admitted he was too lazy, at that early hour of nine a.m., to take coffee before talking to his visitors.

He spoke of the village folk.

"They didn't used to bother me," he smiled, "but last summer a lot of people came here to see us, and they got an idea we were of some account. So, now they've elected me president of the Parent-Teachers' Association."

The reporter remarked about the beauty of the hills (with a silent reservation about having to drive six miles in twelve-degrees-below-zero weather), and through the two small windows of the parlor one could see Mt. Lafayette and the White Notch.

"Yes—we adopted Lafayette long ago. I'm from Massachusetts [and a Californian] by birth, but we have lived in New Hampshire most of our lives, my wife, my four children, and myself."

"Four children, did you say?" gasped the reporter. He hadn't heard any racket, the sure sign of four children.

"Oh, yes; they went to school early this morning. Lesley, my oldest girl, is sixteen; then comes my boy, Carol; then Irma; and then Marjorie, who is nine. Carol does most of the work around the farm."

Carol did the work—what did Papa do? The *Post* reporter intended to find out.

"Who chopped the woodpile that we saw buried in the snow?"

"Oh, I didn't. You know, I like farming, but I'm not much of a success at it. Some day I'll have a big farm where I can do what I please"—he smiled as though he had intended to say "loaf as I please"—"and where I can divide my time between farming and writing.

"I always go to farming when I can. I always make a failure, and then I have to go to teaching. I'm a good teacher, but it doesn't allow me time to write. I must either teach or write: can't do both together. But I have to live, you see?"

"How old are you?"

"I'm forty-three. I suppose I'm just a bit lazy" (again he smiled, knowing that the reporter had guessed it long ago); "so I've had a lazy, scrape-along life, and enjoyed it. I fight everything academic. The time we waste in trying to learn academically—the talent we starve with academic teaching!"[. . .]

"And when do you work?" (In a corner stood a homemade writing table made of two short boards nailed together, which, he explained, he had himself made to set on the arms of the Morris chair, so that he could be more at his perfect ease.)

"Oh, I haven't any set times. I write when I feel like it. Sometimes I write nothing for months. Then I'll work a blue streak, and I rave around all day till it's off my mind. I can't do as many writers do, write to keep my hand in. I write only when I can write—when I must write.

"I hear everything I write. All poetry is to me first a matter of sound.

I hear my things spoken. I write verse that might be called 'free'—the free-versers have accepted me!—but I believe, after all, that there must be a cadence, a rhythm, to all that is to be poetry at all. I don't mean jingle. I hate jingle; I hate rhyme for itself.

"I want drama, too. Some day I may write a play. But I avoid the sublime, the ecstatic, the flights that three hundred—or is it three thousand?—minor poets of America slop into the magazines month after month. Meaningless twaddle, with a few worn-out tones—You know what I mean by tones? I'll explain presently.—and with all kinds of ridiculous extravagances.

"We don't get tones enough into our poetry. Our schools teach us we must do this, must do that; and we do it. Even England isn't tied to academic teaching as we are. That's why they have some real poets, where we have none. We insist on form and on unity and the rest of old stuff.

"Of course, I know there is a crowd of 'emotionalists' who threw all to the winds except emotion. I think they're perhaps worse than the 'intellectualists,' who are the other extreme. But a happy mixture, that's it.

"When a man's young, he's an emotionalist. When he's old, an intellectualist. Only about fifteen middle years are well-balanced. He should do his big works then.

"But the mediocrities, how they do go on! Take, for instance, the expression 'oh.'

"The American poets use it in practically one tone, that of grandeur: 'Oh Soul!' 'Oh Hills!'—'Oh Anything!' That's the way they go. But think of what 'oh' is really capable: the 'oh' of scorn, the 'oh' of amusement, the 'oh' of surprise, the 'oh' of doubt—and there are many more. But these are disdained by the academic poets.

"America must get away from the schools. Forget the books. I don't mean that one should strive for effects. There are people who write poetry as if they said: 'Let's write a shocker.' Others say: 'Let's write a best seller.' 'Let's write a freak.' So they go on, turning out verses that are bad. Some of the free verse—it is just stupid in its striving after sensation, isn't it? It makes one laugh—not with it, but at it, and at the writer."

"What are you writing now?" asked the reporter, trying to lure him to himself.

He blushed. "Well, my publishers say I'm getting out a new book next fall, but—I don't know. . . . They say I'm going to get out a new one each year. That's how they do it in England.[. . .]"

"Will your new poems be also about the country?"

"I shall always write about the country. I suppose I show a sad side to it too often. It only seems sad to those who love the city. I used to think the mill people, scooting home in the dusk, were sad, till I worked in the mill and heard them singing and laughing and throwing bobbins up at me as I stood up on the ladder fixing the lights.

"I used to know a man once whom I'd drag out to the country with me. He'd lean on a fence a moment, then jump up, sit down on the lawn, jump up again, pick a flower, throw it away. . . . In fact, he was insane to be back in the city—just couldn't stand the country. The very people looked sad to him. That was because he himself was sad. The country isn't really sad. . . .

"To get back. If American poets will only try to use all the tones of life and will drop the eternal sublime and see that all life is a fit subject for poetic treatment, they will do better. We must have new subject matter, new treatment of it, and we must employ the neglected tones and forget the overworked ones."

He talked more: of his English friends, of his American co-versifiers (and he mentioned names right out and said things he didn't want printed); how he had been accused of imitating Theocritus—"and I never even read Theocritus, because I'm too lazy to bother with Greek"; how he makes use of subtle psychological suggestions in such poems as "The Fear' and "Home Burial" and "A Servant to Servants"; how a lady had said of one of his poems, "It is nice; but what would Henry W. Longfellow think of it?"; how he and his family just "smouldered" by way of existence, "not really poor or lacking anything, but constantly on the verge of having something"; how the Franconians looked upon him, and he on them; and how he got along, or rather didn't, with his publishers—and much, much more.

It was time to go. He slopped into a pair of overshoes and saw us to the door. As the *Post* reporter clambered into the sleigh, and the driver grasped the reins, he shook hands with a quiet laugh.

"I'll come to see you when I'm in Boston. I'd like to meet some people, because I want to spread my gospel of getting away from those deadly professors! Good-by!"

As the city folks jingled off over the obliterated road, in that twelve-degrees-below weather, the road didn't seem so long, or the weather so cold, or one's ears so frost-bitten, because of Robert Frost. And this came to the reporter:

Some day, long years from now, will there be a Robert Frost Society, whose object it shall be to preserve, as a memorial, the little old house buried in the mountains, which the world of today passes by, and which was the earlier home of one of America's finest poets?

Of Axe-Handles and
Guide-Book Poetry

Anonymous*

Rule Number One for poets who hope some day to duplicate the success Robert Frost, poet of the granite-hilled farms of the White Mountains, has achieved in his *North of Boston* is: "Never larrup an emotion. Set yourself against the moon. Resist the moon. If the moon's going to do anything to you, it's up to the moon."

Mr. Frost has wind-blown cheeks and clear blue eyes. He's a Yankee of Yankees and glad of it, even though eminent critics of the stamp of Edward Garnett haven't hesitated to rank him with Theocritus and Wordsworth as a delineator of pastoral life in such of his poignant poems as "The Death of the Hired Man" and "Home Burial."

Fresh from his farm on Sugar Hill, Franconia, New Hampshire, where Mt. Lafayette towers and the Old Man of the Mountains frowns, Mr. Frost is paying his first visit to Philadelphia. Quite recently he's been skiing over rugged country, tapping maple trees, and shaping up new poems.

Mr. Frost lolled back in a comfortable chair at the Art Club yesterday and talked of one of these new poems—not because he's writing it, for he's very shy in speaking of his work, but because it illustrates his grip on humanity the world over. It's a poem that concerns an axe-handle.

"The thing you hate in poetry is segregated stuff—like love, the moon, and murder," he said.

He lighted a cigarette, commenting that he had learned cigarette smoking in England, where one of his cronies was Rupert Brooke, most promising of young English poets, who lost his life at the front.

"Love, the moon, and murder have poetry in them by common consent. But it's in other places. It's in the axe-handle of a French Canadian woodchopper, and it's in 'poultry-stricken ground' (quoting John Masefield).

"You know the Canadian woodchoppers whittle their axe-handles, following the curve of the grain, and they're strong and beautiful. Art

*From the Philadelphia *Public Ledger*, April 4, 1916. Reprinted by permission.

should follow lines in nature, like the grain of an axe-handle. False art puts curves on things that haven't any curves.

"We think the word 'provincial' is a shameful word here in America. But it is [an] Englishman's pride. You can't be universal without being provincial, can you? It's like trying to embrace the wind."

It wasn't so very many months ago that Mr. Frost "arrived." He is a man of about forty-five years and has a wife and four children living in his little farmhouse on Sugar Hill. Near him are the White Mountain homes of Prof. Cornelius Weygandt of the University of Pennsylvania and Justice Robert von Moschzisker.

The poet is staying here with Dr. Weygandt. He was entertained at luncheon at the Art Club yesterday by the Justice. He spoke last night in Germantown and reads at four o'clock this afternoon before the Arts Association of the University.

The recognition that has come to him as a successful and powerful poet is perhaps best indicated by the fact that he has been selected as this year's Phi Beta Kappa poet at Harvard. The magazines are clamoring for his work, and the colleges and universities want him as much—even more, since he is an American—as they wanted John Masefield or Alfred Noyes.

Mr. Frost is simplicity itself, a strong man, a direct man—a man who believes, as he says, that America needs poets who "get tight-up to things." He detests what he calls "guide-book poetry." He admits that he is a poor farmer. He believes, strange as it may sound, that Puritanism "hasn't yet had its day, and it might be fun to set it up as an artistic doctrine."

Speaking of Puritanism, Mr. Frost has no use for "easy criers and weepers."

"Which is the more terrible," he asks, "a man or a woman weeping? The men, of course. That's Puritanism."

He intends to be "more of a farmer" than he is, but never a "kid-glove or gentleman farmer."

"My country," he says, "is a milk and sugar country. We get what runs from the trees and what runs from the cows. You can't do much real farming, for we have frost every month in the year. You know, the White Mountain farmers say they have nine months of winter and three months of late-in-the-fall!" He laughed as he recalled his struggles with the granite soil.

If anything more than a reading of Mr. Frost's poem "Home Burial" (in which a rugged father buries his child in the yard of his farmhouse) is needed to convince everyone that he's a Yankee to the backbone, he will admit that his ancestors found New Hampshire back in 1630.

"One of them was an Indian fighter, and a cunning one," he says. "He invited the Indians to a barbecue. They stacked their arms, and he promptly killed them. Unfortunately for that ancestor, he didn't kill all of them. A few who were left came back after him on a Sunday morning after he'd finished praying, and got even."[. . .]

Mr. Frost had a very bad grudge against "guide-book poetry" yesterday. It was so bad that he gave a couple of very bad examples of it, dictating them with a Yankee twang, softened somewhat into a drawl by his life in England.

"This is ridiculous, of course," he said, "but it's guide-book poetry—certainly vers libre; you know the White Mountains goes in for vers libre!—and it shows what's the matter with American poets who lay poetry on things. I don't remember who wrote it!

> One of the most deplorable facts about the White Mountains
> Is the lack of legends.
> Imagination, therefore, must be requisitioned
> To supply the story
> That gave a name to this beautiful spot."

He chuckled. Then:

"The point I'm making lies in that line, 'Imagination . . . must be requisitioned.' The curse of our poetry is that we lay it on things. Pocketsful of poetic adjectives like pocketsful of peanuts carried into a park for the gray squirrels! You can take it as gospel, that's not what we want.

"But people say to me: 'The facts themselves aren't enough. You've got to do something to them, haven't you? They can't be poetical unless a poet handles them.'

"To that I have a very simple answer. It's this: Anything you do to the facts falsifies them, but anything the facts do to you—yes, even against your will; yes, resist them with all your strength—transforms them into poetry."

Which, as any one who reads him or talks with him will soon discover, is the secret of Robert Frost's success. He is a Puritan who has fought the soil for sustenance and has fought the world for recognition as a poet. He has won success because he has fought his own emotions, digging into them and behind them, the better to strike the universal note that makes poetry out of axe-handles.

Robert Frost Relieves His Mind

Rose C. Feld*

Have you ever seen a sensitive child enter a dark room, fearful of the enveloping blackness, yet more than half ashamed of the fear? That is the way Robert Frost, poet, approached the interview arranged for him with the writer. He didn't want to come, he was half afraid of coming, and he was ashamed of the fear of meeting questions.

He was met at his publisher's office at the request of his friends there. "Come and get him, please," they said. "He is a shy person—a gentle and a sensitive person—and the idea of knocking at your doors, saying, 'Here I am, come to be interviewed,' will make him run and hide." The writer came and got him.

All the way down Fifth Avenue for ten or fifteen blocks he smiled often and talked rapidly to show that he was at ease and confident. But he was not. One could see the child telling itself not to be afraid.

Arrived at the house, he took the chair offered him and sat down rigidly. Still he smiled.

"Go ahead," he said. "Ask me the questions. Let's get at it."

"There are no questions—no specific questions. Suppose you just ramble on about American poetry, about poets, about men of the past and men of the present, about where we are drifting or where we are marching. Just talk."

He looked nonplused. The rigid smile gave way to one of relief and relaxation.

"You mean to say that you're not going to fire machine-gun questions at me and expect me to answer with skyrocketing repartee. Well, I wish I'd known. Well."

The brown hand opened up on the arms of the chair and the graying head leaned back. Robert Frost began to talk. He talked of some of the poets of the past, and in his quiet, gentle manner exploded the first bomb-shell. He exploded many others.

"One of the real American poets of yesterday," he said, "was Longfellow. No, I am not being sarcastic. I mean it. It is the fashion

*From *The New York Times Book Review*, October 21, 1923. Copyright 1923 by The New York Times Company. Reprinted by permission.

nowadays to make fun of him. I come across this pose and attitude with people I meet socially, with men and women I meet in the classrooms of colleges where I teach. They laugh at his gentleness, at his lack of worldliness, at his detachment from the world and the meaning thereof.

"When and where has it been written that a poet must be a club-swinging warrior, a teller of barroom tales, a participant of unspeakable experiences? That, today, apparently is the stamp of poetic integrity. I hear people speak of men who are writing today, and their eyes light up with a deep glow of satisfaction when they can mention some putrid bit of gossip about them. 'He writes such lovely things,' they say, and in the next breath add, half worshipfully, 'He lives such a terrible life.'

"I can't see it. I can't see that a man must needs have his feet plowing through unhealthy mud in order to appreciate more fully the glowing splendor of the clouds. I can't see that a man must fill his soul with sick and miserable experiences, self-imposed and self-inflicted, and greatly enjoyed, before he can sit down and write a lyric of strange and compelling beauty. Inspiration doesn't lie in the mud; it lies in the clean and wholesome life of the ordinary man.

"Maybe I am wrong. Maybe there is something wrong with me. Maybe I haven't the power to feel, to appreciate and live the extremes of dank living and beautiful inspiration.

"Men have told me, and perhaps they are right, that I have no 'straddle.' That is the term they use: I have no straddle. That means that I cannot spread out far enough to live in filth and write in the treetops. I can't. Perhaps it is because I am so ordinary. I like the middle way, as I like to talk to the man who walks the middle way with me.

"I have given thought to this business of straddling, and there's always seemed to me to be something wrong with it, something tricky. I see a man riding two horses, one foot on the back of one horse, one foot on the other. One horse pulls one way, the other a second. His straddle is wide, Heaven help him, but it seems to me that before long it's going to hurt him. It isn't the natural way, the normal way, the powerful way to ride. It's a trick."

"What is it you teach at Amherst and how?" the writer asked while Mr. Frost was speaking about his students.

"Well, I can't say that you can call it teaching. I don't teach. I don't know how. I talk and I have the boys talk. This year I'm going to have two courses, one in literature and one in philosophy. That's funny. I don't know that I know much about either. That's the reason perhaps that we get along so well.

"In the course in literature we're going to read a book a week. They're not going to be the major authors, the classics of literature, either. They're going to be the minor writers—people that aren't so well known.

"Why do I [insist on] that? For a reason that I think rather good.

Those boys will, in the course of their education, get the first-rank people whether I give it to them or not. That's what education very largely means today—knowing the names that sound the loudest. That's what business means; that's what success means. Well, I'd like to get out of that rut for a while. I'd like to get the boys acquainted with some of the fellows who didn't blow their trumpets so loudly but who nevertheless sounded a beautiful note.

"We're not going to read the works in class; we couldn't do all of that. The boys will do their reading at home. They'll read in class the things that appeal to them most: an incident, a bit of dramatic action. I'll let them read what they wish. And then we'll have some fun in their telling me why they made their choice; why a thing called to them.

"I don't want to analyze authors. I want to enjoy them, to know them. I want the boys in the classes to enjoy their books because of what's in them.

"Here again, perhaps, I am old-fashioned. Youth, I believe, should not analyze its enjoyments. It should live. It doesn't matter what they think Hazlitt thought or tried to do in his works; what matters is the work, the story, the series of incidents. Criticism is the province of age, not of youth. They'll get to that soon enough. Let them build up a friendship with the writing world first. One can't compare until one knows.

"I hope it will work out all right. I don't know. I haven't done just this thing before. I don't like teaching the same thing year after year. You get stale doing that.

"Philosophy—that's another subject that I'm going to teach. Philosophy of what? Of life; of people about you, of course.

"What's my philosophy? That's hard to say. I was brought up a Swedenborgian. I am not a Swedenborgian now. But there's a good deal of it that's left with me. I am a mystic. I believe in symbols. I believe in change and in changing symbols. Yet that doesn't take me away from the kindly contact of human beings. No, it brings me closer to them.

"It's hard to explain this thing; it's hard to talk about it. I don't expect to talk much about it to the boys at college. But I want them to feel that a philosophy of life is something that is not formal, that means delving in books and superimposing on themselves. No, a philosophy of life is an attitude to life.

"Plato doubtless thought that he was discovering something new when he wrote his treatise. He didn't. He gave written expression to an attitude toward life that he had probably found in some of his friends. It wasn't worked out like a problem in mathematics. It grew in men. Men are the important factors to remember. They are the soil which brings forth the fruit.

"One cannot say that the real American poetry is the poetry of the soil. One cannot say it is the poetry of the city. One cannot say it is the poetry of the native as one cannot say it is the poetry of the alien. Tell me what America is and I'll tell you what its poetry is. It seems to me we worry too much about this business. Where there is life there is poetry, and just as much as our life is different from English life, so is our poetry different.

"The alien who comes here for something different, something ideal, something that is not England and not France and not Germany and finds it, knows this to be America. When he becomes articulate and raises his voice in an outburst of song, he is singing an American lyric. He is an American. His poetry is American. He could not have sung that same song in the place from where he hails; he could not have sung it in any other country to which he might have emigrated. Be grateful for the individual note he contributes and adopt it for your own as he has adopted the country.

"America means certain things to the people who come here. It means the Declaration of Independence, it means Washington, it means Lincoln, it means Emerson—never forget Emerson—it means the English language, which is not the language that is spoken in England or her provinces. Just as soon as the alien gets all that—and it may take two or three generations—he is as much an American as is the man who can boast of nine generations of American forebears. He gets the tone of America, and as soon as there is tone there is poetry.

"People do me the honor to say that I am truly a poet of America. They point to my New England background, to the fact that my paternal ancestor came here some time in the sixteen hundreds. So much is true, but what they either do not know or do not say is that my mother was an immigrant. She came to these shores from Edinburgh in an old vessel that docked at Philadelphia. But she felt the spirit of America and became part of it before she even set her foot off the boat.

"She used to tell about it when I was a child. She was sitting on the deck of the boat waiting for orders to come ashore. Near her some workmen were loading Delaware peaches on to the ship. One of them picked out one of them and dropped it into her lap.

" 'Here, take that,' he said. The way he said it and the spirit in which he gave it left an indelible impression on her mind.

" 'It was a bonny peach,' she used to say, 'and I didn't eat it. I kept it to show my friends.'

"Looking back would I say that she was less the American than my father? No. America meant something live and real and virile to her. He took it for granted. He was a Fourth-of-July American, by which I mean that he rarely failed to celebrate in the way considered proper and appropriate. She, however, was a year-round American.

"I had an aunt in New England who used to talk long and loud about the foreigners who were taking over the country. Across the way from her house stood a French Catholic church which the new people of the village had put up. Every Sunday my aunt would stand at her window, behind the curtain, and watch the steady stream of men and women pouring into church. Her mouth would twist in the way that seems peculiar to dried-up New Englanders, and she would say, 'My soul!' Just that: 'My soul!'

"All the disapproval and indignation and disgust were concentrated in these two words. She never could see why I laughed at her, but it did strike me very funny for her to be calling upon her soul for help when this mass of industrious people were going to church to save theirs.

"New England is constantly going through periods of change. In my own state (in Vermont, I mean) there have been three distinct changes of population. First came the Irish, then the French, and now the Poles.

"There are those among us who raise their hands in horror at this, but what does it matter? All these people are becoming, have become, Americans.

"If soil is sacred, then I would say that they are more godly in their attitude to it. The Pole today in New England gets much more out of his plot of ground than does his Yankee neighbor. He knows how to cultivate it so that each inch produces, so that each grain is alive. Today the Pole may not be aware of the beauty of the old Colonial house he buys and may in some cases desecrate it, but three generations from now, two generations, his children will be proud of it and may even boast of Yankee heritage. It has been done before; it will be done in the future.

"And if there are poets among these children, as surely there will be, theirs will be the poetry of America. They will be part of the soil of America as their cousins may be part of the city life of America.

"I am [not] patient with this jealousy of the old for the young. It is change, this constant flow of new blood, which will make America eternally young, which will make her poets sing the songs of a young country—virile songs, strong songs, individual songs. The old cannot keep them back.

"I was amused years ago by the form this jealousy of tradition will take. One of the most brilliant pupils in the class at college was the son of a Polish farmer. Everybody admitted his mental superiority. But the old New Englanders would not swallow the pill as given. They sugar-coated, by backstairs gossip, which insisted that the real father of the boy must have been a Yankee.

"We are supposed to be a broad-minded country, yet in this respect we are so very narrow. Nobody worries about foreign strains in English or French literature and politics. Nobody thinks that England has been tainted by Disraeli or Zangwill or Lord Reading. They are taken as Englishmen; their works are important as English works. The same is true of French writers of foreign strain. We seem to lack the courage to be ourselves.

"I guess that's it. We're still a bit afraid. America, for instance, was afraid to accept Walt Whitman when he first sang the songs of democracy. His influence on American poetry began to be felt only after the French had hailed him as a great writer, a literary revolutionist. Our own poet had to be imported from France before we were sure of his strength.

"Today almost every man who writes poetry confesses his debt to Whitman. Many have gone very much further than Whitman would have traveled with them. They are the people who believe in wide straddling.

"I, myself, as I said before, don't like it for myself. I do not write free verse; I write blank verse. I must have the pulse beat of rhythm, I like to hear it beating under the things I write.

"That doesn't mean I do not like to read a bit of free verse occasionally. I do. It sometimes succeeds in painting a picture that is very clear and startling. It's good as something created momentarily for its sudden startling effect; it hasn't the qualities, however, of something lastingly beautiful.

"And sometimes my objection to it is that it's a pose. It's not honest. When a man sets out consciously to tear up forms and rhythms and measures, then he is not interested in giving you poetry. He just wants to perform; he wants to show you his tricks. He will get an effect; nobody will deny that, but it is not a harmonious effect.

"Sometimes it strikes me that the free-verse people got their idea from incorrect proof sheets. I have had stuff come from the printers with lines half left out or positions changed about. I read the poems as they [stand], distorted and half finished, and I confess I get a rather pleasant sensation from them. They make a sort of nightmarish half-sense."

As he rose to go, he said, "I am an ordinary man, I guess. That's what's the trouble with me. I like my school and I like my farm and I like people. Just ordinary, you see."

Robert Frost

Anonymous*

Robert Frost is what the bucolic Virgil might have been, had Virgil, shorn of his Latinity and born of Scotch-New England parentage, spent most of his life where thermometers remain near and often below zero for three months of each year. If Mr. Frost had lived in classical Italy or Greece, he would probably have tended sheep. And only his flocks would have heard many of his poems, so seldom does he write and so much of his poetry is little more than contemplative conversation. He is a poet of mountain land and of pasture; but how foreign to him would be the mellow temperament of a Virgil! His farms are on rugged hillsides, his meadows too filled with stones. He knows the orchard wall and the mountain, the barn and the birch tree, the Vermont farmer in the fields at haying time or on log roads in winter. All these are not only the properties for his stage set. They are the tools with which he has worked. He *is* a farmer—Massachusetts, Vermont, New Hampshire, what state you will— but a farmer! A poet of the *minutiae* of a locality, a singer of Yankee moods, he yet succeeds in being both national and universal because of his intuitive understanding of the stark motivation of simple minds. His "North of Boston" is a series of dramatic portraits of New England farm folk; but it is more than that, it is an epic of the lives of isolated and lonely people, wherever in the world they may be.

Frost, the man, gives an impression of great force, combined with a sort of tentativeness. Perhaps this is because thoughts are so vital to him. He thinks slowly. He acts slowly. Sensitive, upright, dignified, Mr. Frost is a *good man* moving in a world of wickedness. His New England consciousness of the wicked, he has tried to lay over with a gloss of tolerance. His extreme gentleness of spirit has resulted. He has determined to preserve this gentleness, this freshness of viewpoint in the face of all disillusionment. Consequently he has few prejudices. A tolerant, wise man, with less pity for mankind than willingness to observe people and accept them without superimposing an emotion. His close friends, though not many, are diverse. Among them can be found such contrasting per-

*Excerpt from *The Literary Spotlight* edited by John Farrar, pp. 213–21. Copyright 1924 by George H. Doran Company. Reprinted by permission of Doubleday & Company, Inc.

sonalities as the brittle-minded Louis Untermeyer and the blunt-souled Wilfrid Wilson Gibson. Mr. Frost's life has been filled neither with the physical indecision nor the moral ramblings of undisciplined genius. His ethical firmness partakes of the nature of the hills. His adventures are those of a soul carefully tempered by corporeal decision. Many of the things that are most important to most men are not important at all to him. Of pride of possession he has none. His ambition is the development of his art, not the successful understanding of writing as a possible business. His home is important to him. So is his family. So is his poetry which, in its essence, is a simple facing of the facts of life. Beyond this, he does not go. He fights no glorious combats with existence. He is not a propagandist for God or Puritanism—no, not even for the back-to-the-farm movement.

Frost's body, which is sturdy and square, makes little impression on one who meets him for the first time. It is the eyes: bright blue, steady, gentle yet canny, two vivid lights in a face that is otherwise gray. There is the loose, coarse, now almost white hair, the full but finely cut lips, the nose that is a trifle too broad to allow the characterization "Greek" for the whole head, which is indeed a noble one. Physical movements are casual. In old age, they may become soft and shambling. Loose clothes become the poet. If he were to wear a Snappy Cut suit, it would take on the appearance of homespun. He is a dignified figure as he sits on the back porch of his stone farmhouse on a rise of the road near South Shaftsbury, Vermont. One or two of his four children are usually there with him, and Mrs. Frost, a quiet, beautiful woman of steadfast purpose. A mood of calm industry prevails in her household. The family have made a fountain in the back yard, which slopes by bushy meadowland away to the Green Mountains. Frost works late into the night and sleeps far into the morning. He likes to walk. He likes to sit watching that fountain and letting his mind play along its rising and falling waters. Occasional visitors there are, hospitably received.

For a part of the year now, Frost travels. Recently he returned to his post as professor of English at Amherst College. He speaks occasionally in public, does it well, but does not enjoy it. If he had his own way, he would spend his time alone with his family, thinking and, from time to time, writing. He has never taught himself to write when occasion demands. Apparently he indulges his moods and waits upon them. He has taught his soul to listen too long, to express itself too seldom. In this, he is more poet than journalist. The charge of laziness which has been brought against him seems false. He prefers to write only well, and consequently makes firm demands of his inspiration and his intellect. His control is sometimes a little too studied, his intent too often philosophical rather than lyrical. The body of his work is dryer than need be. You feel that he has often intended a lyric which turned out an eclogue.

The only note of bitterness in his make-up is his attitude toward the writer who despoils his art, and the public which does not countenance comparative indigence in the artist. He feels, perhaps, that the leisure of poets is misunderstood, that periods of contemplation seem times of drought to the average intelligence. The sound of literary claques is annoying to him. If he is intolerant of anything, it is of a certain type of literary personage chiefly to be found in New York clubs.

At various times in his life he has been a teacher; once at Derry, New Hampshire, where his grandfather, despairing of his grandson's business acumen, had bought him a farm. Later he was at the Normal School in Plymouth, New Hampshire, and at the University of Michigan, where he was appointed "poet in residence." His connections with colleges, however, seem irksome. He practically ran away from Dartmouth where he attempted an undergraduate career, and subsequent studies in Latin at Harvard pleased him little. Teaching, in so far as it does not interfere with his real work, is apparently palatable; but the restrictions of academic life beat sadly upon him and he stands puzzled and amazed in the presence of professorial bickering and arraignments. On the campus of the great western university he was ill at ease, though grateful. Not worldly enough to cultivate the manners of a lion, he yet understands those who would lionize him. Though he could actually despise no one, he is at a loss before the self-conscious hero worshiper. Contact with real talent he doubtless enjoys, and as poetry reader for a publishing house he has shown wisdom as a critic; but the merely determined aspirant to literary honors must necessarily fill a true poet with despair.

His ten years in San Francisco, where he was born, seem to have made as little impression on the body of his work as those spent in Beaconsfield, Buckinghamshire, England. He commenced writing poetry at fifteen, and American magazines published his work, but it was during his English stay that his first volume, "A Boy's Will," appeared. "North of Boston," too, was published in England before American publishers awoke to the worth of Mr. Frost. This fact, however, seems to worry him not at all. He has no quarrel either with publishers or public.

There is seldom easy and facile grace in the poetry of Robert Frost. The loveliest of his lyrics are in his latest Pulitzer prize-winning volume, "New Hampshire." An almost rigid adherence to the colloquial prevails; where Lowell and Whittier observed and reported the New England peasant, Frost has become one. He writes stories of their most vivid moments with unswerving power of dramatic presentation. Some of his best pictures are of grim and terrible events, and the whole body of his writing indubitably shows a decaying and degenerating New England. That he fails to see the other side of life is untrue. Passages of great beauty shine from drabness. His events and his characters have moments of warmth and of happiness. Always, however, is manifest the sense of fairness to events as he sees them. He is seldom, if ever, the protagonist. His characters speak for themselves. If he prefers one to another, he conceals his preference with care, as in "Snow," where the reader must be judge between Meserve's impetuosity and the narrowness of the Cole family.

He is a natural dramatist: he sees things as pictures rather than hears them as music. He has written short plays and intends to write longer ones which are still slowly germinating. Soon these projected dramas will become actual plays in Frost's mind. Whether they emerge upon paper or not really matters little to him.

Frost's humor, often of satirical intent, is clumsy. It is intended to catch the dryness and drollery of the Yankee, but it succeeds often in being only very dry. His truest moments of humor are probably accidental and spring simply from his deep understanding of humanity. Like most realists, he is occasionally unconsciously funny. He can write a quatrain that matches Wordsworth's most grotesque ruralism—

> She wheeled the dung in the wheelbarrow
>   Along a stretch of road;
> But she always ran away and left
>   Her not-nice load.

And this is the same hand that pens the following superb lines:

> I'd like to go by climbing a birch tree,
> And climb black branches up a snow-white trunk
> *Toward* heaven, till the tree could bear no more,
> But dipped its top and set me down again.

From "The Black Cottage" there is a passage which typifies Frost. Here is the realist groping for truth, letting the world as it is play upon the character of his work; yet after all fundamentally aware that even the realism of the present may come to be the romance of the future, the truth of the past fade out in the light of new discovery. This would be profound pessimism were it not for the fact that Mr. Frost apparently believes that he has discovered the secret of rotating events. He has found stability in this unstable course.

> It will turn true again, for so it goes.
> Most of the change we think we see in life
> Is due to truths being in and out of favour.
> As I sit here, and oftentimes, I wish
> I could be monarch of a desert land
> I could devote and dedicate forever
> To the truths we keep coming back and back to.
> So desert it would have to be, so walled
> By mountain ranges half in summer snow,
> No one would covet it or think it worth
> The pains of conquering to force change on.
> Scattered oases where men dwelt, but mostly
> Sand dunes held loosely in tamarisk

Blown over and over themselves in idleness.
Sand grains should sugar in the natal dew
The babe born to the desert, the sand storm
Retard mid-waste my cowering caravans—

While Frost permits the world to mold his work, the world can never leave its imprint upon his personality. Let it call him what it will, shiftless, irresponsible, lazy; his primary purpose is as firm as the rocks in his own back-door yard. If Mr. Frost starts out to think a deep thought, the house may burn about his ears, but he will think his thought to the conclusion that satisfies Mr. Frost.

Robert Frost

Percy H. Boynton*

I

The temptation to generalize from Mr. Frost about art and artists is almost too strong to resist, even though there is no subject which so defies abstractions. It is doubtless wiser to write specifically about him, letting the generalizations take care of themselves; and it is beyond question appropriate to do so, because this is his own method in writing about life. He is persistently and cheerfully single-minded about what he wants life to yield him, but common-sensible and almost hard-headed too. To think of the poet who wrote for twenty years on an average literary income of ten dollars as stalking through the world with a somber eye fixed on achievement and fame would be quite to misconceive him. Various pulls have swerved him from the direct path. Until the public came to know him it was the need of daily bread. Since that time it has been the desire of publishers and college presidents to thrust it upon him under distracting circumstances. "They have made a very tempting offer," he said of his first college call. "All the work in three days of the week. But the trouble is that it takes me two days to unscrew, and two to screw up again." He has tried carrying scheduled duties, but now that daily bread can be secured by a little less sweat of brow than formerly, he reverts persistently to his old desire, which is to live relaxed and unhurried, not in indolence—for he likes to work with his hands—and not in solitude—for he is most companionable—but in such quiet circumstances that, as he has said, he can lean against life until it stings him into utterance.

The fact that his first three volumes—two of them quite slender—hold all that he cared to preserve from nearly a quarter of a century of writing, and that it was seven years before a fourth was added to them, shows how free he is from either inward or outward pressure. He seems never to have been impatient for a hearing, and never to have inclined toward putting his own hopes or fears or special convictions into print. He does not plan poetic projects nor preach poetic disquisitions on life. The

*From *Some Contemporary Americans* by Percy H. Boynton by permission of The University of Chicago Press. Copyright 1924 by The University of Chicago.

infrequency of his publishing has led to the comment that he is not really a poet, but only a man who writes poetry. The distinction is a valid one, but the application to Mr. Frost should be exactly transposed. It is only the journalistic versifiers—Walt Mason, Edgar Guest, and the like—who can turn out copy every day. It should be said of the poet what Mr. Crothers said of the average citizen in his *Observations on Votes for Women*, that he is allowed time off occasionally to attend to his daily affairs. Mr. Frost has taken his time, yet, all things considered, it is a surprising fact, for which a prominent publisher is authority, that in point of American sales in recent years, excluding the daily versifiers, Masefield and Masters are the only two poets who have surpassed Mr. Frost, the least prolific of contemporary writers.

II

As a so-called modern poet Mr. Frost is both old-fashioned and new-fashioned in his manner of writing. *A Boy's Will* is composed wholly in established lyric forms, in line, stanza, and rhyme usages. The two later volumes are more generally in an iambic pentameter which carries into effect his definite theory of versification.

In this connection everyone who is interested in modern prosody knows that until recently the theory of versification has been very much obscured by the efforts of critics to prove that every line which was supposed to conform to a certain measure actually did so. In an iambic measure an anapest has been an iambic with another label, and a trochee has been an iambic inverted. Pentameter has had either five stresses and ten syllables or an excuse for shortage or excess. The consequence has been that apologists have had about as much trouble with the conduct of many of Shakespeare's lines as they have had with the domestic vagaries of Henry VIII. Their struggles have been amusing when they came to such an incorrigible as

> Than the soft myrtle. But man, proud man.

Yet rather than surrender, they have forced it into the strait-jacket of

> Te tum, te tum, te tum, te tum, te tum.

Within the last few years the discussion of rhythm has grown to Cyclopean proportions. (A bibliography of rhythm in the *American Journal of Psychology*, 1913–18, has just been characterized as "important but incomplete.") The one definite conclusion to be drawn from all the discussion is that we are probably on the way to a new and sound science of verse. Such being the case, it would be foolish and futile to dogmatize just now on general principles; but it is still reasonable to explain what a particular poet believes about verse, and what he thinks he is doing when he writes it.

Mr. Frost contends that there are two rival factors in every verse product: the absolute rhythm demanded by the adopted pattern, and the flexible rhythm demanded by the accents of the successive words and by the particular stresses needed among the words. The former is illustrated by the mechanical quatrain composed by Dr. Johnson to prove that rhyme and rhythm do not necessarily make poetry (and even in this there is one break from the pattern).

> I put my hat upon my head,
>   And walked into the Strand;
> And there I met another man,
>   Whose hat was in his hand.

The latter is illustrated by the doubts of a young actor in a play within a play who is given a single line for his part, and anxiously wanders about the stage debating whether to say,

> There is a *lady* outside, who desires an audience, or
> There is a lady *outside*, who desires an audience, or
> There *is* a lady outside, who desires an audience.

Says Mr. Frost, admitting these two rival factors, neither should be entirely subjected to the other. In what is called iambic pentameter, most of the feet should be iambic, and most of the lines should have five stresses; but in cases of departure from the pattern, there is nothing to explain away or condone; the rhythm will return to it. There is nothing new in this idea—except among prosodists. The poets have always acted on it. The opening lines of "Thanatopsis" or "The Princess" illustrate it, as does almost any spontaneous blank verse. In the conversational tone of his pentameters, Mr. Frost simply shows that he stands with less formal writers. See how the theory applies to "The Runaway," for example:

> Once when the snow of the year was beginning to fall,
> We stopped by a mountain pasture to say, "Whose colt?"

This is written on an iambic pentameter pattern, but, honestly scanned, the first line opens with four dactyls and the second ends with three stressed syllables in succession:

> **Once** when the **snow** of the **year** was be- **ginning** to **fall**
> We **stopped**   by a **moun**- tain **pas**- ture to **say** "**Whose colt?**"

But he is not solicitous (as are W. B. Yeats or Vachel Lindsay, whose theory and practice are quite different from his). He says to let the spoken word and the verse pattern fight out the issue; and the best poetry results from the nicest compromise between them. So in the forms of all his poems there is a not too insistent design. This appears in rhyme, as well as in rhythm. In "The Runaway" at first glance the rhyme seems to be quite casual; but at second or third glance the twenty-one lines fall into three groups of six and seven and eight, each of which has a nice symmetry of rhyme scheme:

$$a\,b\,a\,c\,b\,c; \quad a\,b\,c\,c\,a\,b\,c; \quad a\,a\,b\,c\,c\,b\,d\,d.$$

However, in a brief discussion such as this, it is easy to place too much emphasis on questions of form, which, though sometimes interesting, are always subordinate in poetry. The main point to remember in connection with this aspect of Mr. Frost's work is that his effects are never accidental. His poems are his expression of a definite theory about poetic form.

III

In its broadest divisions Mr. Frost's work falls into lyrics and sketches—the records of moments of feeling and moments of observation. *A Boy's Will* is made up wholly of the first type, *North of Boston* and *Mountain Interval* largely of the second. The little songs in *A Boy's Will* tell by implication something of a poet's experience in deciding on what life owes him, and what he owes the world. The poet and his bride withdraw into the happy seclusion of the countryside, and here without ecstacizing or sentimentalizing over it they enjoy its quiet and peace and beauty. But they find that care cannot be wantonly thrust forth by happiness, and in the end they come down the hills and into the world again.

> Out through the fields and the woods
> And over the walls I have wended.
> I have climbed the hills of view,
> And looked at the world, and descended;
> I have come by the highway home,
> And lo, it is ended.

Each of the songs was written for itself; they would not have been genuine, the poet has said, if they had been done to measure; and they can be read separately for their beauty. Yet the unity is there, as he discovered it and revealed it in his annotated Table of Contents, and they can be read together for their truth.

Except for the forewords and afterwords the later volumes contain few of these brief lyrics. They in turn, without being too mechanically grouped, may be separated into poems largely on men and women in the presence of nature, and poems largely on men and women in their relation to each other. "Mending Wall," "The Woodpile," and "The Mountain," are of the former sort. Two country neighbors meet each spring to repair the stone walls upset by winter frosts, spring thaws, and the hunters. One of them—the poet—speculates on the fact that every year nature overthrows man's artifice; the other sturdily labors to restore his own handiwork because "Good fences make good neighbors." It is all presented in simplest fashion, with no word of intruded comment or explanation. The pile of wood stands deserted and exposed out in the winter snows. One prop has fallen and vines have covered it in the years since it was laboriously stacked there. Where has the builder gone who stored the fuel that is now wasting "with the slow, smokeless burning of decay"? Again the mystery of nature, "rock-ribbed and ancient as the sun," and man, the transitory. Imagination lingers when the poem comes to an end. The Mountain spreads so wide that on its lower slopes and on the fringe of land around it there are only sixty voters in the township. It looms high in their midst, dominating and limiting life; few have time to go to the top, and fewer still, a surviving curiosity. There is a rigor in the earth north of Boston. Winter is insistent. It frightens the colt who is unused to snow, lets death descend on the autumn, breaks down the birches with its ice storms, overthrows the walls, and reluctantly succumbs to spring. Spring marks rather the departure of the ice king than the coming of plenty; and enjoyment of summer is delegated to the city vacationists.

So the characters presented by Mr. Frost are products of duress and adversity. They live in a country which has come to old age on arid tradition. They are unacquainted with mirth or song or play. Their human contacts have not been varied, for they are far from the main-traveled roads; and the summer visitors, who do not understand them, call them "natives" but think of them as peasants. With little to alleviate life, they have lost the traits of Pauline charity. Hard pride and grim endurance have lined their faces, labor has bowed their backs, and inbreeding has done the rest. They are, in short, the same people today whom Whittier characterized as being a hundred years ago:

> Church-goers, fearful of the unseen Powers,
> But grumbling over pulpit tax and pew-rent,
> Saving, as shrewd economists, their souls
> And winter pork, with the least possible outlay
> Of salt and sanctity; in daily life
> Showing as little actual comprehension
> Of Christian charity and love and duty
> As if the Sermon on the Mount had been
> Outdated like a last year's almanac.

Such people are not to be found only in New England. Similar conditions produce the same type anywhere in Anglo-Saxondom; but their characters are like their speech, which has the general features of the English tongue, with a local twang and idiom. And Mr. Frost has fixed them in his pictures.

IV

As a poet Mr. Frost is no more concerned with the world of affairs than Mr. Robinson is. He does not discuss institutions, movements, tendencies. He has no reforms to advocate, or theories to advance. He does not even propound a philosophy of life. On the whole, if we are to deduce one from his collected work, it is the philosophy that a cheerful, persistent man of hard-headed common sense might be expected to have. His convictions have not grown so much from what he has thought as from what he has felt; and because they are the fruit of his temperament rather than the children of his mind, he has very little to say about them—just takes them for granted. He feels that while this is not the best of all possible worlds, it is the best one that he knows, and that as far as his life in it is concerned it is pretty much a world of his own making. If he has misgivings at the actual ugliness of life he admits them and records them, but he is reassured by its actual and potential beauties. Of all that life has to give he finds nothing to rival sympathetic companionship—between neighbors, friends, parents and children, husbands and wives.

He has very seldom drawn open analogies from nature, or written openly about himself; but he has done both in the last stanza of "Birches," and it goes far toward explaining his reticent optimism:

> So was I once myself a swinger of birches;
> And so I dream of going back to be.
> It's when I'm weary of considerations,
> And life is too much like a pathless wood
> Where your face burns and tickles with the cobwebs
> Broken across it, and one eye is weeping
> From a twig's having lashed across it open.
> I'd like to get away from earth awhile
> And then come back to it and begin over.
> May no fate wilfully misunderstand me
> And half grant what I wish and snatch me away
> Not to return. Earth's the right place for love:
> I don't know where it's likely to go better.
> I'd like to go by climbing a birch tree
> And climb black branches up a snow-white trunk
> *Toward* heaven, till the tree could bear no more,
> But dipped its top and set me down again.
> That would be good both going and coming back.
> One could do worse than be a swinger of birches.

Soil of the Puritans

Carl Van Doren*

The Puritans dreamed their dream on an island, but they carried it to a continent. That high city they were to build without hands, that tower which was to touch heaven, that commonwealth of all the virtues—these phases of the dream in some way or other took for granted a barrier around England as powerful as the sea. The barrier did not hold. Animosity awoke in neighbor kingdoms and struck at the Puritans for their daring. Contention at home grew so keen that many of those who were stoutest in the new faith broke the barrier outward and went across the Atlantic to establish a New England more congenial to their doctrine. Here also there was no wall to protect the sacred commune. The colonies and states of New England might bind themselves together with a thousand chains of unity and pride and hope, but a continent yawned behind them. As the generations fell away from the radiance of the first vision, they turned to more and more secular undertakings. They sailed off to the ends of the earth in busy ships; they drifted off into the Western wilderness. The original stock was constantly diminished and diluted. The more adventurous spirits begot their children upon the women of distant regions. The dissenters from the native code of the region enriched other communities with the heat and stir of their dissent. Those who remained tended to be either the most successful or the least successful, the gentry for whom Boston set the mode or the gnarled farmers who tugged at the stones of inland hillsides.

The gentry found its poetical voice first: the sharp-tongued satirists of the Revolution; Holmes, the little wit of the Puritan capital; Longfellow, the sweet-syllabled story-teller and translator; Lowell, learned and urbane, who stooped to the vernacular; Emerson, whose glowing verses had to preach. The Yankee subsoil long resisted the plow. Thoreau, hired man of genius, read Greek in his hermitage; Whittier, born to be the ballad-maker of his folk, was half politician. And when, after the Civil War, rural New England was rediscovered by poetry and

*From *Many Minds*, 1924. Copyright 1924 by Alfred A. Knopf. Reprinted by permission of the estate of Carl Van Doren.

romance, it was valued largely because it seemed quaint, because it was full of picturesque remnants of a civilization. For half a century too many of those who sang its charms looked at them as if from the cool verandas of summer boarding-houses, touched by an antique fashion and tickled by an angular dialect. They collected episodes and characters as they collected brass knockers and hooked rugs and banister-back chairs and walnut high-boys. As time went on there were so many summer visitors that they forgot the natives. The rock-bound coast echoed to the cries of jolly bathers; up and down the solid hills dashed motor-cars filled with bright boys and girls as pagan as the youth of Greece; hunters in an alien scarlet took stone walls which it had broken backs to build; somber farm-houses blossomed into pleasant villas; oak-raftered barns turned into studios; churches which had once enshrined the aspirations of devout parishes were kept up by the donations of men and women who valued them chiefly for the quality they gave the landscape. No wonder the elder Yankees had no voice. Inarticulate themselves, both by principle and by habit, they invited obscurity. Overwhelmed by the rush of the new world which had poured over them, they took to the safer hills.

But there were flesh and blood beneath their weather-beaten garments, as there was granite beneath the goldenrod and hardhack about which the visitors babbled; and in time the flesh and blood and granite were reached. If it seems strange that Robert Frost, born in California, should have become the voice of those left behind, it actually is natural enough. New England was in his blood, bred there by many generations of ancestors who had been faithful to its soil. Some racial nostalgia helped draw him back; some deep loyalty to his stock intensified his affection. That affection made him thrill to the colors and sounds and perfumes of New England as no poet had done since Thoreau. He felt, indeed, the pathos of deserted farms, the tragedy of dwindling townships, the horrors of loneliness pressing in upon silent lives, the weight of inertia in minds from which an earlier energy has departed; but there was in him a tough sense of fact which would not let him brood. He drew life from the sight of the sturdy processes which still went on. Unable to see these upland parishes as mere museums of singular customs and idioms, he saw them, instead, as the stages on which, as on any human stage however small or large, there are transacted the universal tragedies and comedies of birth, love, work, hope, despair, death. The same sun shines upon New Hampshire as upon Arcadia or Sicily or Provence or Wessex; the same earth rolls under the feet of men. Suppose, Mr. Frost may be imagined as having thought, New England had a poet who, in the Yankee way, was willing to work with the tools he had upon the materials which lay at hand. Suppose, further, he did not forever apologize for his tools or comment upon the quaintness of his materials, but gave his time to fashioning poems which should be shrewd or wise or beautiful in their own right.

2

To compare Robert Frost, as he has often been compared, with Robert Burns, is to call attention at the outset to a difference between the Yankees and the Scots which has had a great effect upon the difference between these two poets. Burns grew up among a peasantry which sang. Not only were there ballads of the traditionary sort in every chimney-corner, but there were also gay tunes in the air ready for the new words of any new versifier. Even a genius like Burns in even his most characteristic lyrics was likely to owe some of his lines and the mold in which he cast them to old songs of love or laughter or defiance; and he was sure in such cases to owe to the fame of the older songs some part of the prosperity of his own. The ears of his hearers were already prepared for him. In rural New England Robert Frost had no similar advantages. Almost the only tunes which had ever been lifted there had been the dry hymns of the churches. Ballad-making had died out; hilarious catches had rarely been trolled in cheerful taverns; youth did not sing its love, but talked when it did not merely hint. New England since the Revolution has had but one great popular orator; since *Yankee Doodle* only one popular patriotic song has come out of New England. The voice of that region is the voice of reason, of the intellect, of prose, canny or noble; it walks, not flies. There was nothing to teach or to encourage Mr. Frost to ride on the wings of established melodies.

He would not have heeded any such teaching and encouragement, perhaps, being so much an individualist in his speech; but that very individualism was in part a Yankee trait. Yet if he could not lean upon accepted habits of song, he could lean upon accepted habits of talk. Behind all that his poems have to say there is to be heard the sound of a shrewd voice speaking. Here, for instance, is a farmer saying that he has never climbed a mountain at the foot of which he lives:

> "I've always meant to go
> And look myself, but you know how it is:
> It doesn't seem so much to climb a mountain
> You've worked around the foot of all your life.
> What would I do? Go in my overalls,
> With a big stick, the same as when the cows
> Haven't come down to the bars at milking time?
> Or with a shotgun for a stray black bear?
> 'Twouldn't seem real to climb for climbing it."

Though the passage is full of significant reference to the unadventurous and utilitarian attitude of the Yankee rustic, it does not raise its voice to point the reference, but hugs the ground of understatement and casual syntax.

Nor does Mr. Frost leave the idiom or rhythm of common speech behind when he rises to the pitch of aphorism. In *The Death of the Hired Man* the wife is telling her husband that the old laborer has come back:

> " 'Warren,' she said, 'he has come home to die:
> You needn't be afraid he'll leave you this time.'
>
> 'Home,' he mocked gently.
>
>   'Yes, what else but home?
> It all depends on what you mean by home.
> Of course he's nothing to us, any more
> Than was the hound that came a stranger to us
> Out of the woods, worn out upon the trail.'
>
> 'Home is the place where, when you have to go there,
> They have to take you in.'
>
>   'I should have called it
> Something you somehow haven't to deserve.' "

These definitions of home, as profound as were ever spoken, fall from the lips which utter them without one symptom of rhetorical or poetical self-consciousness. They have the accents of folk-speech clarified and ennobled, but clarified and ennobled by no other art than a poet may learn from folk-speech itself.

Even when Mr. Frost touches his peaks of elevation he still talks, not sings.

> "So was I once myself a swinger of birches.
> And so I dream of going back to be.
> It's when I'm weary of considerations,
> And life is too much like a pathless wood
> Where your face burns and tickles with the cobwebs
> Broken across it, and one eye is weeping
> From a twig's having lashed across it open.
> I'd like to get away from earth awhile
> And then come back to it and begin over.
> May no fate willfully misunderstand me
> And half grant what I wish and snatch me away
> Not to return. Earth's the right place for love:
> I don't know where it's likely to go better.
> I'd like to go by climbing a birch tree,
> And climb black branches up a snow-white trunk
> *Toward* heaven, till the tree could bear no more,
> But dipped its top and set me down again.
> That would be good both going and coming back.
> One could do worse than be a swinger of birches."

Though at such moments he has become so much himself that the rhythm is of course personal more than it is sectional, it still suggests, in its cadences, the sly, shy Yankee tongue.

3

If Robert Frost talks as becomes a Yankee poet, so does he think as becomes one. In particular there is his close attention to the objects he sees in his chosen world. He seems never to mention anything that he has merely glanced at. Whether it is a bit of "highway where the slow wheel pours the sand"; or "windfalls spiked with stubble and worm-eaten"; or ice-coated branches that "click upon themselves as the breeze rises"; or an "instep arch [that] not only keeps the ache, [but] keeps the pressure of a ladder round"; or the frost

> "that doesn't love a wall,
> That sends the frozen-ground-swell under it,
> And spills the upper boulders in the sun"

—no matter what the thing is that Mr. Frost's eye has seen, he has seen it with his undivided mind and heart. Moreover, he speaks of mowing, for instance, not as a man might who had seen such work done in another's meadow or picture, but as a mower who has done it himself, alert for stones in the grass and tired at the end of the day. He speaks of a cow in apple time or of a colt left out in the weather not as a member of a humane society, but as a farmer who knows the unruly ways of cows and the nervous ways of horses. He speaks of the dislike of Yankees for being told how they shall do their tasks or of the plight of a woman who faces the coming of madness in a life of unrelieved toil, not as a cynic or a spectator or a philanthropist, but as a neighbor of similar persons, well enough aware of their eccentricities, yet still held close to them by the bonds of a neighborly knowledge and affection.

Now, such knowledge and such affection, characteristic as they may be of Robert Frost as an individual, are also characteristic of his Yankee community. In a neighborhood left behind as this is, deserted by its more ambitious members, overrun by outsiders of another culture, the people have been united by a natural increment of passion for their nook of land. They may complain of the hardships they endure, but they would hunger and sicken if they went away. Thus circumscribed, they have grown ardently familiar with the details of their world. Thus disciplined by loneliness and nearness, they have learned to live together. Thoreau himself, the sharpest observer and the sharpest critic of the common life, was eager to be a good neighbor: he was willing to help work the roads that all men used; he would have been prompt to keep up his fences if he had had any. So Mr. Frost, a good neighbor, has drawn from daily Yankee examples a good deal of what he knows about the practice of poetry and the conduct of life.

In either matter he refuses to be vague. If rapture visits him, it must come in the company of something that can be seen or felt. What is it, he asks himself as he is mowing, that his scythe whispers?

"It was no dream of the gift of idle hours,
Or easy gold at the hand of fay or elf:
Anything more than the truth would have seemed too weak
To the earnest love that laid the swale in rows,
Not without feeble-pointed spikes of flowers
(Pale orchises), and scared a bright green snake.
The fact is the sweetest dream that labor knows."

And the fact, he might add, is the truest dream that poetry knows. Ideas, after all, are but dim lines drawn through unmapped regions from fact to fact; when all the facts shall have been found out, there will be no further need for ideas. Meanwhile poets understand that the love of reality is the root of most poetry. Diffuse love too much, and it loses meaning as well as power; fix it upon specific things, and they become first important and then representative. Always Mr. Frost reaches his magic through the door of actuality. "Sight and insight," he says, are the whole business of the poet. Let him see clearly enough, and understanding will be added.

A single short poem will serve to illustrate Mr. Frost's poetic method. Two generations of prose have labored to express the loneliness of New England winters, the pathos of empty houses, the desolation of old age, the cruelty of the cold. All this, and more, Mr. Frost, selecting one case only and omitting generalization or commentary, has distilled into fewer than thirty lines.

"All out of doors looked darkly in at him
Through the thin frost, almost in separate stars,
That gathers on the pane in empty rooms.
What kept his eyes from giving back the gaze
Was the lamp tilted near them in his hand.
What kept him from remembering what it was
That brought him to that creaking room was age.
He stood with barrels round him—at a loss.
And having scared the cellar under him
In clomping there, he scared it once again
In clomping off;—and scared the outer night,
Which has its sounds, familiar, like the roar
Of trees and crack of branches, common things,
But nothing so like beating on a box.
A light he was to no one but himself
Where now he sat, concerned with he knew what,
A quiet light, and then not even that.
He consigned to the moon, such as she was,
So late-arising, to the broken moon
As better than the sun in any case
For such a charge, his snow upon the roof,
His icicles along the wall to keep;
And slept. The log that shifted with a jolt
Once in the stove, disturbed him and he shifted,

> And eased his heavy breathing, but still slept.
> One aged man—one man—can't fill a house,
> A farm, a countryside, or if he can,
> It's thus he does it of a winter night."

The bare details are sufficient. They draw no sword, they wave no banner; but they steal upon the reader of the poem as if he were the observer of the scene, and stir him to insight into the essential drama of the situation by making his sight of it so vivid.

As sight and insight are connected in Mr. Frost's procedure, so are the practice of poetry and the conduct of life. He is neighbor, in a Yankee fashion, both to the things he sees and to the beings he sees into. He can smile, as he does in *Mending Wall*, at the peasant-witted farmer who keeps on repeating that "good fences make good neighbors," even though the maxim is something he has inherited, not discovered, and though at the moment the wall he is working at is useless; yet Mr. Frost only smiles, neither condescending nor philosophizing. He approaches his fellows through the fellowship of labor. In *The Tuft of Flowers* he tells how, once turning the hay in a meadow which another man had mowed before him, he thought with pain that men always are alone, "whether they work together or apart." But coming shortly upon a tuft of flowers which the mower had spared out of his delight in their beauty, the poet could

> "feel a spirit kindred to my own;
> So that henceforth I worked no more alone.
>
> But glad with him, I worked as with his aid,
> And weary, sought at noon with him the shade;
>
> And dreaming, as it were, held brotherly speech
> With one whose thought I had not hoped to reach.
>
> 'Men work together,' I told him from the heart,
> 'Whether they work together or apart.' "

In this lyrical apologue Mr. Frost is more explicit than almost anywhere else in his work. As a Yankee he may have too little general humanitarianism to be a patriot of the planet, but he is so much a neighbor that he can strike hands of friendship with the persons whom he encounters in his customary work. Other men may make wider acquaintances; other men may have, or feign, wider sympathies; for himself, he will continue to study what lies nearest him, confident that though remoter things may be larger, nearer things are surer.

4

Once Robert Frost's Yankee rhythm and Yankee attitude have been detected, his other qualities become less elusive. Has he failed to represent the whole of humanity in his work? He has not undertaken to do that. He has written about the things that interest him most. Has he found much of life drab and lonely? He has merely set down what he saw. At least, he has not been morbid. He is full of quiet fun, of the sense of windy pastures, of spicy roadside smells, of hardy souls busily at work, of drama unfolding naturally out of the movements of life. He dives into the Yankee back country and brings up fierce tales of sin and witchcraft; he dives into the Yankee character and brings up a cranky humor as well as a stern gravity, a longing for freedom and beauty and love as well as a deliberate endurance of hard fate. Puritan as his tradition may be, he singularly lacks the Puritan modes of judgment, and he sets forth departures from the common codes of Yankee life without rancor. He manages to seem to be a poet talking about his neighbors and still to be minding his own business. He is, to risk a paradox, both closer to his folk than are the summer visitors and further from it. That is, he is so close as not to think of explaining Yankees to the world, and so far as not to be sentimental about them.

Or, to put the matter in more literary terms, Robert Frost has given little of his power to commentary and much of it to creation. For this reason he suffers with that larger audience which a poet can hardly catch without doing something to digest his own work for it. In the long run, however, he has taken the better road. The New England temper has ordinarily thought that in literature it is better to comment than to create; it has produced more sermons than poems. Even Thoreau, whom Mr. Frost most resembles among New-Englanders, though he lived a life as clear-cut as that of some hero in a book, did not create such a person. He talked about his time without bodying it forth; he believed that he could tell the world more about Concord by discussing it and the world at large than by portraying some typical Yankee character or mood or drama. Mr. Frost has gone back of this discursive habit to the true way of the old Yankees themselves, as if he were the last of the Yankees and their essence; he has as a poet taken a leaf out of the book of men and women who would rather talk than sing, but who would also rather work than talk.

Science Can't Dishearten Poets, Says Robert Frost

Allen Shoenfield*

Has the scalpel of science within recent years probed so deeply into the mysteries of the air, the earth, and the waters beneath that all the phenomena of nature, stimulating the imagination of man from time immemorial, are at last reduced to "laws" and formulae? Is the unknown now so knowable that the poetic genius must seek in vain for the free play of his fancy?

Robert Frost, reckoned among the great of the world's living poets, who has returned to Ann Arbor to assume his unique position as Fellow in Letters on the University of Michigan faculty, would answer both questions with an emphatic negative.

Recently acquired knowledge, he declared in a chat following his arrival and marked with all his boyish enthusiasm, so far from clipping the wings of Pegasus has but spurred on the poet's classic steed to loftier flights. What if cold science has reduced the Jovian thunderbolt to a charge of electricity tearing earthward from the skies? What if the Homeric legend of a Cyclops is found based on the discovery by an ancient and ingenuous race of a mastodon's skull and the great blank socket of the one-eyed giant merely the trunk-cavity of the prehistoric beast? "Still, science offers just compensation," says Dr. Frost.

"Think of the great abysses opened up by our study of the atom. Think of the strange and unaccountable actions of the hurrying winds experienced by our travelers of the skies. Think of the marvels of marine life lately brought to us by the explorers of the distant oceans, each more wonderfully wrought than ever mermaid or water sprite of which the poets dreamed.

"Life has lost none of its mystery and its romance. The more we know of it, the less we know. Fear has always been a great stimulus to man's imagination. But fear is not the only stimulus. If science has expelled much of our fear, still there is left a thousand things from which to shape our dreams.

"Keats mourned that the rainbow, which as a boy had been for him a magic thing, had lost its glory because the physicists had found it resulted

*From *The Detroit News*, October 11, 1925. Reprinted by permission of the newspaper.

76

merely from the refraction of the sunlight by the raindrops. Yet knowledge of its causation could not spoil the rainbow for me. I am so sure that it is not given to man to be omniscient. There will always be something left to know, something left to excite the imagination of the poet and those attuned to the great world in which they live.

"Only in a certain type of small scientific mind can there be found cocksureness, a conviction that a solution to the riddle of the universe is just around the corner. There was, for example, Jacques Loeb, the French biologist, who felt he had within his grasp the secret of vitality. Give him but ten years and he would have it fast.

"He had the ten and ten more, and in ten more he was dead. Perhaps he knows more of the mystery of life now than ever he did before his passing.

"I have heard it cried that America has become a standardized nation and that Americans have long ago ceased to seek expression for their individuality. I do not believe it.

"It may be true that our breakfast food is made in one city, that our clothes are of the same cut and fashion and made by three or four clothiers, that we live in virtually the same sort of houses, possess the same general type of furniture, seek the same sort of amusements, drive the same makes of motor car, utter the same conversational idioms, and, it is said, think the same thoughts. I say this may be true and it may not. But even if it were, I am not fearful of uniformity, even though it led to external monotony. For this monotony can not go beyond externals. The ultimate things are too spiritual for that.

"Look at the sea. Where in all the world is there anything more monotonous—sky, water, wind, and a few boats perhaps? Yet, consider the literature that has come from the ocean, its mass, its kind, and its infinite variety. The very monotony of the sea has driven man in upon himself. Finding no variation in nature, he sought and found it in himself. That is why all our science, all our so-called civilization—our standardization, if you will—need never give the poet pause.

"Monotony? Have we not always had the same stars and the same sky above us, changing only in its shades of blue and gray and purple black? And who shall say that such themes are exhausted? Have we not always had love and passion, war and peace, summer and winter and spring and fall with us? And are these things unable longer to impel us to spiritual variations?"

The poet has only good-natured pity for the shortsightedness of those near-literati who bemoan the passing of "the good old days" and believe the nation committed to hopeless Babbitry because of its flivvers, radios, phonographs, motion-picture theaters, railroads, breakfast foods, ready-made clothes, telephones, newspapers.

"Why," he said with a laugh, "all these things are merely mixing machines. The nation owes to them its preservation.

"For one thing, you cannot have a fairly homogeneous people without presupposing some sort of uniformity. For another, you cannot have a people as far-flung as this, practising efficient self-government, without providing them first with rapid means of communication.

"In the days of the stagecoach some very well-grounded fears were entertained for the continued existence of the Republic. Since then our territory has expanded from ocean to ocean, and were it not that the people of California and Texas are as closely in touch with their representatives at Washington as are the citizens of New York and Florida, we might have good reason to fear for the worst."

Dr. Frost has spent his first days in Ann Arbor renewing old friendships made in 1921 and 1922 while holder of the University Fellowship in the Creative Arts. With Mrs. Frost he has engaged a charming house on the edge of town and, pending its complete furnishing, is living with Joseph A. Bursley, Dean of Students. During the present semester he plans to give a few open readings and to gather together a group with which to form a seminar in writing, starting next semester.

"This will have to be limited to about a dozen upperclassmen, I suppose," he said. "But I shall only want those people who would be writing anyway. There will be no assignments. I am just going to sit and listen to what they have written and talk things over with them.

"Please don't call this a course in 'creative' writing. I hate that word. Writing's writing and that's all there is to it."

Good Greek out of New England

Elizabeth Shepley Sergeant*

Robert Frost's spirit is native to all high, sweet-smelling, lonely slopes which command, as from a remove, the homes and the graves of men. Of such places he has seemed to me, ever since I first read *A Boy's Will*, the *genius loci*. If I watched long enough he might put off his trick of invisibility and show his head above a blueberry bush or a boulder. No doubt I have searched for him most persistently in the pastures below the ledgy shoulder of Chocorua, but I once thought I spied him in a sun-burned cliff city of New Mexico, and his elusive figure is associated with the high glare of Delphi, and with those jagged little peaks of southern France whence the scent of herbs rises like incense. Those who mistake his verse for a product local or provincial have been too literal. They have failed to catch the poet in his game of hide-and-seek. Frost does hide, if he can, in verse or out. The language of his poetry, though so markedly that of New England speech, is symbolic; his subject-matter, for all its clear geographical limits, is universal. Through the realism of the lines, stars and "charted meteors" are always piercing. Like his friend the Star-splitter, Frost seems once for all to have burned down his house for the in-surance, and spent the proceeds on a telescope,

> To satisfy a life-long curiosity
> About our place among the infinities.

He has been interrogating the heavens ever since. That may be the reason why he is still, as he puts it in "New Hampshire"—the most openly autobiographical of his poems—"a rascal," instead of the learned doctor or the celebrated bard he might be if he chose.

A kind of professor he has had to be in spite of himself, since most good Greeks—Frost almost admits himself one in "New Hampshire," as well as a plain farmer—from Socrates on have needed to add youth to their star-gazing. Frost affirms that he has "never earned a cent, save from and through verse. But for my first twenty years at it I earned a total of two hundred dollars." Farming and teaching, those two subsidiary occupations with which he has had almost as lifelong a connection as with the infinities, grew somehow out of his poems, as poems so surely grew out of them. In the early days it was more farming than teaching. Latterly it has been the other way about. Frost is too suspicious of formal learning to have become a pedagogue easily. It was not, so he tells, until he found the store-keeper at Derry, New Hampshire—where by the grace of a grandfather with no faith in the Muses he had that first farm of his—appraising his horse for the grocery bill that he decided to apply (with a poem) at Pinkerton Academy. He would prove to the world of men that he could have as much practical success as he wanted. But there was more for Frost in teaching than a solution of household economics, or we should not find him still trailing, in the Amherst hills or the Michigan flats, his troop of college boys.

Even when he consents to sit on a platform he has a vanishing and peripatetic look, and the doctrine he enunciates in his dry, sly, halting way is very different from the glib aestheticism his students might expect of a poet. Perfectionist and polisher of words though he is, he proclaims words to be "less than nothing unless they amount to deeds, as in ultimatums and battle cries." In poetry, as in life, there is no worth in being unless it is allied to doing. And what kind of professor is this who gives you no synthetic appreciations, and forces you to speculate? The day I saw him on an Amherst platform he was steering his class towards the reading of Emerson by asking it to define an "idealist." Is he a man who measures up from nothing, or one who measures down from everything? Might he be, especially if an artist, somewhere between the two? "I believe in what the Greeks called synecdoche: the philosophy of the part for the whole; skirting the hem of the goddess. All that an artist needs is samples. Enough success to know what money is like; enough love to know what women are like." Enough time, he might have added, for creative puttering; enough thin books of verse to fill half a foot of shelf. Frost is always bedevilling his students with questions, but never with one—this is his cardinal principle as an educator—which he can answer himself. For example this poser: How many things can you do to a poem besides read it or write it? The class found one hundred and eight. Compare the passage in "A Fountain":

> How had the tender verse escaped their outrage?
> By being invisible for what it was,
> Or else by some remoteness that defied them
> To find out what to do to hurt a poem.

One of the outstanding facts about Robert Frost is that he and his verse were buried for twenty years in the rocky quietude of New Hampshire. It is not so sure that even now college students—or for that matter college teachers, publishers, editors, critics, and friendly readers—know what to make of the cast of mind and spirit of a good Greek disguised as a Yankee sage.

The cast of feature bears out the cast of mind. If I could choose a sculptor from the antique world to mould Frost's head, I should vote for Skopas, who added shadows of human passion to calm Greek faces. In certain moods, this Frost face with its musing eyes, so deeply hollowed and shaded by sharp-drawn brows, seems touched by that pathetic hand. But again the poet's dream grows unified, grave, mystical-religious, and one says, here are a brow and eyes like Dante's. At the dinner in honour of Frost's fiftieth birthday at the Hotel Brevoort, in New York, he wore at first this marble Dantesque mask; coloured really like Carrara marble, with mauve and golden shadows, and shining with a clear Renaissance beauty of the Christian sort. Frost should have wrapped himself in a white Dominican gown to celebrate his half century. For he carried almost visibly the consecration and weight of his ascetic priesthood.

Yet it took only a featherweight of affection—all that the friends dared offer, since they had come, for the most part, with the hands that bore gifts tied behind their backs—to make tenderness flicker like flame over the still features, and shape itself in facial line; only a quip of New England humour to bring a gentle cynic out of hiding. Or shall I say a rustic deity? Eyebrows arch roundly, cheeks draw into shrewd, satiric wrinkles, eyes turn to flashes and darts of blue light, malicious or rejoicing, and as an unruly lock is tossed, one hears the stamp of a hoof—

> Pan came out of the woods one day.
> His skin and his hair and his eyes were grey . . .

Frost's skin and his rebellious hair have now a fine harmony of tone, "the grey of the moss of walls," a young and living greyness that, like a delicate lichen, softens without hiding the hard and eternal shape of the rock beneath.

> —a new-world song, far out of reach.

that is what the rascally Pan of the haunting Yankee pipe came out of the woods to play. Poetry has not flowed in a swelling stream from the pipe of Robert Frost; it has been distilled within him preciously, like heart's-blood, drop by drop. The verse reveals a keen warfare between the Puritan who thought shame of revelation, and the artist who had to speak out, a battle never wholly won or lost, yet probably serving him well. For the inhibitions and reticences of the Dantesque or Puritan Frost have imposed on the sensuous singing Frost that austere and elegant poetical outline of his. It is not as enigmatic as it seems to some of the young intellectuals that he should have preferred frugality to luxury in many realms of culture, knowledge, and experience. His anti-aesthetic prejudices, for instance, are essential to him. He does not want superlatives. A rather bare world suits him. His doubt of the trappings and self-indulgences of the artist, which has in it more of judgment than he usually allows himself (think how little there is in his New England narratives,) is a sort of armour to preserve his poetry intact. He will not talk of art in his poetry except in symbolic terms, as in "The Axe-helve," where he endows a French workman with desires and aims he can scarcely admit. And how deliberately he makes his artistic ego the butt of his malice:

> I'm what is called a sensibilitist,
> Or otherwise an environmentalist;
> In other words, I know wherever I am,
> Being the creature of literature I am,
> I shall not lack for pains to keep me awake.

("Not so you'd notice it," appends a Frostian note in pencil, "but still too much so for self-approval." *Self-approval*—there the Puritan shows his spots. The sensibility is, however, allowed.)

The satiric wrinkle that lifts the corner of his long upper lip tells the whole story. In the heart of his starkest tragedy we find the old New England effort to compromise ideals and facts, escaping either in shy tenderness and beauty or in a whimsical humour that often verges on irony. Consider for tenderness "An Old Man's Winter Night"—one of Frost's ultimates in the union of form and substance; for humour "A Hundred Collars," and you will see that what looks like fancy is no more nor less than a fact. Yes, there is something strong and steady in Frost's spirit which takes account of his compromises, and holds the twisted strands of his life together for one central purpose. The claim one makes for him of first-rateness—he will make few claims for himself—rests in part on his sureness and continuity of poetic development. In life he has turned from one task to another, but in verse he has stuck with piety to the clarification of his own tone of voice, his own form and matter. If he is "Greek" it is not that he is truly pagan, but only that he has known how to choose from the world exactly what he needed for himself and his song—for himself as a singer.

One of the things he needed and found was a normal human destiny. Born in San Francisco; brought up from the age of ten by a mother and a grandfather in Lawrence, Massachusetts; looking in—no more—at Dartmouth College; he married young a very true New England girl—a marriage preserved like treasure through the years—retired to his rustic isolation of farming and teaching, and had in time four children, now launched in their own life paths. In all these level solitary seasons Frost was writing poetry with solid faith in his mission, though editors seemed to make little of it. When he stole away with his family on his decisive voyage to England in 1912, at the age of thirty-eight, the world where reputations are made was none the wiser, and he himself was far from conceiving that triumphant return two years later after the English publication of *A Boy's Will,* and *North of Boston.* Yet here were the editors drawn up on the dock, hailing him as a leader of his generation in the "new poetry"; here were rewards and successes which made farming somewhat vicarious and gave teaching a privileged academic form; here was leisure to produce *Mountain Interval* and *New Hampshire.* These books reveal that neither the "new poetry" nor the new opportunity have taken Frost farther from his native base than the stride to Michigan. You can find just one English poem—if you look hard: "The Sound of Trees." Frost recognized early that, like his Census-taker, he wanted life to go on living; but he has sought it where he stood.

The life he found, as revealed in his books, has a pattern, a colour, above all a sound, that must vanish like mist in the prose telling. Its background is a landscape, pearly in tone, lonely to those who do not recognize its friendliness; northern New England, broken in outline, with views but not giant views, mountains but not too high ones, pastures, swamps, farms deserted and farms occupied. This land, to the spare human figures who move across it, is an extension and explanation of themselves, as the Irish country to the fairy folk. And these New Englanders are somehow "folk" in addition to being real people and even local "characters." They are planted here by necessity, their roots are tangled in the roots of elm and cedar, their wisdom is all garnered from natural things. Those who find Frost's poetry sad and grey probably cannot bear the sheer clarity he gives to human lives in this thin northern atmosphere of his, shut in by a moral and physical solitude, yet escaping through their barriers to grapple together in situations of love and hate and suffering typical and inevitable of New England but also of "the world in general."

The landscape background is already sharply etched in *A Boy's Will,* that slender lyrical volume that gives off, through its changing subjective moods, a delicate aroma of young happiness, all mingled with the sensuous love of earth. The exile of Derry Farm, his shadowy reliant bride beside him, meets the seasons and their tasks alone, with no soul to interfere. Though one notes a few uncertainties which the older Frost has left behind, here, already at his height, is the visual Frost, Frost the "gloater"—"poetry is gloating"—who has the power to look so hard at things that they come to life—as in "The Vantage Point":

> My breathing shakes the bluet like a breeze,
>   I smell the earth, I smell the bruiséd plant,
>   I look into the crater of the ant.

And here is Frost of the "concrete vocal image," already finding his own tones of speech—as in "Mowing," the first "talk song" he was aware of, or in "My November Guest." And Frost the artificer of tight and subtle verse form—in this respect he has never surpassed "Storm Fear":

> When the wind works against us in the dark,
> And pelts with snow
> The lower chamber window on the east,
> And whispers with a sort of stifled bark,
> The beast,
>   "Come out! Come out!"—
> It costs no inward struggle not to go,
> Ah, no!
> I count our strength,
> Two and a child,
> Those of us not asleep subdued to mark
> How the cold creeps as the fire dies at length,—
> How drifts are piled,
> Dooryard and road ungraded,
> Till even the comforting barn grows far away,
> And my heart owns a doubt
> Whether 'tis in us to arise with day
> And save ourselves unaided.

The book tells how a youth "was scared away from life and came back to it through a poem." The youth was "consumed with stars at fifteen, with flowers at twenty," as he tells elsewhere, "matter of history," and the poem was "The Tuft of Flowers":

> A leaping tongue of bloom the scythe had spared—

the scythe of an unknown reaper who thus restored Frost to his comradeship in the gregarious universe. On such fragilities do the lives of poets hang in literal fact. "Got me my first real job. Whole family owe their life to this poem and they'd better believe it."

"Mending Wall," the first poem in *North of Boston*, takes up the psychological theme where "A Tuft of Flowers" laid it down:

> Something there is that doesn't love a wall,
> That sends the frozen-ground-swell under it,
> And spills the upper boulders in the sun;
> And makes gaps even two can pass abreast.

Here is an older and more objective Frost, who has squarely accepted his human fate and seen himself for only a half-rustic, questioning, as he works on his side of the gaps, the true farmer's aphorism: "Good fences make good neighbours."

> My apple-trees will never get across
> And eat the cones under his pines, I tell him.

A characteristic accent, which would be recognizable at the Antipodes as Robert Frost. And how profoundly imagined the neighbour, symbol of a whole country race:

Bringing a stone grasped firmly by the top
In each hand, like an old stone savage armed.
He moves in darkness as it seems to me,
Not of woods only and the shade of trees.
He will not go behind his father's saying,
And he likes having thought of it so well
He says again: "Good fences make good neighbours."

And so a conversation between two men about stone walls is really concerned with the life force, always building and breaking down, and serves as introduction to a book of searching human revelation.

The New England narratives in *North of Boston* established Frost's poetic majority. They were too fresh, mordant, unsentimental, to be read without a shock of recognition. Frost illumines character not by comment or explanation but through crisis. He is a dramatist rather than a story-teller. "Drama is all; a poem must create situation as much as a play"—and he lives up to it, even in a lyric of a butterfly. The diverse crises in marital relations summarized in "Home Burial," "The Death of the Hired Man," "The House-keeper," "A Servant to Servants,' might be dealt with at the pace of *Jude the Obscure*. Frost epitomizes them, without sacrificing that flavour of talk which helps to give the poems their air of pastoral leisure. He has transformed blank verse into a fluid instrument of his own idiomatic speech, pungent and taciturn, a speech sharpened and mellowed with a humour that strikes always through its mark of literal fact. In these and the similar narratives of people in later volumes the verse is an element of the originality inherent in spirit and structure alike. Another is Frost's oblique method of dealing with grim realism. However unescapable the horror—recall, for instance, the superb passage of "A Servant to Servants," where the woman who is losing her own hold on reality tells how for her mother as a bride "love things" were involved with the madness of her husband's brother, in his cage in an upper room—a tenderness as generic as sunshine, and as uncritical, seems to play about the bitter truths. In the same way the homespun background, the bucolic detail, is transformed and sublimated by a kind of abstract beauty and detachment, like the abstract quality of Frost's sculptured head as rendered in Du Chêne's fine bust, reproduced in the books. If Virgil had been a plain dirt farmer he could hardly have written the Eclogues. So with Frost and his dramatic pastorals at Derry, Franconia, and South Shaftesbury, Vermont.

The analogy with Virgil was made by Frost himself. In my copy of the *Selected Poems*—a volume which should be more familiar to the public—he writes: " 'Black Cottage,' 'The House-keeper,' 'The Death of the Hired Man,' date from 1905" (his thirtieth year); "Virgil's Eclogues may have had something to do with them." And again, in the section containing "Mending Wall," "The Mountain," and other definitely pastoral poems: "First heard the voice from a printed page in a Virgilian Eclogue and *Hamlet*. Influenced by what I have supposed *Piers Plowman* to be. Never read it." To ladies who claim that they are "interested in the 'new poetry' but cannot understand it"—"That gives me a feeling in my arm, just in my arm!" Frost is likely to explain that Barnyard Verse goes back at least to the first poem in *The Oxford Book of English Verse*. He also enjoys the story of the agricultural college which pronounced "Good-Bye and Keep Cold"—a poem of an orchard—"pomologically accurate," while offering to amend the verse. His irony would spurn any over-estimation of "influences." Yet consider the opening of "The Mountain":

> The mountain held the town as in a shadow.
> I saw so much before I slept there once:
> I noticed that I missed stars in the west,
> Where its black body cut into the sky.
> Near me it seemed: I felt it like a wall
> Behind which I was sheltered from a wind.

Here is a spacious mood established in a few lines, a love relation predicated between a man and a mountain; and as the rhythmic pattern unfolds, the reader is transplanted into a realm of brooding tranquillity. The poem was written "with one stroke of the pen," as were three other favourites from the later volumes—Frost hopes one day to publish the four together—"Birches," "Two Look at Two," and that perfect lyric, "Stopping by Woods on a Snowy Evening." In all the same exquisite inter-transfusion between man and nature, the same allusiveness which starts long whispering echoes in the mind and heart, the same cherishing of an objective image in a poet's dream and fantasy until it is ready to flow out upon the page at last in calm and eternal shape.

Let those who will debate Frost's place in the old poetry or the new: what makes him, as I believe, one of the few authentic poets of his age is that he is (as I began by saying) a star-gazer, who writes for the satisfaction of his own curiosity. Every poem is a fresh discovery. The general shape of his curiosity was fixed in those first two volumes. Frost has not tried to change it—indeed he has tried not to, since the aim of an artist, to him, is the "undrossing" of himself. *Mountain Interval* and *New Hampshire* are not pioneering but fulfilment; they extract new and rich treasure from known veins of ore, lyrical and narrative, as the poet's life has been enriched and eased but not basically altered by success and geniality. Greater preoccupation with the vocal side of verse we do find: here Frost intuitively feels himself to be most himself. To translate the actual shape and sound of living speech into poetry is the chief aim of his prime.

> All the fun is how you say a thing.

Comment: "And the chance it gives you for tones of voice."

Frost is theorizing about poetry. See him stretched out in the sweet-fern, under a bountiful August sun, eyes and shirt coloured like juniper, hair shaded like grey bark, eyebrows of a rogue, lips of a caustic wit. He is soliloquizing to one of those projections of his wandering self—maybe the Gum-gatherer.

They call me a New England dialect poet. . . . Not so you'd notice it. It was never my aim to keep to any special speech unliterary, vernacular or slang. I lay down no law to myself there. What I have been after from the first, consciously and unconsciously, is tones of voice. I've wanted to write down certain brute throat noises so that no one could miss them in my sentences. I have been guilty of speaking of sentences as a mere notation for indicating them. I have counted on doubling the meaning of my sentences with them. They have been my observation and my subject-matter.

I know what I want to do most. I don't do it often enough. In "The Runaway" I added the moral at the end just for the pleasure of the aggrieved tone of voice. There are high spots in respect of vocal image in "Blueberries":

> There *had* been some berries—but those were all gone.
> He didn't say where they had been. He went on:
> "I'm sure—I'm sure"—as polite as could be.

Frost the shrewd, lounging rascal, has vanished behind the junipers. In his place I fancy I see an austere, hieratical figure, serving a rustic altar with a ritual of his own making. And these are some of the ritualistic words:

Imagery and after-imagery are about all there is to poetry. Synecdoche and synecdoche——My motto is that something has to be left to God.

In making a poem you have no right to think of anything but the subject-matter. After making it, no right to boast of anything but the form.

A poem must at least be as good as the prose it might have been. A poem is a box with a *set* or assortment of sentences that just fit together to fill it. You are rhyming sentences and phrases, not just words. They must go into it as unchanged in size and shape as the words.

A straight crookedness is most to be desired in a stick or a line. Or a crooked straightness. An absolutely abandoned zigzag that goes straight to the mark.

See him standing on his hill-top, this Virgilian who, for all his crooked, New England speech has made the ancient renunciation, and for all his love of earth left earth behind. Remember "Into My Own," the first poem in A Boy's Will, which is also the last in the Selected Poems:

> One of my wishes is that those dark trees,
> So old and firm they scarcely show the breeze,

Were not, as 'twere, the merest mask of gloom,
But stretched away unto the edge of doom.

I should not be withheld but that some day
Into their vastness I should steal away,
Fearless of ever finding open land,
Or highway where the slow wheel pours the sand.

I do not see why I should e'er turn back. . . .

Against this Robert Frost has written: "This began it. *Exeo*."

The World of Robert Frost

Granville Hicks*

In one of the poems in his "West Running Brook," Frost says,

> I have been one acquainted with the night.
> I have walked out in rain—and back in rain.
> I have outwalked the furthest city light.

He has known, he would tell us, what the world has to offer of pain and sorrow. He is not unfamiliar with the experiences that make men grieve and despair. If he has kept his sanity, it is not because he has blinded himself to the elements in life that make men mad. But to him as a poet the most important result of his acquaintance with sorrow has been the realization that the exercise of the creative faculties is independent of circumstance—

> And further still at an unearthly height
> One luminary clock against the sky
> Proclaimed the time was neither wrong nor right.
> I have been one acquainted with the night.

This is vigorous doctrine in an age that has been fertile in self-analysis and self-commiseration. Frost's credo, however, runs counter to the consensus of opinion of the critics of all ages as well as to the temper of his own era. Matthew Arnold summarized the verdict of most students of letters when he said, "For the creation of a master work of literature two powers must concur, the power of the man and the power of the moment, and the man is not enough without the moment." Wordsworth said something of the same sort, and perhaps came closer to the difficulties of our own time, when he pointed out that facts and ideas have to become familiar to mankind, have to become part of common human experience, before the poet can use them. The poet cannot accept them until they are "ready to put on, as it were, a form of flesh and blood." So much in modern life has not been assimilated to organized human experience, so many of our acts and thoughts are unrelated to any central purpose or unifying hypothesis,

*Review of *Collected Poems*. From *The New Republic*, December 3, 1930. Copyright 1930 by *The New Republic*.

89

so many obstacles stand in the way of the much-discussed modern synthesis, that the poet must grow desperate who looks for the order of ideas, the intellectual and spiritual atmosphere, that Arnold says he needs. It is no wonder that most poets and critics would say that a time may indeed be either wrong or right and that the present time is decidedly wrong.

So strong is the case for this view of literature that we may omit the task of defending it in detail, and, instead, ask ourselves how it is possible for Frost to hold the contrary opinion. The answer is to be found, of course, not in any critical writings of his but in his poetry. "Collected Poems" shows and shows clearly that Frost has written as fine poetry as any living American and that the proportion of first-rate poetry to the whole is greater than that in the work of any other contemporary. This last point is important, not because quantity matters, but because so many American poets, after a brief productive period, have slipped into silence or mediocrity. The fact that Frost's power is not only intense but also sustained forces us either to accept his theory or find some other explanation of his achievements.

What the other explanation may be is suggested when we realize how compact and unified Frost's work is. Instead of writing about this aspect of our civilization and that, instead of yielding himself to the casual inspirations of unrelated phenomena, he has occupied himself with a limited body of experiences. He has, in short, found, for poetic purposes, a world of his own. In so doing he is not, obviously, alone among contemporary poets: Robinson, Aiken, Eliot, each has his own world. But Frost's world is different from the world of any of these other poets, in that it is related to a real world with definite boundaries in time and space. That is why his poetry is more substantial than the poetry of any of the others, why his people are three-dimensional, why his figures of speech are always concrete and non-literary. His world is not an artificial, intellectual abstraction from the real world; it is set apart from the rest of the world by geographical and historical facts. Of course his world is not to be completely identified with the rural New Hampshire of the maps and books of statistics; it is, after all, his world. But it is directly related to rural New Hampshire, as Dante's world was directly related to medieval Europe and Shakespeare's to Elizabethan England.

Let us enter Frost's world and examine its advantages for the poet. What we do not find is perhaps more important than what we do. We find, in the first place, nothing of industrialism, and since at present so many of both the demands and the accomplishments of the machine are unrelated to the permanent hopes and impulses of the human heart, the absence of this phenomenon is significant for the poet. In the second place, we look in vain for evidences of the disrupting effect that scientific hypotheses have had on modern thought. The natives may have heard that

> "The trouble with the Mid-Victorians
> Seems to have been a man named John L. Darwin."

But the fundamental problems of conduct and destiny are still considered in terms older and richer in emotional connotations than the phraseologies of Darwinian biology and Einsteinian physics:

> "Go 'long," said I to him, he to his horse.

Frost, living in that world, can afford to look with amusement on the bewildered modern—

> A baggy figure, equally pathetic
> When sedentary and when peripatetic.

Finally, to take a third example of the absence in Frost's world of some of the less assimilable factors in our civilization, there is the matter of Freudianism. He is still free to treat love in the language of an era before psychoanalysis was known. When he is in New York he may be told,

> "Choose you which you will be—a prude, or puke,
> Mewling and puking in the public arms."

But he can reply,

> "Me for the hills where I don't have to choose."

It remains to summarize briefly some of the things that can be found in Frost's world. For purposes of his narrative verse he can find not merely pathos but also, because there are certain standards implicit in that world, something close to tragedy. He can find subjects for comedy there, dramatic conflicts, objects of natural beauty. He can treat abnormality and yet keep it in its place, or he can find a theme for as illuminating a commentary on failure as Robinson ever wrote. In the contemplation of nature he can, as scores of lyrics show, find the beginnings of paths that lead straight to the problems that have perennially perplexed the mind of man. He can, in short, find opportunity and stimulus to exercise to the full the poetic imagination.

There is one thing, of course, Frost cannot do: he cannot contribute directly to the unification, in imaginative terms, of our culture. He cannot give us the sense of belonging in the industrial, scientific, Freudian world in which we find ourselves. The very limitations that are otherwise so advantageous make it impossible. That is why no one would think of maintaining that he is one of the great poets of the ages. To that extent the time, even though he refuses to lay the responsibility at its door, is not right. But, if the time is so completely wrong as there is reason to suspect, no poet, however great his genius, could render that ultimate service of the imagination. Every poet today is necessarily a limited poet. Frost's relative greatness lies in the fact that, endowed with the power, he discovered a way to make the time as favorable for the exercise of that power as it could possibly be. He told the story himself when he said of the star in the stone boat—

> Such as it is, it promises the prize
> Of the one world complete in any size
> That I am like to compass, fool or wise.

He compassed it, and we should be considerably the poorer if he had not.

Robert Frost's New Poems

Horace Gregory*

For the past five or six years. Mr. Frost's critics have done him a curious disservice. They have insisted, both by implication and emphatic reassertion, that his poetry is the work of a major poet; they have assured us that Mr. Frost must take an embarrassed stand as the inheritor of a New England tradition which at its best includes the names of Emerson, Whittier and the recently rediscovered metaphysical poet, Jones Very. I doubt if Mr. Frost pretends to any such eminence, for to do so would place his work at singular disadvantage. If he were to step at any point crossing the paths of Emerson and Whittier he would be forced to carry an unwelcome load of social responsibility—and even, God save him!—give up forever "My own strategic retreat" and an obscure desire for a "one-man revolution."

No, Mr. Frost is not the kind of poet, major or otherwise, that his critics have imagined him to be. I prefer to think of him in another set of associations where his virtues are more positive and his gains more genuine. I think of him as the last survivor of the "Georgian movement" which ran its course in England from 1911 to 1921. Of the poetry published during the first years of that period "A Boy's Will" was easily the best; it was Robert Frost, the American, who was to compress into one short line the philosophy of the entire movement: "Turn the poet out of door." His great advantage over his English contemporaries (such poets as Edward Thomas, Wilfred Gibson and W. H. Davies) was a quick ear for the use of the common words in everyday speech that are the property of uncommon poetry; and he has never lost his skill in using them, retaining even in his present book the familiar tang of Yankee vernacular.

Perhaps the title of his new book, "A Further Range," is half ironic; if not, I believe that he has heard too clearly the siren call of his unwise critics. It has always been Mr. Frost's particular virtue to make molehills out of mountains, to dig sharply, clearly and not too deeply into New England soil; so far as he has done this well, his integrity remains unquestioned. Beyond this range, however, he becomes self-defensive and ill in-

*Review of A Further Range. From The New Republic, June 24, 1936, p. 214. Copyright 1936 by The New Republic.

formed; I refer to "Build Soil—A Political Pastoral," "To a Thinker," "A Lone Striker" and those thinly disguised platitudes in "Ten Mills"—all included in the present volume. If Mr. Frost sincerely wishes to identify himself with "A Drumlin Woodchuck" (one of the better poems in the book), to be "more secure and snug," why does he trouble his head about further ranges into politics, where his wisdom may be compared to that of Calvin Coolidge?

There are two poems in this collection of fifty-one that are memorable examples of Mr. Frost's happiest insights and abilities: they are "The Master Speed" and "Provide Provide."

Frost: A Dissenting Opinion

Malcolm Cowley*

I

Robert Frost has been heaped with more official and academic honors than any other American poet, living or dead. Although he was never graduated from college, having left Dartmouth after two months and Harvard after two years (and more credit to his dogged independence), he holds by the last count seventeen honorary degrees. He was twice made a Master of Arts (by Amherst and Michigan), three times a Doctor of the Humanities (by Vermont, Wesleyan and St. Lawrence) and twelve times a Doctor of Letters (by Yale, Middlebury, Bowdoin, New Hampshire, Columbia, Williams, Dartmouth, Bates, Pennsylvania, Harvard, Colorado and Princeton). He has been chosen as a Phi Beta Kappa poet by Tufts, William and Mary, Harvard (twice) and Columbia. He has been a professor at Amherst; a poet in residence and a fellow in letters at Michigan; a Charles Eliot Norton professor, a Ralph Waldo Emerson fellow and a fellow in American civilization at Harvard, all these being fairly lucrative appointments. He has been awarded four Pulitzer Prizes, one more than E. A. Robinson and two more than Stephen Vincent Benét, the only other poets to be named more than once. He has also received the Loines Prize for poetry, the Mark Twain medal, the gold medal of the National Institute of Arts and Letters and the silver medal of the Poetry Society of America. His work has been the subject of at least two full-length critical studies, many brochures, pamphlets, bibliographies and a memorial volume, "Recognition of Robert Frost," not to mention hundreds of essays which, with some discordant notes in the early years, have ended as a vast diapason of praise.

And Frost deserves all these honors, both for his poetry in itself and for a long career devoted to the art of verse. In a country where poets go to seed, he has kept his talent ready to produce perfect blossoms (together with some that are misshapen or overgrown). It is a pleasure to name over

*From *The New Republic,* September 11, 1944, pp. 312–13 and September 18, 1944, pp. 345–47. Copyright 1944 by *The New Republic.*

the poems of his youth and age that become more vivid in one's memory with each new reading: the dramatic dialogues like "The Death of the Hired Man" and "The Witch of Coös," besides half a dozen others almost equally good; the descriptions or narrations that turn imperceptibly into Aesop's fables, like "The Grindstone" and "Cow in Apple Time"; and, best of all, the short lyrics like "The Pasture," "Now Close the Windows," "The Sound of the Trees," "Fire and Ice," "Stopping by the Woods on a Snowy Evening" (always a favorite with anthologists), "To Earthward," "Tree at My Window," "Acquainted with the Night," "Neither out Far Nor in Deep," "Beech," "Willful Homing," "Come In" . . . and I could easily add to the list. One of his best lyrics was written in 1892, when Frost was a freshman at Dartmouth; three or four others were included in his latest book, "The Witness Tree," published just fifty years later; and these recent poems show more skill and density of expression than almost anything he had written before. This same volume and the one that preceded it—"A Further Range," published in 1936—also contain bad poems that have been almost equally admired: long monologues in pedestrian blank verse, spoken as if from a cracker barrel among the clouds, and doggerel anecdotes directed (or rather, indirected) against the New Deal; but a poet has the right to be judged by his best work, and Frost at his best has added to our little store of authentic poetry.

If in spite of this I still say that there is a case against him and room for a dissenting opinion, perhaps I chiefly mean that there is a case against the zealous admirers who are not content to take the poet for what he is, but insist on using him as a sort of banner for their own moral or political crusades.

We have lately been watching the growth in this country of a narrow nationalism that has spread from politics into literature (although its literary adherents are usually not political isolationists). They demand, however, that American literature should be affirmative, optimistic, uncritical and "truly of this nation." They have been looking round for a poet to exalt; and Frost, through no fault of his own (but chiefly through the weaker qualities of his work), has been adopted as their symbol. Some of the honors heaped on him are less poetic than political. He is being praised too often and with too great vehemence by people who don't like poetry. And the result is that his honors shed very little of their luster on other poets, who in turn feel none of the pride in his achievements that a battalion feels, for example, when one of its officers is cited for outstanding services. Instead Frost is depicted by his admirers as a sort of Sunday-school paragon, a saint among miserable sinners. His common sense and strict Americanism are used as an excuse for berating and belittling other poets, who have supposedly fallen into the sins of pessimism, obscurity, obscenity and yielding to foreign influences; we even hear of their treachery to the American dream. Frost, on the other hand, is depicted as loyal, autochthonous and almost aboriginal. We are told not only that he is "the purest classical poet of America today"—and there is some truth in Gorham B. Munson's early judgment—but also that he is "the one great American poet of our time" and "the only living New Englander in the great tradition, fit to be placed beside Emerson, Hawthorne and Thoreau."

But when Frost is so placed and measured, his stature seems greatly diminished; it is almost as if a tough little Morgan horse, the best of its breed, had been judged by the standards that apply to Clydesdales and Percherons. Height, breadth and strength: he falls short in all these qualities of the great New Englanders. And the other quality for which he is often praised, his utter faithfulness to the New England spirit, is not one of the virtues they knowingly cultivated. They realized that the New England spirit, when it stands alone, is inclined to be narrow and arithmetical. It has reached its finest growth only when cross-fertilized with alien philosophies.

Hinduism, Sufism, Fourierism and German Romanticism: each of these doctrines contributed its own share to the New England renaissance of the 1850's. Even Thoreau, who died almost in sight of his birthplace, said that he had traveled much in Concord; he spoke of bathing his intellect "in the stupendous and cosmogonal philosophy of the Bhagvat-Geeta. . . . The pure Walden water," he said, "is mingled with the sacred water of the Ganges." And Hawthorne, who told us that "New England is quite as large a lump of earth as my heart can really take in," was eager for any new ideas that might help to explain the nature of New Englanders as individuals or as members of society. The books he borrowed from the Salem Athenaeum during the ten lonely years he spent at home included the complete works, in French, of Rousseau, Voltaire (several times), Pascal, Racine (several times) and the "Essais" of Montaigne, as well as a great number of volumes on science, philosophy, general history and the past of New England. [These facts about Hawthorne are taken from F. O. Matthiessen's "American Renaissance," a book that has never been sufficiently praised—M. C.] Some of his weaker contemporaries were quite unbalanced by the foreign learning with which they overloaded their minds; but the stronger ones assimilated everything and, in the end, reasserted their own New England natures, which had become immensely richer.

And even Frost, as purely Yankee as his character seems today, was partly formed by his three years abroad. The turning point in his life was when he sold his first New Hampshire farm (which his grandfather had bought for him on condition that he live there at least ten years) and when, in 1912, his wife said, "Let's go to England and live under thatch." In England he made the reputation that enabled him to continue his career as a poet (and also as a "poet in residence"). In England, too, he had the experience of meeting other poets who understood what he was trying to say: Lascelles Abercrombie, Rupert Brooke, Wilfred Wilson

Gibson and Edward Thomas. They were willing to learn from him, and Frost, in a sense, learned even more from them: that is, he learned to abandon the conventional language of the Late Victorians and to use his own speech without embarrassment. It is interesting to compare "A Boy's Will," published in London but written in New Hampshire before his English journey, with "Mountain Interval," published after his return to this country in 1915 but written chiefly in England. The poems in "A Boy's Will" gave his own picture of the world, but in the language of the genteel poets; they were full of "maidens pale," "sweet pangs" and "airy dalliance." The poems written in the English countryside used the language that is spoken north of Boston. Once it had been regarded as a mere dialect only to be used in ballads like "Skipper Ireson's Ride" and in satirical comments like "The Biglow Papers"; but Frost in England had done what Hemingway would later do in Paris: he had raised his own idiom to the dignity of a literary language.

It was after his return that he carried the process further. Having learned to write New Hampshire, he also began to think New Hampshire, in the sense of accepting its older customs as immutable laws. But this subject of Frost as a social philosopher and, at his worst, a Calvin Coolidge of poetry is one that I should like to discuss next week.

II

In spite of his achievements as a narrative and lyric poet—some of which I mentioned last week—there is a case against Robert Frost as a social philosopher in verse and as a representative of the New England tradition. He is too much walled in by the past. Unlike the great Yankees of an earlier age, he is opposed to innovations in art, ethics, science, industry or politics. Thus, in one of his longer blank-verse monologues, he bridles when he hears a "New York alec" discussing Freudian psychology, which Frost dismisses as "the new school of the pseudo-phallic." Elsewhere he objects to researches in animal behavior (which he calls "instituting downward comparisons"), to new inventions (saying that ingenuity should be held in check) and even to the theory of evolution—or at least he ridicules one farmer who speaks of it admiringly, whereas he sympathizes with another who stops him on the road to say:

> The trouble with the Mid-Victorians
> Seems to have been a man named John L. Darwin.

New ideas seem worse to him if they come from abroad, and worst of all if they come from Russia. He is continually declaiming against the Russians of all categories: the pessimistic Russians, the revolutionary Russians, the collectivistic Russians, the five-year-planning Russians: he seems to embrace them all in a global and historical dislike that extends from Dostoevsky to Dnieperstroy. He is horrified by the thought that New

England might be exposed to the possibility of adopting any good or bad feature of the Russian program. Thus, after reading about a project for rural rehabilitation, he hastened to write:

> It is in the news that all these pitiful kin
> Are to be bought out and mercifully gathered in
> To live in villages next to the theatre and store
> Where they won't have to think for themselves any more;
> While greedy good-doers, beneficent beasts of prey,
> Swarm over their lives, enforcing benefits
> That are calculated to soothe them out of their wits,
> And by teaching them how to sleep the sleep all day,
> Destroy their sleeping at night the ancient way.

Sometimes Frost decides that it would be a relief "To put these people at one stroke out of their pain"—these people being the marginal farmers; then next day he wonders how it would be if someone offered to put an end to his own troubles. The upshot is that he proposes to do nothing whatever, being satisfied with the New England countryside as it is—or rather, as it was in his early manhood—and outraged by anyone who tries to improve it.

Yet there are other poems in which he suggests that his faithfulness to "the ancient way" is more a matter of habit than conviction. In "The Black Cottage," he remembers an old woman who had lost her husband in the Civil War and who used to say (in her "quaint phrase," as Frost calls it) that all men were created free and equal. The old woman was also an orthodox Christian, and her presence in church kept the minister from changing any phrases in the Creed. The minister says, recalling "her old tremulous bonnet in the pew":

> I'm just as glad she made me keep hands off,
> For, dear me, why abandon a belief
> Merely because it ceases to be true.
> Cling to it long enough, and not a doubt
> It will turn true again.

Although the minister is speaking, he seems to express Frost's attitude toward the old New England standards. The poet is more conventional than convinced, more concerned with prudence than with virtue, and very little concerned with sin or suffering; you might say that he is more Puritan, or even prudish, than he is Christian. All the figures in his poems are decently draped; all the love affairs (except in a very late narrative, "The Subverted Flower") are etherealized or intellectualized; and although he sometimes refers to very old adulteries, it is only after they have been wrapped in brown paper and locked away in cupboards. On the other hand, there is little in his work to suggest Christian charity or universal brotherhood under God. He wants us to understand once and for all that he is not his brother's keeper:

> I have none of the tenderer-than-thou
> Collectivistic regimenting love
> With which the modern world is being swept

—and the ancient world was also swept, in the first centuries after Christ. There is one of his narratives, "Two Tramps in Mud Time," that has often been praised for the admirable lesson with which it ends; and yet a professor told me not long ago that his classes always seemed vaguely uncomfortable when they heard it read aloud. It was first published in 1934, and it deals with what seems to have been an incident of the depression years. The poet tells us that he was working in his dooryard on an April day between winter and spring; he was splitting great blocks of straight-grained beech with a lively sense of satisfaction. Two tramps came walking down the muddy road. One of them said, "Hit them hard," and then lingered by the roadside, suggesting wordlessly that he might take the poet's job for pay. The poet assumed that they had spent the winter in a lumber camp, that they were now unemployed and that they had slept "God knows where last night." In life the meeting may have had a different sequel. Perhaps the poet explained to the homeless men that he liked to split his own wood, but that he had other work for them to do; or perhaps he invited them into the kitchen for a slab of home-baked bread spread thick with apple butter. In the poem, however, he lets them walk away without a promise or a penny; and perhaps that explains why a college class—west of the Alleghanies, at least—cannot hear it read without feeling uneasy. Instead of helping these men who wanted to work, Frost turns to the reader with a sound but rather sententious sermon on the ethical value of the chopping block:

> But yield who will to their separation,
> My object in living is to unite
> My avocation and my vocation
> As my two eyes make one in sight.
> Only where love and need are one,
> And the work is play for mortal stakes,
> Is the deed ever really done
> For heaven and the future's sakes.

The meter and tone of the passage remind us of another narrative poem written in New England almost a hundred years before; but "The Vision of Sir Launfal" had a different moral to point:

> Now what we give but what we share,
> For the gift without the giver is bare;
> Who gives himself with his alms feeds three,
> Himself, his hungering neighbor and me.

What Frost sets before us is an ideal, not of charity or brotherhood, but of separateness. "Keep off each other and keep each other off," he tells us in "Build Soil." "We're too unseparate out among each other. . . . Steal away and stay away." In some of his poems he faintly suggests Emerson, and yet he is preaching only half the doctrine of self-reliance, which embraced the community as well as the individual. Emerson said, for example, "He only who is able to stand alone is qualified for society," thus implying that the self-reliant individual was to use his energies for social ends. Frost, on the other hand, makes no distinction between separateness and self-centeredness. In his poems, fine as the best of them are, the social passions of the great New Englanders are diverted into narrower channels. One cannot imagine him thundering against the Fugitive Slave Law, like Emerson; or rising like Thoreau to defend John Brown after the Harper's Ferry raid; or even conducting a quietly persistent campaign against brutality on American ships, as Hawthorne did when he was consul at Liverpool. He is concerned chiefly with himself and his near neighbors, or rather with the Yankees among his neighbors (for although his section of New England is largely inhabited by Poles and French Canadians, there are only two poems in which these foreigners are mentioned). He says when splitting his straight-grained beech blocks:

> The blows that a life of self-control
> Spares to strike for the common good
> That day, giving a loose to my soul,
> I spent on the unimportant wood;

—and one feels that these blows might symbolize the inward or backward turning of energies in a region that once had wider horizons.

And Frost does not strive toward greater depth to compensate for what he lacks in breadth; he does not strike far inward into the wilderness of human nature. It is true that he often talks about the need for inwardness. He says, for example, in "Build Soil," which for all its limitations of doctrine is the best of his long philosophical poems and perhaps the only one worth preserving:

> We're always too much out or too much in.
> At present from a cosmical dilation
> We're so much out that the odds are against
> Our ever getting inside in again;

—yet still he sets limits on the exploration of himself, as he sets them on almost every other human activity; here again he displays the sense of measure and decorum that puts him in the classical, or rather the neoclassical, tradition. He is always building defenses against the infinite, walls that stand "Between too much and me." In the woods, there is a pile of rocks and an iron stake to mark the limit of his land; and here too:

> One tree, by being deeply wounded,
> Has been impressed as Witness Tree
> And made commit to memory
> My proof of being not unbounded.

The woods play a curious part in Frost's poems; they seem to be his symbol for the uncharted country within ourselves, full of possible beauty, but also full of horror. From the woods at dusk, you might hear the hidden music of the brook, "a slender, tinkling fall"; or you might see wood creatures, a buck and a doe, looking at you over the stone fence that marks the limit of the pasture lot. But you don't cross the fence, except in dreams; and then, instead of brook or deer, you are likely to meet a strange Demon rising "from his wallow to laugh." And so, for fear of the Demon, and also because of your moral obligations, you merely stand at the edge of the woods to listen:

> Far in the pillared dark
> Thrush music went—
> Almost like a call to come in
> To the dark and lament.
>
> But no, I was out for stars:
> I would not come in.
> I meant, not even if asked,
> And I hadn't been.

But Hawthorne before him, timid and thin and conventional as he was in many of his tales, still plucked up his courage and ventured into the inner wilderness; and Conrad Aiken's poems (to mention one example of New England work today) are written almost wholly from within that haunted mid-region. To explore the real horrors of the mind is a long tradition in American letters, one that goes back to our first professional novelist, Charles Brockden Brown. He said in one of his letters, quoted in a footnote by Van Wyck Brooks, "You, you tell me, are one of those who would rather travel into the mind of a plowman than into the interior of Africa. I confess myself of your way of thinking." The same tendency was continued by Poe and Melville and Henry James, and it extends in an almost unbroken line into the late work of Hemingway and Faulkner. But Frost, even in his finest lyrics, is content to stop outside the woods, either in the thrush-haunted dusk or on a snowy evening:

> The woods are lovely, dark and deep.
> But I have promises to keep,
> And miles to go before I sleep,
> And miles to go before I sleep.

If he does not strike far inward, neither does he follow the other great American tradition (extending from Whitman through Dos Passos) of standing on a height to observe the panorama of nature and society. Let us say that he is a poet neither of the mountains nor of the woods, although he lives among both, but rather of the hill pastures, the intervales, the dooryard in autumn with the leaves swirling, the closed house shaking in the winter storms (and who else has described these scenes more accurately, in more lasting colors?). In the same way, he is not the poet of New England in its great days, or in its late-nineteenth-century decline (except in some of his earlier poems); he is rather a poet who celebrates the diminished but prosperous and self-respecting New England of the tourist home and the antique shop in the abandoned gristmill. And the praise heaped on Frost in recent years is somehow connected in one's mind with the search for ancestors and authentic old furniture. You imagine a saltbox cottage restored to its original lines; outside it a wellsweep preserved for its picturesque quality, even though there is also an electric pump; at the doorway a coach lamp wired and polished; inside the house a set of Hitchcock chairs, a Salem rocker, willow-ware plates and Sandwich glass; and, on the tip-top table, carefully dusted, a first edition of Robert Frost.

The Critics and Robert Frost

Bernard DeVoto*

Mr. Richard Thornton's anthology, "Recognition of Robert Frost," will be useful to admirers of Mr. Frost's work and to everyone who is interested in the generation of American literature of which that work is the highest achievement. It is most useful in that it brings together a representative selection of early notices and reviews and many biographical details and personal sketches never before collected. It is less useful as criticism. Intended as a tribute on the twenty-fifth anniversary of the publication of "A Boy's Will," it naturally omits the derogation which two groups of critics have written in obedience to fashion, and what it contains is a miscellany of opinion, rather than an articulated attempt either to examine Frost's poetry or to judge it in relation to its time. Nevertheless, this shapelessness works out usefully in the end. If it makes indifferent criticism it makes excellent archeology, and it enables the reader to contemplate in tranquillity the fetishes and mores of literary thinking over a generation.

Not all the criticism in the book makes sense to anyone who tends to keep his mind fixed on poems and let theories go, who thinks of what Mr. Frost has written rather than what this or that theory would have preferred to have him write. Probably only Mr. Untermeyer, Mr. Lewisohn, and Mr. Kreymborg would appear in an anthology which set out to describe what Mr. Frost's poetry really is. The rest is divided unequally among Ph.D. analysis, the cosmically vague, and various kinds of nonsense. Of the last, Amy Lowell's review of "North of Boston" is easily the first—though Ezra Pound's presbyopia would have run close if Mr. Pound had used as much space as he was currently giving Latvian and Esthonian geniuses in *Poetry*, or as he had given Rabindranath Tagore a year or so before. When Miss Lowell reworked her piece in "Tendencies in Modern American Poetry" she brought it down from the higher to the middle strata of the inane, but in the review you get the pure stuff and it is one of the most idiotic pieces written about poetry in this generation. It is screamingly silly. Nothing approached it until the publication of "A Fur-

*From *The Saturday Review of Literature*, January 1, 1938. Copyright 1938 by *Saturday Review*. All rights reserved. Reprinted by permission.

ther Range" impelled a group of muddled minds to tell us about Mr. Frost without bothering to read him. At that time Newton Arvin and Horace Gregory crowded Miss Lowell hard, only to lose in the end to Mr. Blackmur. His piece in the *Nation* may not be quite the most idiotic review our generation has produced, but in twenty years of reading criticism—oh, the hell with scholarly reservations, Mr. Blackmur's *is* the most idiotic of our time. It is one of the most idiotic reviews since the invention of movable type. The monkeys would have to tap typewriters throughout eternity to surpass it, and Mr. Blackmur may regard his immortality as achieved.

But already I am falling into the habits of criticism. It is not true that Messrs. Blackmur, Gregory, and Arvin did not read "A Further Range." They read it carefully, but interposed between their eyes and the page were systematic theories about the nature of poetry. They could not see what this poetry is because they knew in advance what it ought to be. That has been the principal trouble with the criticism of poetry throughout our generation. All literary criticism is basically an exercise in autobiography, but poetry provides far fewer restraints than prose to keep it in touch with the objective world. In the criticism of poetry, the abstract and systematic theory is usually everything; what a poet actually writes becomes nothing more than a solution into which the critic thrusts his litmus paper. Less than that, even, for critical theory is not like litmus paper which, after all, is capable of rendering two colors, but a mathematical scheme something like the benzene ring. Usually a critic finds in poetry just what mathematical prediction has told him he ought to find there, or he verifies a mathematical prediction that he won't find there what he ought to find. The striking thing is that not honest human prejudices or preconceptions but mathematical processes have told him. He has not got to his judgment by instinct, he has worked it out: he knows by logic, which is far stronger than experience, what poetry ought to be, and so it doesn't much matter to him what poetry actually is.

This subjective absolutism is abundantly illustrated in Mr. Thornton's book. Something like a third of the critics quoted see Mr. Frost escaping from reality into nature or idea or distance or the unknown. Another third assert that he never escapes but instead holds fast to the fact which is the sweetest dream that labor knows. Mr. Freeman says that he has a larger share of the English tradition than any other American of his time; Mr. Untermeyer says that "North of Boston" is one of the most intensely American books ever printed. Miss Lowell says that he has no sense of humor: half the essays say that humor is part of the cell-structure of his work. (Miss Lowell also says that he has no imagination, that his New England is decadent, that he is incapable of subtle undertones of expression or meaning.) To Mr. Munson he is the purest classicist of our time, to Mr. Lewisohn a pure specimen of the naturalistic revolt; Mr. Blankenship calls him a pure realist; Mr. Freeman finds no rebellion in him. Mr. Pound finds his poetry a bit slow, and Mr. Newdick finds it strained to the bursting point with dramatic tension. Mr. Pound says it is not "accomplished"; Mr. Muir decides that it is as deeply, severely, and intricately wrought as one of Plato's dialogues. (But Mr. Munson says that Frost lacks the common sense deliberately aimed at that Socrates achieved, whereas three or four find that he elevates common sense into metaphysical vision.) And so on: he has practically no emotion but he has intense and passionate emotions, there is no color in him save only black and white but he has a magnificent color sense, he is minor but major, he is all on the surface but you have to look for him in the depths. . . . Meanwhile Mr. Frost has remarked that he thinks of poetry as the renewal of words and that a complete poem seems to him one where an emotion has found its thought and the thought has found its words—and has gone about his business. You can get out of that just as much as you can get out of it. Thoreau also spoke in such phrases, and critics have succeeded in identifying the hound, the bay horse, and the turtle dove to which he once alluded. As you might guess, it turns out that the turtle dove is the girl who threw him down.

Mr. Thornton's book omits the two fashions in mathematical analysis which rejected Mr. Frost's poetry some years after its first full fame, but does contain the four essays from the English battle line that so embarrassingly repealed the rejection. Those two fashions were mutually contradictory but yet mystically one, and a glance at them will be instructive.

Mr. Frost's poetry was first awarded critical approval because it was thought to be in revolt against something, at a time when poetry must be in revolt. (To be sure, the best way was to revolt as Imagism, while Amy Lowell was active and Mr. Pound—who has invented many of the fashions and most of the theories that rationalize them—was still an Imagist.) A period of anarchy followed, when poetry must be so many different things that it could be practically anything and criticism could still accept Mr. Frost, but order was again imposed with a metamorphosis of Mr. Pound and the rise of Mr. Eliot. Poetry now must not be anything like Imagism and must not even revolt, but must be the kind of poetry that Mr. Pound or, more purely and quintessentially, Mr. Eliot wrote. This kind of poetry took a lot of explaining—about a hundred pages of theory to one page of text—but a brief statement of its imperatives was contained in Mr. MacLeish's "A poem should not mean, But be." A poem, that is, must not crudely carry "meaning"; it must communicate by direct experience. To be sure, Mr. MacLeish presently doubled on his theory and has ever since done his damnedest to make his own poems mean rather than be; and at the height of the imperative Mr. Eliot supplied footnotes and explanatory treatises on his work which showed that it was at least intended to mean a lot, whereas Mr. Pound has published glosses on his work which prove it so full of meaning that you are lost unless you are equipped with anthropology, philology, half a dozen other sciences and pedantries, a half-knowledge of half the ancient and modern tongues, Major Douglas's economics, and the theory of Fascism.

Obviously Mr. Frost's poems neither looked nor sounded like Mr. Eliot's and Mr. Pound's. If Mr. Eliot's way was the right way to write poetry, then it followed that Mr. Frost's poetry must be pretty bad or pretty minor; and with that mathematical demonstration his decline among the theorists began. But just when a new crop of critics bottlefed on Mr. Eliot's theories (which, happily, have had little effect on his poetry) had mastered this mathematical integration of a new phase of symbolism, another imperative suddenly shattered it to bits. Mr. Eliot was discovered to be not only an antique esthete approximately on a level with Richard LeGallienne, Lionel Johnson, Austin Dobson, or the Sweet Singer of Michigan, but also decadent, Catholic, and dangerously fascistic as well. The only right way to write poetry now was to revolt in it against private ownership of the means of production and saturate it with the emotions, experience, and aspirations of the workers of the world, though you must also somehow depersonalize it till it had the passionless beauty not of a worker but of the machine he operates. The conflict thus produced in minds conditioned to the secrecies of the not-mean-but-be theory bred a neurotic kind of poetry which was allegedly proletarian in feeling but could be read with understanding only by decadents idle and corrupt enough to afford a long initiation in symbolism. The conflict was finally resolved with a decision that the only right way to write poetry was the way Messrs. Auden, Spender, and Day Lewis wrote it. Clearly Mr. Frost didn't write that way, either, and so he was doubly damned. . . . Alas, the neurosis was to be reactivated when Auden and Lewis, as well as Edwin Muir, wrote prefaces to a new edition of "Selected Poems" and not only expressed a profound admiration for Mr. Frost's poetry but also, most charitably, conceded that its kind was right. Equations to harmonize this finding with theory are under way, and the sound you hear offstage may be interpreted as Mr. Blackmur reëxamining Mr. Frost.

In such ways literary theory chases its tail among meaningless absolutes. It is a harmless occupation which has no reference to poems, the people who write them, or the people who read them. What gave these particular theories piquancy, however, was the fact that they sanctioned Mr. Frost's practice quite as much as Mr. Eliot's or Mr. Spender's. For if it mattered, as it doesn't, you could prove Mr. Frost a complete not-mean-but-be poet and a complete proletarian poet. Whereas the surface of a Pound poem is usually roiled and that of an Eliot poem usually opaque, the surface of a Frost poem is usually limpid and clear. One kind of critic has concluded that therefore the surface is all there is to it, and has scornfully turned from it to dredge for the Golden Bough and the castration complex in "The Waste Land." If you got meaning from the surface, obviously there could be nothing underneath. Yet the communication of a Frost poem is always by experience—the shrieking truism is that you can peel off layer after layer of meaning so long as your intelligence and your knowledge last, and at the end still more than you can phrase has been experienced. More than one contributor to Mr. Thornton's book calls Frost a symbolist, and in the critical meaning of the term he is as thoroughly a symbolist as Laforgue, yet that is only a small part of the truth about him. And if the necessity of grace is to write out of the experience of laborers, then Mr. Frost is, as he once outraged a group of literary feeble-minds by admitting, the only pure proletarian poet of our time. His is the only body of poetry of this age which originates in the experience of humble people, treated with the profound respect of identification and used as the sole measure of the reality and value of all experience.

All this, however, is irrelevant. "Pressed into service means pressed out of shape." It is quite true that Frost does not write like Eliot, Pound, Auden, or Spender. Fools may conclude that he is therefore a bad or an unimportant poet, but intelligent people look at the poetry he has written. When you do that, unless your nerves are sealed with wax, you immediately and overwhelmingly perceive that it is the work of an individual and integrated poet, a poet who is like no one else, a major poet not only in regard to this age but in regard to our whole literature, a great American poet.

The most immediately recognizable attribute of any great artist is his authority. He dominates both his materials and his methods till they are inseparable from each other and from his will. (An emotion has found its thought and the thought has found its words.) To perceive the authority of Frost's later lyrics at first glance requires the reader to possess some subtlety, but surely the most forthright reader, or the most theory-bound, can perceive it in the dramatic poems—in such poems as "The Death of the Hired Man," "The Black Cottage," "A Servant to Servants," "Snow," "The Self-Seeker," "In the Home Stretch." Whether unmitigated tragedy or grounded on that spiritual security which is its triumphant opposite, they are a memorable experience of human life immediately and wholly known—and made known. They are written with a mingled harmoniousness and tenseness which completely occupies our attention, focussing it wholly on the individuals before us, and yet at the same time, by means of them, leading out as far as we are capable of following toward universals.

You know these people as completely as any in literature. You are always amazed to find the poem so short because it has told so much. A packed and surcharged economy of the lines, an absolute mastery of words, strips everything to the granite. And at the same time a simple vernacular speech altogether appropriate to the people uttering it has somehow been transformed to a fresh poetic imagery, like no other in literature. You find that the simplicity was deceptive; here is a tune and orchestration of old words now heard and felt for the first time. It is subtle enough here, and it is subtler still in the lyrics, where it is translating privacies and demands more prescience of the reader. The hair which divides the false and true will not divide them if the reader is dull, as some critics seem to be. If he is not, then he will find the pure poetic glory, the fire and ice, of a language remade and a new, unique harmony created. Well, what is poetry?

"Something there is that doesn't love a wall." That is the first line of Frost's second book. There is authority in its dramatic suddenness and directness. There is authority of another kind in the suddenness with which, wholly and instantly, the full truth about the lives embodied in his poems is made known. I have shown that some very strange things indeed have been written about Frost's poetry. Surely the strangest of them was the notion voiced by Amy Lowell (and by a number of her contemporaries, among them several who have since generated a considerable sympathy for the poor) that the New England farmers in his poems were decadent and even degenerate. . . . That was the form—it has since changed—that literary snobbery took in the early 1920's. You see, these people did not have much money. . . . The decadence exhibited in his poems is that some of his characters suffer a grief which is hopeless and whose rebelliousness is futile: it is called tragedy when the Greeks do it. Such a poem as "The Death of the Hired Man" is as sharp an assertion of human kindness, and of the finality of human feeling, as has ever been made anywhere. That assertion is basic in his work, and it is all but unique in this generation: the serenity of an integrated mind which rests on a clear knowledge of human experience and an unflawed belief in its dignity. Frost's poetry is a new assertion of eternal things—that, whether in tragedy or in fulfillment, life *counts*, is worthy, can be trusted, has dignity. On that infrangible dignity, the worth of the individual's experience, he has based the stubborn singularity that has made him a variegated assortment of enemies in the last quarter-century, and all his poetic practice as well. It is the only major affirmation that modern American literature has made.

It will be the central occupation of whoever first bothers to write intelligently about the poetry of Robert Frost—rather than the ways in which that poetry differs from Eliot's. Because of it and the serenity that flows from it he has been able to maintain his prime lightness. "I want one to go with me only so far as he will go playfully." Much of the impatience that one kind of critic feels for him comes from his antic willingness to make jokes about the verities. The pure literary thinker will permit truth no handmaiden but solemnity—recall what horrid pain has been voiced in rebuke of Mark Twain. Yet God may be worshipped with conundrums, the Church was founded on a pun, and truth accepts familiarities from her familiars. It is besides a traditional habit of Yankees to say less than they mean, to say it lightly, and to let any fool go uncorrected who therefore takes them for fools. Thoreau will say the most hopelessly frivolous things, and some part of his purpose has been accomplished as soon as you show that you lack wit to plumb them. One of Frost's poems describes what happens when you look down a well with your head at the wrong angle to the sun. It is recommended to critics: look, boys—a well.

In "A Further Range" the title prefixed to some jokes, aphorisms, and wisecracks is "Ten Mills." Anyone could see that they were humorous and they therefore annoyed a number of the thoughtful, who protested at some length. But I saw no review which unraveled so much as the first obvious layer of the cocoon, the glance at "Pomes Penyeach." It is characteristic of the Yankee mind to spin the cocoon most thickly across the ports that open most directly on itself, and you will find Frost most frivolous, or most cryptic and sibylline, when he is speaking from the deepest wisdom his own experience has deposited on his heart. I hope that criticism will some day examine the lyrics. In such fairly transparent ones as "Good-Bye and Keep Cold" and "Two Look at Two" it will find some surprising things, if it applies to them a decent tenth of the exploration it has devoted to "The Hollow Men." If it then moves on to such more difficult ones as "The Lovely Shall Be Choosers," it will have to repudiate some judgments it has made in print or make absurd its own description of the poetic process. When Frost was annoying the thoughtful by describing himself as a sensibilitist, he was considerate enough not to add that he is also an atomist. If he had, literary confusion would have been increased, but Nils Bohr would have known what he meant.

It is not by chance that even so brief a summary as this has had to allude twice to Thoreau. There is such a thing as continuity in literature, and behind Frost are the generations of men in New England. In his perceptions, in his humor, in his accent, in the undeluded clarity of his vision, in his lifelong concentration on the individual and on the rights, dignities, and sanctities of the individual, he is a neighbor of Thoreau's— who had traveled much in Concord, as Frost in Derry, Franconia, and South Shaftsbury. Nearly a century apart, they would have known each other by the same genius of the place, the same instant assertion of human dignity, the same cadence of thought, a rhythm deeper than consciousness, of the bloodstream itself. "I do not see how he can ever die; nature cannot spare him." "He was prince of heartachers amid countless achers of another part." "Rescue the drowning and tie your shoe-strings. Take your time, and set about some free labor." "By throwing away patience and joining the impatient in one last rush on the citadel of evil, the hope is we may end the need of patience." "In Arcadia, when I was there, I did not see any hammering stone." "Sand grains should sugar in the natal dew the babe born to the desert." "I did not wish to take a cabin passage but rather to go before the mast and on the deck of the world, for there I could best see the moonlight amid the mountains." "You can't sail by the north star at the south pole." "I wonder if something isn't due the victor in a war." "Our inventions are wont to be but pretty toys which distract our attention from serious things. They are but improved means to an unimproved end." "May I live to the end in premises and rest in processes.". . . If you are quite sure you can tell Frost from Thoreau in these sentences casually chosen from five contexts, you must nevertheless recognize that both minds are oriented by the same map.

It has been the curious folly of criticism in our time to stand constantly at the passages of Jordan and require poets to pronounce a password. One year it has been Shibboleth and another year Sibboleth, but in both years those who spoke it a different way were slain. Unquestionably Eliot's poetry is not like Auden's, and Frost's is different from both. But intelligence is content to find beauty and wisdom in poetry wherever they exist, no matter who the poet or by what theory he may—idiotically—be supposed to have written. "The utmost of ambition is to lodge a few poems where they will be hard to get rid of." Frost has lodged a good many poems there. They will be hard to get rid of—harder, I believe, than any others written by an American in our time. Steeped in Whitman, knowing my Eliot by heart as well as commentary, admiring Robinson as most of my colleagues once did but do no longer, I nevertheless think of Frost as the finest poet, living or dead. That, of course, is subjective; you do not prove "best" and "finest," and no one need adopt my judgment. But to ignore the attributes of greatness briefly glanced at here is to make a fool of yourself in public. Lovers of poetry have not committed that asininity.

Tenderness and Passive Sadness

Randall Jarrell*

Reading through Frost's new book one stops for a long time at "Directive."

> Back out of all this now too much for us,
> Back in a time made simple by the loss
> Of detail, burned, dissolved, and broken off
> Like graveyard marble sculpture in the weather,
> There is a house that is no more a house,
> Upon a farm that is no more a farm
> And in a town that is no more a town . . .

One climbs there along a road quarry-like with glacier-chiseled boulders, not minding the "serial ordeal" of the eye-pairs that watch from forty cellar-holes, not minding "the woods' excitement over you/That sends light rustle rushes to their leaves. . . ."

> Where were they all not twenty years ago?
> They think too much of having shaded out
> A few old pecker-fretted apple trees.

Finally, on "the height/Of country where two village cultures faded/Into each other. Both of them are lost," you too are lost, "pull in your ladder road behind you," and make yourself at home with the only field left, "no bigger than a harness gall," with the shattered "playthings in the playhouse of the children." ("Weep for what little things could make them glad.") Then, passing the "house in earnest" that has become "only a belilacked cellar hole," you go to your destination, "a brook that was the water of the house,/Cold as a spring as yet so near its source,/Too lofty and original to rage," and at last you find

> . . . hidden in the instep arch
> Of an old cedar at the waterside
> A broken drinking goblet like the Grail
> Under a spell so the wrong ones can't find it,
> So can't get saved, as Saint Mark says they mustn't.
> (I stole the goblet from the children's playhouse.)

*Review of *Steeple Bush*. From *The New York Times Book Review*, June 1, 1947. Copyright 1947 by The New York Times Company. Reprinted by permission.

> Here are your waters and your watering place.
> Drink and be whole again beyond confusion.

There are weak places in the poem, but these are nothing beside so much longing, tenderness, and passive sadness. Frost's understanding that each life is tragic because it wears away into the death that it at least half-welcomes—that even its salvation, far back at the cold root of things, is make-believe, drunk from a child's broken and stolen goblet hidden among the ruins of the lost cultures. Much of the strangeness of the poem is far under the surface, or else so much on the surface, in the subtlest of details (how many readers will connect the "serial ordeal" of the eye-pairs with the poem's Grail-parody?), that one slides under it unnoticing. There are no notes in the back about this Grail.

There is nothing else in "Steeple Bush" like "Directive"; probably the nearest thing is the dry mercilessness of "The Ingenuities of Debt." But most of the poems merely remind you, by their persistence in the mannerisms of what was genius, that they are productions of somebody who once, and somewhere else, was a great poet. The man who said that he learned from Marlowe to say his prayers: "Why, this is Hell, nor am I out of it"; who could be annoyed at a hornet for not recognizing him as "the exception I like to think I am in everything"; who in poems like "A Servant to Servants," "The Witch of Coös," or "Home Burial," had a final identifying knowledge of the deprived and dispossessed, the insulted and injured, that one matches in modern poetry only in Hardy—this poet is now, most of the time, an elder statesman like Baruch or Smuts, full of complacent wisdom and cast-iron whimsy. (Of course there was always something of this in the official role that Frost created for himself; one imagines Yeats saying about Frost, as Sarah Bernhardt said about Nijinsky: "I fear, I greatly fear, that I have just seen the greatest actor in the world.")

"Steeple Bush" is no book to convert intellectuals to Frost. Yet the ordinary "highbrow" reader is making a far greater mistake when he neglects Frost as commonplace, than the academic reader makes when he apotheosizes him, often on the basis of his most complacent or sentimental poems.

Frost is one of the subtlest and saddest of poets; and no other living poet has written so well about the actions of ordinary men. But anyone should know this after reading "Home Burial," "Two Witches," "A Servant to Servants," "Neither Out Far Nor In Deep," "Design," "Acquainted with the Night," "Provide, Provide," "Desert Places," "Directive," "The Gift Outright," "An Old Man's Winter Night"; or guess at it after reading

> But now he brushed the shavings from his knee
> And stood the axe there on its horse's hoof,
> Erect, but not without its waves, as when
> The snake stood up for evil in the Garden. . . .

A Visit to 35 Brewster Street

John Mason Potter*

The spring afternoon was coming to a graceful end, and the lights were already on in the living room at 35 Brewster Street, Cambridge. The bard of New England's north country, Robert Frost, portly, white-haired, pleasant-faced, with the charm of many years and much accomplishment, sat in a book-lined corner and talked.

It was gladsome talk, rich with a feeling for being an American, a New England countryman—for Robert Frost is that, even though he has a home in Cambridge—for being a poet and a spiritual being. It was serious talk, seasoned here and there with a bit of humor.

It was [as] though the atmosphere of the purposeful, albeit gay, spring afternoon had reached into the room and touched him. Probably it had, for he has recorded many such instances where the spirit of places and hours and things has touched the antenna of his soul.

"The arts are important, but they do not stand alone. They are a part of something bigger, a part of a nation's enterprises. Those enterprises are all sorts of things: business, science, politics, manufacture, and the arts. They all go together, are all part of each other. You can't separate them from each other.

"People sometimes say that America is too commercial, too energetic in its efforts for prosperity. I get very impatient with that sort of talk. Other nations are commercial too, and they seek to prosper. Without prosperity the arts suffer. I don't know why it is, but the periods of prosperity are also the periods of our greatest strides in art.

"The arts serve as a permanent record of a nation. What we know about our past, about a country, we learn from the written word and from architecture. They record permanently. You can't separate them from the things they record.

"If the arts become separated from these other things, they fail. If the arts get left out, there is no record. They say that Carthage had everything except the arts, so now no one knows anything about it."

It is the belief of many persons that in future ages people will be able

*From the *Boston Post Magazine*, April 27, 1952. Copyright 1952 by the *Boston Post Magazine*.

to know what life was like in America—in the part of America formed by the northern half of New England—by reading the poetry of Robert Frost. There are many who esteem him as America's greatest living poet and one who within his own lifetime has taken his place beside Bryant and Whitman and Emerson and the other immortals of verse.

It is the country life that Robert Frost loves and of which he writes—of farms and trees and rural lanes and of birds and small animals and of country people.

"There are people who don't write such things, and sometimes they are. . . . Well, you mustn't call them Communists because then they can sue you, but I know what they are.

"Sometimes I hear someone say that he does not like poetry about nature, the country, that it should be about the city and machines and man-made things. When he says that I know what's inside of him. He is as clear as can be to me then, and I know what he is, whether he does or not."

The poet has little patience, either, with the obscurantists in art.

"I met a young man from South America recently, an Argentine, and he asked me if I had ever read any of the works of a certain Argentine poet. I hadn't. (I don't read much in translation, because you lose so much.) He said to me, 'He writes in code.' I asked him, 'Who supplies the code?' 'Another man,' was the answer."

Mr. Frost chuckled, and several times after he referred to writing poetry in code as a big joke.[. . .]

"I've only written one book, really. It has come out in sections, but it is really only one book. You know I'm really not much of a writer. I've been writing poetry for sixty years now, and the book has six hundred pages, and so I have averaged only ten pages of poetry a year. That is not very much.

"I write when I feel like it. Sometimes I can sense that feeling coming on for a couple of days, and then I find that I have to versify.

"I do it sitting down in a chair with a piece of paper lying on a book on my knee. I never use a desk. I write wherever I happen to be. Once I wrote a poem in a hotel in Wilkes-Barre. It was the only time I was ever there. It was 'The Heart Begins to Cloud the Mind.' It was a sort of reflection of myself and the New Deal.

"I usually do a poem in one sitting, and the longest ones in never more than two sittings. You either go ahead or you get stuck. If I am exhausted from doing it at twelve or one o'clock, I stop, if I am not near the end of it."[. . .]

"I don't like to stop for fear that I won't come back to it. But I have got back to it in every case. I am always afraid that I will get distracted and break the back of it.

"I always use a pen. I have never learned to typewrite and have never used one."[. . .]

At seventy-five he still reads his Poe, declaring, "I have never outgrown anything that I ever liked. I have never had a hobby in my life, but I have ranged through a lot of things. I have a cursory interest in life."

As for the poetry that has been his life, he says, "I don't like a too technical interest in verse, even though I am a versifier. It is the tune that I am interested in."

[Freedom and the Poet]

"Meet the Press"

SPIVAK: Mr. Frost, few words have had their meaning so distorted as freedom and liberty. It seems to mean different things to different people in different countries. Now will you tell us what freedom means to you, a poet?

FROST: First of all it means the freedom my country gives me and I suppose the freedom that everybody's country gives him. There ought to be, of course, no comparative freedoms, but I like mine best; and I think [. . .] the reason for it probably is that it's like old clothes or old shoes. Mine fits me, and that's as far as I can go.

SPIVAK: Mr. Frost, do you think there is any relationship between freedom and great poetry, or do you think that a great talent expresses itself regardless of the political climate of a country?

FROST: I don't believe the political state of affairs matters too much. I think that the personal freedom that you get from the country is something you assume. Your real anxiety day by day is your own freedom of your own material, your own condition, your own mental condition and physical condition that gives you command of what you want to think of when you want to think of it. And then I'm more interested in the liberties I take than in the big thing you call freedom or liberty: the little liberties socially, in poetry, art and little trespasses and excesses and things like that.

FADIMAN: What you are saying perhaps ties down to the question I wanted to ask you.

We hear a good deal these days about economic and political freedom, the kind of freedom guaranteed to us by law. Do you think economic and political freedom in itself is very much good without the kind of freedom that's inside your head? I mean the mental freedom that comes from having enough character and intelligence to make proper choices?

FROST: The economic freedom of course is something. . . . You're

*From the transcript of "Meet the Press," December 23, 1956; participants: David Brinkley, Ned Brooks, Clifton Fadiman, Inez Robb, and Lawrence Spivak. Copyright © 1956 by the National Broadcasting Company. Reprinted by permission.

117

asking me do I think it makes any difference to a poet whether he hears the wolf at the door all the time, and I don't believe it makes too much difference.

If you are talking about poverty and wealth I think sometimes wealth has its bad things and poverty has its bad things and limits to our freedom. Poverty has done so much good in this way in the world that I should hesitate to abolish it.

ROBB: In the world in which we live, Mr. Frost, there is a great yearning for what people think of as security, and that usually means economic security. Do you feel that you would have written any better poetry if you had been endowed from the beginning with an ample income?

FROST: I don't think so, no. You see, I'm on the other side. I know what you're talking about, what you're leading up to. I'm on the side of adversity.

I once drew up a little story about that. It said just how many disadvantages does a person need to get anywhere in the world—disadvantages. And I said here's a man born to too much money, and that's disadvantage number one. Then his mother is a very dominant person, very fond of him. That's disadvantage number two. No father in it; that's disadvantage number three.

He goes to Groton, and that's disadvantage number four. Then he goes to Harvard, and that's disadvantage number five. Then he begins to kick around among the politicians in Albany and Washington. That's disadvantage number six. (Have I got six?)

And then God says, "I'm going to make something of that boy; I set my heart on him." And, "He hasn't amounted to anything yet, but I'm going to give him one more disadvantage." And He gives him polio, and then he sits on top of the world along with Stalin and Churchill!

That row is forever in my mind.

ROBB: May I ask another question?

You once wrote, Mr. Frost, "Originality and initiative are what I ask for my country." Are those the two things that you still ask for your country?

FROST: Say those again.

ROBB: "Originality and initiative."

FROST: Yes. That's what I want in art, and I want that so much that I am inclined to favor young poets and artists too much. It's their funeral you know, not mine; but I make their funeral mine.

BRINKLEY: Mr. Frost, I think most of us tend to think of the poet as being a kind of agent of the free spirit. I wonder how you in that light would feel about the increasing pressure in this country toward conformity, toward having people think and act and dress and live alike?

FROST: I don't know how to answer that, because I don't feel that pressure. I think we're the freest people that ever were free. I don't know what the pressure is.

Take this pressure of haste, you know, that they talk about: the pace. If you want to see the opposite from haste come up to Ripton, Vermont. We live on "procrastinity" up there, I call it. We just put everything off.

FADIMAN: You do have a lot of haste down here, Mr. Frost; we have a monopoly on it.

FROST: But you don't have to join in it. I didn't meet any last night in the hotel where I am. And I used to visit my daughter in Bank Street, and I couldn't even hear the murmur of the city down there. It was as quiet as it is in Vermont.

BRINKLEY: I'd like to ask one more brief question on the same line.

Do you think non-conformity is as much admired in this country today?

FROST: Yes, I think we're paid for it.

SPIVAK: Mr. Frost, do you seek to do anything through your poetry or do you just write because you must, or because you love to do it?

FROST: I do it because I like to do it. I have always done what I liked to do. I never did anything I disliked to do very long at a time.

SPIVAK: Which of your poems do you like the best?

FROST: The one that was last praised by some friend.

SPIVAK: Which one is that?

FROST: The last one that was praised very much by people was too long for me to recite to you so I can't help you there; but it was called "One More Brevity."

SPIVAK: Have you a short one that's been praised?

FROST: Yes, I have one on this subject of freedom. (What gives us our freedom is having a territorial basis, belonging to the land.) That's one of my favorite poems. Because other people seem to like it. Shall I recite it? It's short.

SPIVAK: Yes, if you will.

FROST:

The land was ours before we were the land's. . . .

It all lies in that first line.

The land was ours before we were the land's.
She was our land more than a hundred years
Before we were her people. She was ours
In Massachusetts, in Virginia,
But we were England's, still colonials,
Possessing what we still were unpossessed by,
Possessed by what we now no more possessed.
Something we were withholding made us weak
Until we found out that it was ourselves

> We were withholding from our land of living,
> And forthwith found salvation in surrender.
> Such as we were we gave ourselves outright
> (The deed of gift was many deeds of war)
> To the land vaguely realizing westward,
> But still unstoried, artless, unenhanced,
> Such as she was, such as she would become.

It all lies in the first line.

FADIMAN: It's a beautiful poem you just quoted and is of course a severely limited thing that it is bound by the rules of meter or measure. And people talk about freedom in poetry as if that were a thing very much to be desired; but isn't it true that great poetry becomes great in part because of its limitations, and may it not be true that freedom, even politically and socially, emerges the same way?

FROST: And that's no paradox that we gain in freedom on a higher plane by sacrificing agents on the next plane below it. All the way up. That's our freedom.

When it says "the truth will make you free" it means that you get a new enslavement that will free you from all your other enslavements.

FADIMAN: The notion of unfettered, unrestricted freedom is really a Utopian and windy idea, is it not?

FROST: Excuse me?

FADIMAN: I say, the notion of unfettered freedom some people talk about—complete freedom—is meaningless.

FROST: To me it's unchartered freedom. You want something in balance, form. It comes to everything. It's just as much in the phrase as it is in the verse, isn't it? You need your freedom by phrase, and that's a kind of formality.

The dictionary is a limitation, isn't it? I'm awfully limited by the dictionary, and I'm awfully limited by the need of phrase and grammar; and I just have the feeling I can take all that and then some. Freedom of rhyme and meter.

ROBB: What we are saying then, Mr. Frost, is that both poetry and freedom have their own discipline?

FROST: Absolutely. And in limitation, yes. But one rises above another to higher and higher freedom all the way to the freedom of the spirit.

BRINKLEY: You are a teacher. You know, of course, there's a great cry in this country now that we should train more scientists in our schools, because the Russians are. I wonder if you see in this any danger we might train too many people to split atoms and not enough to write sentences?

FROST: No, no, I'm not afraid. They're advertising for those boys in the *Scientific American* and all around all the time. They don't seem to be able to get them. I don't know where they are. I should think that's been drawn that way. My imagination would have been caught by all that's going on in there, and I wonder that we don't—that they don't swamp that.

Where do they go? Do you know?

FADIMAN: Do you think they are going into the humanities more, Mr. Frost?

FROST: I'm afraid not so much into the humanities as into sociality. Humanity in another sense of the word. The humanities means, you know, the Latin, Greek, and all that sort of thing.

BROOKS: Right along that line, Mr. Frost, we seem to find a great many people in the world today who are deeply depressed by all the conditions we find around us, but you seem to be very much of an optimist, and I wonder how other people can acquire the same optimism that you seem to have?

FROST: I do not believe I am quite an optimist, but I believe there is a lot that is so good in it that it is worth going on with. There is a lot of bad about it.

This matter of confusion. I think the thing that confuses the mind is loss of a sense of form, and if you lose the sense of form, the doctor can restore it by teaching you how to make a horseshoe or a basket or something like that, or to blow smoke rings or anything to restore your sense of form. And as long as so many of us, nearly all of us, have a chance to make a little rounding out of something—of family life or a magazine or an article or a poem or a basket or a horseshoe or a tumbler—that is what keeps the sanity and that is what keeps and saves us from the sense of confusion.

When I hear people talk about confusion—at commencement addresses, you know—I just think it is getting into a bad habit. They don't mean it. Someone said it that was confused probably, and the rest of them are not confused but just go on saying it.

SPIVAK: Mr. Frost, in the minds of most of us, Christmas has come to be a happy season, and yet very few of us believe we are really happy. Do you consider yourself a happy man?

FROST: That would be self-praise, if I said it.

SPIVAK: Well, what then does happiness mean? I am trying to find out what you think happiness means.

FROST: It is an expression that lost its ancient English meaning; it is inward happiness. It is very hard to tell you. You can judge better of it than I can. I cannot even tell what I look like except in a looking glass, and that does not seem to persuade me. And I cannot tell how happy I am. I rather you tell me.

SPIVAK: Let me put it this way: What are the things in life that really count to you?

FROST: Well, this feeling of everyday that you can handle it, that you can give it shape, you know. Every morning I make up my bed. (I live alone.) Every morning I make up my mind a little bit before I begin to read the morning papers. Then I alter it a little bit, but that is going on all the time. What a busy world it is that way. How attractive it all is to have so much to re-handle day by day—the question of international affairs.

About this question of poetry and prose, you have not asked me if poetry has half a chance in a world like this—the making of poems and giving them their shape.

FADIMAN: I often wonder whether we have an audience for poetry. I know your books are widely read, Mr. Frost, but is it not true that many other poets are [not] equally fortunate? Have we lost the great audience that Whitman said was necessary for great poets?

FROST: I think the best audience the world ever had, probably, is the little town-and-gown audience that we get in the little college towns in the U.S.A.—two thousand towns, very pretty towns, too. They may not teach anybody anything, those colleges, but they do make pretty towns, and they do make a nice town audience!

FADIMAN: Along that line. . . .

FROST: Better than Homer ever had or Ossian ever had or 'the troubadours ever had. I am just a wandering bard myself.

FADIMAN: You are a wandering educator, too, Mr. Frost. Do you feel that poetry can [be] taught?

FROST: In this loose way: I made up some lines the other day—

> It takes a lot of in and outdoor schooling
> To get adapted to my kind of fooling.

Poetry is a kind of fooling that you got to get the hang of, and I go around playing that. You cannot preach about it; you get in a little wisecrack and you read a poem and so on.

There is a certain amount of teaching; that is, from the teacher's desk, too. At the same time, it cannot be too direct. It is shooting all around it and playing all around it, and it is outdoors and indoors, in school and out of school.

You can say a snobbish thing about it, if you want to, but St. Mark said, "These things are said in parables" (that is, poetry, figures of speech), "so the wrong people cannot understand them, and so get saved."

BROOKS: Mr. Frost, you must at various times have had young ambitious poets come to you for advice. Perhaps some of them had talent. What encouragement do you give these people?

FROST: Well, I always say to them, "This is what we want, but you have to have a snout for punishment. You are going to take a lot of punishment for it." And then I would say, "I wish you the greatest things for my country and for you and for me, but it is your funeral, not mine."

ROBB: In other words, the way of the poet is still hard?

FROST: Yes, it is meant to be. The way of everything is still hard. I have heard people quote me as saying that one thing will never change in the world no matter how easy we make it with all sorts of science and everything else. One thing will always be hard. That is saving your soul, Inez, saving your decency.

ROBB: One other question. This is the question that you yourself asked, Mr. Frost, and I am going to ask you to answer it.

It is a quatrain and is called "A Question," and you say:

> A voice said, Look me in the stars
> And tell me truly, men of earth,
> If all the soul-and-body scars
> Were not too much to pay for birth.

FROST: You bring up another thing, the mood. That is a mood, when you sometimes wonder if it is worth it, all the pain.

ROBB: Well, was it?

FROST: Sometimes I feel one way, and sometimes I feel the other. In the many movements of a poet's mind you do not have to have one doctrine running all through the work, optimism or pessimism. Sometimes it seems too bad.

I made a prayer the other day. (You say things against God and the whole thing sometimes.) I made a prayer like this: "O God, if You'll forgive our little jokes on You—all our little jokes on You—we'll forgive Your one great big joke on us."

BRINKLEY: I have one short question, Mr. Frost.

I believe I have seen you quoted as saying that a poem in one respect is like a love affair, in that it begins in delight and ends in wisdom. I wonder if you have found any other similarity?

FROST: Yes, that is true about everything. You know what God's great big joke on us is? The answer is the spring of the year. It begins in delight and ends in we don't know what kind of a crop.

SPIVAK: You once wrote that courage is the human virtue that counts most. Why did you say that?

FROST: I said that to tease the lady, so she would say: "Isn't it a sad world where courage has to be the chief virtue."

SPIVAK: You do not quite believe that?

FROST: I don't think it is sad. I do believe it, yes; I think it is. But I wanted to hear her say it is a sad world where the chief virtue had to be courage; that is, in all things—the daring.

SPIVAK: Do you believe that virtue, courage, is the human virtue that counts most, though?

FROST: Yes, I will stick to that, tonight.

SPIVAK: Only for tonight?

FROST: I will stick to that.[. . .]

Frost and Emerson: Voice and Vision

Alvan S. Ryan*

It is reliably reported that Robert Frost once called Ralph Waldo Emerson his favorite American poet. According to Reginald Cook, he has even called Emerson "the greatest Western poet." The same writer also quotes Frost as calling Emerson "a great disturber of the peace" and "profoundly subvertive." While these and numerous other statements by Frost attest his concern with Emerson's work, they furnish only fragmentary and peripheral evidence as to Frost's relationship to Emerson. What vision emerges from the total work of each writer? This is the significant question, yet it has been answered by critical judgments that are often flatly contradictory. G. R. Elliott, for example, interprets Frost's poetry as rejecting "the Emersonian anarchy." In defining the relation between Frost and poetic tradition, Elliott contrasts the romantic sentimentality of much nineteenth century poetry with Milton's "vision of a just and charitable Will, human but supernaturally given, alone able to subdue our Satanic selfishness and to build for us some greatness of society," and holds that Frost's poetry moves in the arc of this tradition. More recently, Yvor Winters has called Frost "a disciple without Emerson's religious conviction: Frost believes in the rightness of impulse. . . ." He is, says Winters, the spiritual drifter as poet, believing "that impulse is trustworthy and reason contemptible. . . . The principles which have hampered Frost's development, the principles of Emersonian and Thoreauistic Romanticism, are the principles which he has openly espoused. . . ."

Such disagreements are typical. Charles H. Foster writes that in Frost "there live on many of the central Emersonian convictions. . . . One misses in Frost the intellectual complication and the mystical intensity, but Frost is Emersonian." (Out of context, Foster's position seems close to that of Winters, but Foster's evaluation of both Frost and Emerson is fundamentally opposed to the notion that either substitutes impulse for reason, or that Frost is the spiritual drifter as poet.) Joseph Warren Beach, on the other hand, after devoting a chapter in his *Concept of Nature* to "Emerson's Nature-Poetry," quotes Frost's "West-Running

*From *The Massachusetts Review*, October, 1959, pp. 5–23. Copyright © 1959 by The Massachusetts Review, Inc. Reprinted by permission.

Brook" as expressing a view of nature far different from Emerson's. "Surely never was nature," he writes, "invoked in more sober fashion; never was more modest claim made on the Power so awesomely regarded by Shelley and Emerson."

If one thinks of the divergent interpretations of each writer to be found in very recent statements, these earlier judgments are understandable. I think, for example, of Newton Arvin's "The House of Pain: Emerson and the Tragic Sense," in the Spring, 1959 issue of the *Hudson Review*, which goes far toward reconciling the older view of Emerson as bland optimist with the newer one that he resolutely faced the problem of evil. At the center of Emerson's vision Arvin discerns "perhaps the fullest and most authentic expression in modern literature of the more-than-tragic emotion of thankfulness." And in the most recent issue of the *Partisan Review* (Summer, 1959), Lionel Trilling prints in full the text of the address which last March roused—and why? one wonders—such a storm of protest. Trilling, with an engaging candor, told those assembled at Frost's eighty-fifth birthday dinner that he was one of Frost's most recently won admirers, and that *his* Frost was "a terrifying poet." At least Trilling's Frost, so much like the Frost that Jarrell gave us in his brilliant essay twelve years ago in the *Nation*, is another refreshing corrective to Malcolm Cowley's "case against Mr. Frost": the poet "who celebrates the diminished but prosperous and self-respecting New England of the tourist home and the antique shop in the abandoned gristmill."

I

Are Frost and Emerson poets in the same tradition? There are superficial similarities. They agree on the central importance of symbol and metaphor. They have a common preoccupation with rural subjects. They share a basic sense of "correspondences," though the differences here are also important. Their experiments with various meters and verse forms, their use of dialogue, their fondness for epigrammatic statement—both have written a great deal of gnomic verse—are also evident. The very titles of some of Frost's poems ("Mending Wall," "Storm-Fear," "The White-Tailed Hornet," "I Could Give All to Time," "Spring Pools") carry the mind back to Emerson's "The Snow-Storm," "Give All to Love," "Two Rivers," "The Humble-Bee," "The Rhodora." But all this may indicate no more than that they turn to similar subject matter. The question still remains—and must be answered, however briefly: What of their poetic theories and practice of poetry?

For Emerson the poet's role is essentially bardic and prophetic; invariably the definitions have religious overtones. Before he is maker, the poet is prophet, priest and seer. Through his imagination and intuitive powers he penetrates the hidden mystery of things, apprehends their transcendent or inner reality and announces his findings to men. All this is characteristic of the nineteenth century view of the poet's role. According to Emerson the poet "has no definitions, but . . . is commanded in nature, by the living power which he feels to be there present. . . . It is nature the symbol, nature certifying the supernatural . . . which he worships. . . ." These lines from Emerson's essay "The Poet" are echoed in "Nature," the essay in which the whole section on language reveals his sense of the poet's role:

> It is not words only that are emblematic; it is things which are emblematic. Every natural fact is a symbol of some spiritual fact. . . . Who looks upon a river in a meditative hour and is not reminded of the flux of all things?

This is one side of Emerson's theory, the quintessentially transcendental or romantic note. Granting the need for further distinctions, it links him with Wordsworth, Shelley, Arnold and Whitman, and with others, such as Carlyle, who also claim for the poet the role of prophet, priest or seer.

There is nothing about Frost's conception of the role of the poet that is close to Emerson's. Frost has made few statements in prose on the poet's role, and when in his poetry he invokes the bardic attitude, as in "To a Thinker," it is with wry humor: "But trust my instinct, I'm a bard." He prefers to talk about the making of poems. As Lawrance Thompson remarks, "He has frequently suggested that he is particularly wary of hydra-headed Platonic idealism and of all those glorious risks taken by any who boldly arrive at transcendental definitions." Frost's comment on E. A. Robinson's Platonism is too well known to need quoting. But there is one passage in his "Education by Poetry" that brings Frost close to Emerson:

> Greatest of all attempts to say one thing in terms of another is the philosophical attempt to say matter in terms of spirit, or spirit in terms of matter, to make the final unity. That is the greatest attempt that ever failed. We stop just short there. But it is the height of all poetry, the height of all thinking. . . .

Where Emerson's emphasis is on mysticism, or on some natural analogue of mystical experience closely allied to poetic intuition and inspiration, Frost is content to make a more modest and yet evocative statement:

> The figure a poem makes. . . . It begins in delight, it inclines to the impulse, it assumes direction with the first line laid down, it runs a course of lucky events, and ends in a clarification of life—not necessarily a great clarification, such as sects and cults are founded on, but in a momentary stay against confusion.

The difference in tone is not only indicative of the fuller commitment of Frost to poetry as first of all the craft of words; it also shows what has happened to the poet's sense of his role since the nineteenth century.

It is in the stress on emblem, symbol, and analogy that the theories of

Emerson and Frost really meet. For Emerson the perception of analogy lies at the very root of poetry: "man is an analogist, and studies relations in all objects." The vehicle in poetry of this analogical habit is the symbol. Frost is essentially in agreement with this and he says so in his own way:

> Poetry begins in trivial metaphors, pretty metaphors, "grace metaphors," and goes on to the profoundest thinking that we have. Poetry provides the one permissible way of saying one thing and meaning another.

But he goes on to say that "All metaphor breaks down somewhere. That is the beauty of it. It is touch and go with the metaphor. . . ." Emerson, on the other hand, is less suspicious of metaphor. His whole theory is characteristically less guarded than Frost's. He speaks of the poet's "intoxication" with symbols, and sees the poet not only as using symbols, but as perceiving "the independence of the thought on the symbol, the stability of the thought, the accidency and fugacity of the symbol." In that one phrase, "the stability of the thought," there is a note that will account for one of the major differences between Emerson's poetry and Frost's. Just as in his theory Frost sees the poet as somehow "riding" the metaphor to see where it will carry him, so, in his best poetry, the thought is too deeply implicated in the metaphor to be called independent.

But the similarities evident in the two poets are not so important as the differences, which go deep into their artistic vision. There is a far greater difference, for example, between Emerson's and Frost's poetry than between their theories. And if organic structure and symbol are central to Emerson's theory, then paradoxically Frost's poetry embodies the theory far more fully than Emerson's. Nothing makes this clearer than a comparison of the structure, the use of image and symbol, and the handling of meter and rime in much of their poetry.

Emerson's poems do not often achieve immediacy. This is so in great part because of the *a priori* nature of many of them or because of their "panoramic" quality. As a result their impact is frequently vague and general as, for example, in "The Rhodora." On the other hand, many of Frost's poems, from no matter what period, achieve an immediacy through the poet's permitting his persons not merely to speculate or muse about experience but to see and to move through the medium of literal action—action which more often than not turns finally into symbolic representation or significant generalization. "Birches," "After Apple-Picking," "Tree at My Window," "Come In," "Directive" are clear examples of this procedure.

Whereas Emerson prefers to be suggestive, to develop a few images or a series of briefly sketched scenes, Frost characteristically structures a poem around a single symbolic event. Emerson's unifying principle is ideational, Frost's metaphorical. Emerson's "The Humble-Bee," while symbolic, is also generic; Frost, in contrast, focuses on a particular "White-Tailed Hornet" whose antics demonstrate to the eye-witness the fallacy of the theory of nature's unerring aim and instinct and the danger lodged in man's worship of such illusion:

> As long on earth
> As our comparisons were stoutly upward
> With gods and angels, we were men at least, . . .
> But once comparisons were yielded downward,
> Once we began to see our images
> Reflected in the mud and even dust,
> 'Twas disillusion upon disillusion.
> We were lost piecemeal to the animals,
> Like people thrown out to delay the wolves.
> Nothing but fallibility was left us. . . .

"Woodnotes" offers a good example of Emerson's use of the panorama or catalogue, as in these lines:

> He saw the partridge drum in the woods;
> He heard the woodcock's evening hymn;
> He found the tawny thrushes' broods;
> And the shy hawk did wait for him.

This double brace of birds is the game of an eclectic hunter who scatters his shot. But Frost, whether in "Dust of Snow," "A Minor Bird," or "The Oven Bird," prefers one bird at a time.

> There is a singer everyone has heard,
> Loud, a mid-summer and a mid-wood bird,
> Who makes the solid tree trunks sound again.
> He says that leaves are old and that for flowers
> Mid-summer is to spring as one to ten.
> He says the early petal-fall is past
> When pear and cherry bloom went down in showers
> On sunny days a moment overcast;
> And comes that other fall we name the fall.
> He says the highway dust is over all.
> The bird would cease and be as other birds
> But that he knows in singing not to sing.
> The question that he frames in all but words
> Is what to make of a diminished thing.

The habit of Frost's imagination is, in short, not like Emerson's. Rather, it is much closer to Thoreau's in its tenacious adherence to the inscapes of his world.

Stephen Whicher is right when he says that Emerson's poems "tend to slide off quickly from the fact to the idea—the cloying literariness of too much of his imagery and diction seems to represent an unsuccessful attempt to make up this deficiency of the sensuous in his verse—and they typically lack the organic, musical structure of the modern symbolist poem, since they can result only from playing off one symbol or meaning against another in a pattern of contraries." It is only in a very few of Emerson's poems that a single metaphor or symbolic action is made into a tightly organized and dramatic experience comparable to the best of Frost's. "Days" is an outstanding example.

> Daughters of Time, the hypocritic Days,
> Muffled and dumb like barefoot dervishes,
> And marching single in an endless file,
> Bring diadems and fagots in their hands.
> To each they offer gifts after his will,
> Bread, kingdoms, stars, and sky that holds them all.
> I, in my pleachéd garden, watched the pomp,
> Forgot my morning wishes, hastily
> Took a few herbs and apples, and the Day
> Turned and departed silent. I, too late,
> Under her solemn fillet saw the scorn.

Here is a poem of which Frost might say the "words comb the idea all one way." The scene, the slow stately movement of the verse, and the exquisitely appropriate language all work together superbly—in a way not common in Emerson's poems.

II

The question to which I now wish to turn concerns the vision or interpretation of experience that emerges from the total work of each writer. This is the question that has excited the sharpest critical debates in recent years. To compare the whole vision of Emerson and Frost we must have a sense of the "center" of each writer's work, yet recent criticism shows how difficult it is to find this center. For example, any attempt to interpret Emerson's whole vision, or to assess the major emphasis in his work, hinges on how one sees the relation between the two Emersons—the early Emerson of "Nature," "The Divinity School Address," "The American Scholar" and "Self-Reliance," and the later Emerson of such essays as "Experience" and "Illusions." The current critical practice is to stress the Yankee realism throughout his work, or to stress the later phase, in which there is a much profounder sense of the complexities of human experience, a recognition of evil and of limitation and a less ecstatic sense of the possibilities open to the active soul. If this new reading of Emerson is valuable it should not obscure the fact that it was the earlier Emerson of the stirring and oracular affirmations who made so strong an impact on his contemporaries. Even if he was, as Austin Warren penetratingly suggests in his essay "Emerson, Preacher to Himself," really counseling himself in such utterances, trying to compensate for the opposite bent in his own nature, he did make them in public, and they are at the root of what we have come to think of as Emersonianism. Had the dialogue we find in his early journals been conducted in public,

Emerson's impact would have been far different. The stress in the public lectures and the essays is on intuition, the moral sentiment, immediate religious experience without mediation of history, institution (church), or sacraments, and on obeying the law of one's own nature—these affirmations gave him his central place among the transcendentalists.

Nor is it quite true to say that the total interpretation of Emerson shows us a man who holds opposing truths in dialectical tension and presents his thought in the form of dialogue. If there is a dialectic, it has to be in the mind of the reader who moves through the whole body of Emerson's work and becomes aware of the differing emphases in the early and the late essays. I do not find this dialectic in the early essays and lectures. The interpretation of Emerson by Stephen Whicher is immensely illuminating; he has recovered for us a whole facet of Emerson's work that adds a new dimension to his genius. But development in a writer does not equate with a rhetorical strategy or with a philosophical view that sees in a single vision the complexities of experience and conveys this vision throughout the body of his work.

To turn to a contemporary novelist, I would say that Robert Penn Warren has precisely the type of vision that Whicher attributes to Emerson, but this to me is an unromantic and unEmersonian vision. To take another example, Carlyle's *Sartor Resartus*—which contains so many of the doctrines found in "Nature," "The Divinity School Address" and "Self-Reliance"—is not, I grant, a genuinely dialectical work. Carlyle's voluntarism and his super-charged rhetoric scarcely allow room for consideration of opposing claims. Yet in *Sartor*, Carlyle is in some ways more dialectical than Emerson. Carlyle at least creates the fiction of an English editor commenting on Teufelsdröckh's clothes philosophy, however incomplete the fiction may be.

Newton Arvin's essay on Emerson, already cited, and the remarks of Trilling's at Frost's birthday dinner further dramatize the problem. Arvin's essay in one sense corroborates Whicher's recognition that there is far more awareness in Emerson of the problem of evil than has usually been admitted, but Arvin's final conclusion—in this sense corrective of Whicher's—is that Emerson's vision at its best is in a great religious tradition, a tradition which sees beyond tragedy to affirm the ultimate meaning even of pain and suffering. Arvin, like Pollock in his excellent essay "The Single Vision," finds unsatisfactory the view that Emerson merely reiterated the importance of intuition and spontaneity. Yet he cannot agree that Emerson can justly be reinstated for modern readers as a writer with a tragic vision. Hence Arvin affirms, in the passage already quoted, that in Emerson we find "the more-than-tragic emotion of thankfulness." Here, to put it briefly, we find Arvin recognizing the modern demand that a writer deal adequately with the problem of evil, but also affirming the possibility of a vision which views evil and suffering in a larger perspective.

At about the time Arvin's essay appeared, Lionel Trilling made the address that precipitated so much criticism. What did Trilling mean by calling Frost a "terrifying poet"? Clearly, in the context, he meant a tragic poet. Opening with a reference to Frost's "Sophoclean birthday," he ended by saying directly to Frost: "When I began to speak I called your birthday Sophoclean and that word has, I think, controlled everything I have said about you. Like you, Sophocles lived to a great age, writing well; and like you, Sophocles was the poet his people loved most. Surely they loved him in some part because he praised their common country. But I think that they loved him chiefly because he made plain to them the terrible things of human life: they felt, perhaps, that only a poet who could make plain the terrible things could possibly give them comfort."

It would seem difficult to give any modern poet greater praise than to compare him favorably with Sophocles, and as one reads Trilling's address and remembers his authoritative book on Matthew Arnold, two lines of Arnold's praise of Sophocles come to mind: first, the familiar line referring to him as one "who saw life steadily and saw it whole," and second, the reference to him as "Singer of sweet Colonus and its child." It is on these two notes—in Trilling's words, the praise of "their common country" and the making plain "the terrible things"—that Trilling rests his comparison of Frost and Sophocles. If Trilling's view was to be questioned, one might expect it to be questioned most strenuously by admirers of Sophocles who find Frost not of such stature. Yet, ironically, it was certain admirers of Frost who repudiated what they incomprehensibly took as Trilling's attempt to minimize Frost's significance. By their interpretation, Frost is an optimistic and benevolent singer of the emotional joy to be felt in the presence of nature, and not a "terrifying poet" at all. Moreover, one of Trilling's critics suggested that he "come out of the Freudian wood" and that he might better have invoked Emerson as one who would move familiarly in Frost's world. The comment is in line with a widely-held view that both Emerson and Frost are amiable, inspiriting, optimistic writers, who prefer to look on the pleasanter aspects of life. It is a view most effectively turned against the admirers of the two poets by a critic like Winters who holds that both Emerson and Frost turn away from the darker side of experience and abrogate their responsibility in favor of embracing a nostalgic vision of perfection.

Since it is clear that just as the more conventional estimates of the two writers bring them close together as optimists, and the severe criticism of them by Winters denigrates them for the same reason, so the more recent stress on their serious confronting of evil and limitation also brings them together, but in a very different way. To strike the balance among these three perspectives, and variations of them, is not easy. I only hope to make a start by taking a few focal points—their views of nature, of man in relation to society, of evil and suffering—for comparing Emerson's vision with Frost's.

Any understanding of Emerson's response to nature must begin with the religious attitudes central to all his thought. Rejecting the Calvinistic doctrine of total depravity and the rational theology of Unitarianism, he fastens on that same distinction between the transient and the permanent in religion made by Theodore Parker in America, Carlyle in England and numerous others in the mainstream of Transcendentalism. Like them, he fashions an eclectic synthesis of his own and turns to nature for the religious experience or sentiment. To this extent he is a transcendentalist. He rejects institutional Christianity in all its forms, while simultaneously affirming an intuitive religious experience open to all men. The most intense manifestation of this experience occurs when we attune ourselves to spiritual meanings in the contemplation of nature. This note leads, in Emerson's theory of poetry, and in much of his poetry and prose, to those sudden leaps from things, from actuality, to metaphysical affirmations. It is the flash of meaning, not the full steady confrontation of complex and ironic reality, that marks Emerson's whole attitude. And the flash of meaning he waits for is often for him a kind of "good news" which is no longer told in the churches. The affirmation, "God speaks, not spaketh" of the "Divinity School Address" is a clear link between all that he says of religion and all that he says of nature.

For Emerson the natural world mediates between man and spiritual realities. Nature is a revelation of the eternal in the things of sense, an avenue to the world of spirit. Granted that many passages in his writing seem to merge God and nature in a pantheistic way, there are numerous passages, from "Nature" on, where he makes a clear distinction between the creative God and His created universe. He calls the woods "the plantations of God"; he sees a farm as a "mute gospel." It is "a sacred emblem from the first furrow of spring to the last stack which the snow of winter overtakes in the fields."

The early essays emphasize the beneficence of nature; they are directed against an arid rationalistic theology that cuts man off from the rhythms of the natural world. The intuitions of joyous contemplation outweigh the cognizance of the darker side of nature. Even in the essay "Nature" there is, to be sure, the section on "Discipline" in which nature is seen as a discipline of the understanding, but the major stress is on an emotional and intuitive response. With the essay "Experience" the more rational response to the complexities of nature begins to dominate. Nature "is no saint." "She comes eating and drinking and sinning." And in "Fate," nature is "no sentimentalist. . . . The habit of snake and spider, the snap of the tiger and other leapers and bloody jumpers . . . these are in the system, and our habits are like theirs." In short, there is a clear shift in emphasis between Emerson's early and later interpretation of nature, and in the search for correspondences between man and nature which is one of his major concerns.

Between Frost's early and late poetry there is no such shift of emphasis from impulse or spontaneity to the recognition of evil and limitation as is found in Emerson's essays. Frost has kept the dialogue between feeling and thought circulating through nearly all of his poetry, most fully in his dramatic narratives, but also in his briefer lyrics. It is chiefly because of this that he is not Emersonian; his interpretations of experience—in his own words, his momentary stays against confusion—are not those of either Emerson, though they are nearer to Emerson's later than to his earlier phase.

Consider the whole theme of the correspondences between man and nature, which is so important in Emerson's prose and in his poetry. Many of Frost's poems center on this theme, and while several of them simply celebrate a brief moment of contemplation, transmuting an actual experience into a significant form, the most characteristic are those which pose a dilemma and resolve it. In one of the two or three most illuminating essays yet written on Frost's work, Robert Penn Warren traces this double attitude of acceptance and rejection in "Stopping by Woods," "Into My Own," "Come In," "After Apple-Picking" and "Birches." In each poem, as Warren shows, the speaker is strongly moved by an impulse to identify himself with nature, yet there is also the drawing back toward a properly human self-definition. In "Stopping by Woods" there is the attractiveness, the seductive and dark beauty of the woods filling up with snow. But there are also the promises to be kept. The speaker shows his humanity by his full awareness of this beauty, but he defines it finally by returning, as Warren says, "to the world of action and obligation." "We can accept neither term of the original contrast, the poem seems to say; we must find a dialectic that will accommodate both terms." Warren shows that the same conflict runs through the other poems he discusses, and that their common theme is "the idea that the reward, the dream, the ideal, stems from action and not from surrender of action."

There is a similar tension and resolution in many of Frost's other poems, especially those which recognize the mutability of nature. This mutability theme is pervasive in Romantic poetry. Romantic identification with nature oscillates between joyful celebration of nature's beauty and melancholy awareness of its transience. The ecstasy is apparent in Emerson's "Nature" and in many of his poems. The melancholy is familiar in many of the poems of Shelley, Keats and Coleridge. Frost, unlike the Romantics, defines a human attitude in the face of nature's mutability and transience either by opposition, or by seeking in nature itself a type of analogy which the Romantic poets ignore. He does not invest so heavily in nature as they do. He watches the whole curve and rhythm of the natural world and builds the human response on the minor chord in nature, and often by the very opposition Warren stresses in his essay.

The minor chord is the suggestion even in nature itself of refusal to ac-quiesce in mutability. "The Oven Bird" may know that "mid-summer is to spring as one to ten," yet he continues to sing when other birds have ceased:

> The question that he frames in all but words
> Is what to make of a diminished thing.

Again, "Hyla Brook" flows loud and swift from melting snows and early rains, but by June has "run out of song and speed." Then there is left only the dry stream-bed asking, one might say, what to make of a thing diminished to nothing.

> This as it will be seen is other far
> Than with brooks taken otherwhere in song.
> We love the things we love for what they are.

In "West-Running Brook" the central symbol is not the brook spending itself to nothingness, but the white wave that resists the lapsing away of the water:

> It is from this in nature we were from
> Long, long before we were from any creature.

A similar theme is expressed in small compass in the sonnet, "The Master Speed," in which the speed is, paradoxically, the capacity for thought and meditation, the ability to stand aside from contingency and reflect upon its meaning:

> You can climb
> Back up a stream of radiance to the sky,
> And back through history up the stream of time.
> And you were given this swiftness, not for haste
> Nor chiefly that you may go where you will,
> But in the rush of everything to waste,
> That you may have the power of standing still—
> Off any still or moving thing you say.

This same definition of a human response through opposition to nature's mutability is also found in "A Leaf Treader." The speaker in the poem has been treading leaves until he is "autumn-tired." He momentar-ily entertains the impulse to identify his own mood with the decay of nature, but only to reject the impulse:

> They tapped at my eyelids and touched my lips with
>   an invitation to grief.
> But it was no reason I had to go because they
>   had to go.
> Now up my knee to keep on top of another year
>   of snow.

Turning from the nature themes to the dramatic poems, we find a difference in the whole approach of Emerson and Frost to the meaning of human personality—a difference that is of great significance, however difficult it may be to sum it up briefly. To deal with their conceptions of the person and society, to estimate the extent to which Frost's "individualism" is like Emerson's would require a separate essay. Certainly Frost's attitude as expressed in his poetry is closer to what is called in contemporary thought "personalism" than it is to the nineteenth century type of individualism that Emerson represents.

This difference in attitude toward personality is apparent in the very style and technique of the two writers. The essay as a form in the hands of Emerson becomes a monologue in which we overhear him conversing with himself, or a sermon in which he exhorts us to a life of virtue and of sensitivity to the ever new meaning of the universe. He can be oracular and epigrammatic, can sum up his findings on Intellect, Love, Heroism, Self-Reliance, Character, without opposition. Frost, on the other hand, has put much of his finest poetry into the form of dialogue. By so doing, he achieves the full dialectical quality that Emerson misses or, at best, achieves but partially in his essays and in his poetry. Frost is willing to sacrifice "conclusions" for dramatic immediacy and realism. He is more tentative but also more objective; the play of other personalities and the tone and cadences of other voices than his own run through all his work. The search for conclusions, for resolutions of conflicting thoughts and emotions, the impact of grief and loneliness, all are dramatized by Frost through the interplay of individual human beings.

The difference in their understanding of personality is also apparent in the contrast between Emerson's recurrent exhortation that we must transcend personality and Frost's tenacious adherence to the particularity of things as well as of people. Emerson's essay on "Love" follows Plato's "Symposium" in describing love as ultimately transcending personality and becoming love of the universal. Platonism can, to be sure, be harmonized with the Christian concept of love of God and of neighbor, but Emerson's essay does not succeed in harmonizing them. It is a cold theoretical performance, one with which even Emerson was dissatisfied. It represents a form of Platonism which Frost rejects both explicitly in prose statements and implicitly in his poetry. Love in Frost's poetry is the love of men and women for one another, for beauty, for knowledge, for things made well and with an eye to function.

It is in Frost's dramatic narratives, notably those of *North of Boston*, that his attitude toward experience is seen to be least Emersonian. There is in these poems such a full confrontation of disappointment, frustration, and failure as is not to be found in Emerson's work. In tone they have usually been called pathetic rather than tragic, yet in most of them there is a movement toward self-definition and self-knowledge that is tragic or close to the tragic. Few of Frost's protagonists are passive victims, nor do they escape into a romantic dream-world; we see them at a moment of crisis confronting the existential situation in all its ironic reality. And they have the integrity that comes with the awareness, however dim, that more than circumstance is involved in their trials. Somehow they have chosen, and would not have it otherwise. The title of Frost's early poem, "The Trial by Existence," suggests the underlying theme of many of these poems. The fact is that the mode of these poems is closer to that of the metaphysicals than to that of the romantics. The "ideal" is entangled and interfused in the seemingly commonplace and fortuitous. For example, the action of "In the Home Stretch," from *Mountain Interval*, is simply the delivery of the furniture and belongings of a middle-aged couple from the city to the farm, where they intend to settle down for good. But the banter, the gestures, the implied criticism of their action by the furniture movers arouse second thoughts, doubts, and forebodings in the two moving to the darkness and solitude of the country. The poem lays bare the possibility of their resigning themselves to despair. The wife is tempted to; the husband keeps interposing possibilities for the future, and looks forward to inspecting "pasture, mowing, well, and brook" the next morning. The theme might be stated somewhat as follows: contentment and happiness require a certain activity of the will, a refusal to let mood drive one toward despair. The husband and wife have fashioned for themselves an image of the personal meaning of this moving to the country, but the scorn of the young city boys for country life, the oncoming darkness, the bleakness and emptiness of the house make them suddenly question the reasons that have led them to their choice. But when the men have left, they regain their composure, though the husband confesses: "They almost shook me." What is significant in such a poem is Frost's full confronting of this sense of isolation in men, and his recognition of the human need to master the imagination in its shifting moods.

Consideration of such poems as Frost's "A Servant to Servants," "The Witch of Coös," "Design," "Acquainted with the Night," "Once by the Pacific" would give a fuller awareness of that element in his work which Trilling calls "terrifying." Insofar as this aspect of Frost's work has been minimized, Trilling did a great service to criticism in emphasizing it so effectively and so movingly. Yet these poems and others similar in tone and theme are not the whole of Frost. His poetry spans a wide spectrum. Celebration of form, radiance and design in the natural order, and the lyric or dramatic evocation of those moments when man discovers joy and reward in his work are at one end of the spectrum. At the other end are those poems which Trilling has in mind as being the most significant work of "his Frost." My own Frost would be closer to R. P. Warren's than to either of these extremes. The interplay and the tension between the human and the non-human, the sense of a goodness in the natural order which evokes and challenges human response without fulfilling the need for a properly human self-definition—this is the vision, as it seems to me, that subsumes, or perhaps connects, both extremes. And largely because it has the dialectical and dramatic quality which Warren emphasizes, it is an unEmersonian vision. Or to speak more accurately, if this Frost bears some resemblance to Emerson, it is not at all to the Emerson most critics have in mind when they compare the two. Rather, Frost is, in the poems of the darker vision, like the Emerson recovered by such critics as Stephen Whicher, and, in the more serene lyrics, like Arvin's Emerson of "the more-than-tragic emotion of thankfulness." This constitutes the poetic ground on which Frost and Emerson really meet.

Robert Frost's "Directive" out of *Walden*

S. P. C. Duvall*

By emphasizing idea and aphorism, those who evaluate Robert Frost's indebtedness to his literary antecedents in New England too often guide us away from rather than back to his poetry.[1] Yet Frost's own insistence on "poem as metaphor" might be a more reliable signpost for his readers.[2] An examination of Frost's metaphors, in one important poem certainly, not only reveals Thoreau as a genuine inspiration (so far only glancingly noted), but by doing so drives us even deeper into the poem. For "Directive," a widely acclaimed Frost poem, bears the unmistakable imprint of Thoreau—or at least of *Walden*.

"Directive," published first in 1946 and later included in the collection *Steeple Bush*, is a gathering of traditional and authentic New England images formed to a metaphor of quest. Using by extension Grail allusions, along with others, the poet (in the literal imagery) leads us, fearful, upwards and back along an abandoned road, past abandoned houses or, more fearfully, past abandoned cellar holes—mere "dents in dough" marked now only by the surging lilacs—to seek out and reclaim at one homestead a drinking goblet consecrated in the play of children. With this cup we are led then to the long abandoned brook and thus directed:

> Here are your waters and your watering place.
> Drink and be whole again beyond confusion.[3]

The poem's imagery, not only in its detail but, crucially, in its extensions and its ultimate meaning, may be traced to autochthonous origins in *Walden*. As Randell Jarrell has suggested, we need no Grail notes for this poem.[4]

Frost is on record in specifying *Walden* as one of his favorite books, as "everything from a tale of adventure . . . to a declaration of independence and a gospel of wisdom."[5] It has for him, he says, "something of the same fascination" of *Robinson Crusoe* (another favorite) in showing him "how the limited can make snug in the limitless."

*From *American Literature*, January, 1960, pp. 482–88. Copyright © 1960 by *American Literature*. Reprinted by permission.

Cruso was cast away; Thoreau was self-cast away. Both found themselves sufficient. No prose writer has ever been more fortunate in subject
than these two. I prefer my essay in narrative form. In *Walden* I get it and
always near the height of poetry.[6]

With "Directive" in mind, let us consider one small segment of this
narrative essay. Self-cast away at Walden, Thoreau in "House-warming"
prepares to make snug in the winter, going a "step or two beyond instinct"
by boxing up in the hut the vital heat of his fireplace. The fireplace fire
was also a companion—"you can always see a face in the fire"—and
Thoreau hints his sorrow during the second winter beside the "compact
utilitarian heap" of a stove where, without the dim flitting shadows, "The
present may sit down and go to sleep,/Nor fear the ghosts who from the
dim past walked,/And with us by the unequal light of the old wood fire
talked."[7] "Housewarming" ending on this note, we are prepared for the
succeeding chapter, "Former Inhabitants; and Winter Visitors," by the
ghosts from the dim past.

For human society in that fireside winter, Thoreau "was obliged to
conjure up the former occupants of these woods" (p. 414), conjurations
out of his own sufficiency. Along a former road by Walden Thoreau
wanders, his firelit imagination repeopling the deserted dwellings: the
shacks of Cato Ingraham, Zilpha the witch, and Brister Freeman—slaves
or former slaves; the Stratton farm "whose orchard once covered all the
slope of Brister's Hill, but was long since killed out by pitch pines . . ." (p.
416); Breed's location, the tavern; and the huts of Nutting, Le Grosse,
Wyman, and Hugh Quoil. Thoreau even remembers visiting Quoil's
house before it was pulled down: "His pipe lay broken on the hearth, instead of a bowl broken at the fountain. The last could never have been the
symbol of his death, for he confessed to me that, though he had heard of
Brister's Spring, he had never seen it. . . ."[8]

Now, remarks Thoreau, "only a dent in the earth marks the site of
these dwellings, . . . cellar dents, like deserted fox burrows, old
holes, . . . all that is left where once were the stir and bustle of human
life, and 'fate, free will, foreknowledge absolute,' in some form and
dialect or other were by turns discussed."

> Still grows the vivacious lilac a generation after the door and lintel and
> the sill are gone, unfolding its sweet-scented flowers each spring, to be
> plucked by the musing traveller; planted and tended once by children's
> hands, in front-yard plots—now standing by wallsides in retired pastures,
> and giving place to new-rising forests;—the last of that stirp, sole survivor
> of that family. Little did the dusky children think that the puny slip with
> its two eyes only, which they stuck in the ground in the shadow of the
> house and daily watered, would root itself so, and outlive them, and
> house itself in the rear that shaded it, and grown man's garden and or-
> chard, and tell their story faintly to the lone wanderer a half-century after
> they had grown up and died. . . . (p. 419)

Why, asks Thoreau finally, did this small village fail? "Were there no natural advantages—no water privileges, forsooth? Ay, the deep Walden Pond and cool Brister's Spring—privilege to drink long and healthy draughts at these, all unimproved by these men but to dilute their glass" (pp. 419–420). But these waters are now Thoreau's privileges, and "again, perhaps, Nature will try, with me for a first settler, and my house raised last spring to be the oldest in the hamlet." Thus, with such imaginings, he "repeopled the woods and lulled [himself] asleep" (p. 420).

Surely such an extravagant excursion is adventure near the height of poetry. Snugly withdrawn against the unlimited confusion of winter, Thoreau still leads us to the spirit's watering places, to Brister's Spring and Walden Pond and, ultimately, to the Ganges. And what, he had asked earlier, do we want most to dwell near to? To our watering places, "to the perennial source of our life, whence in all our experience we have found that to issue, . . . this is the place where a wise man will dig his cellar" (p. 333). This then is our directive.

Frost's poem, similarly, is a directive to the perennial source of our life, for our ultimate goal, our destination and our destiny, is the brook near the belilacked cellar hole. To begin the journey we must get "Back out of all this now too much for us"—the equivalent of Thoreau's advice to simplify, to "work and wedge our feet downward through the mud and slush of opinion, and prejudice, and tradition, and delusion, and appearance, that alluvion which covers the globe, . . . till we come to a hard bottom and rocks in place, which we can call *reality*, and say, This is, and no mistake. . . ."[9]

But the poem is not only directive, it is conjuration too. There is an edge of fear in the journey, a suggestion of ghosts, of "being watched from forty cellar holes/As if by eye pairs out of forty firkins," so that Frost advises the quester:

> Make yourself up a cheering song of how
> Someone's road home from work this once was,
> Who may be just ahead of you on foot
> Or creaking with a buggy load of grain.

This is a kind of "whistling in the dark" as we progress, to protect ourselves against the serial ordeal, the complications of time—the eye pairs now increased forty-fold from the original puny slip planted by the children.

And of course this is adventure. In this excursion under the poet's direction, simplified by the gradual sloughing of detail, by stripping life to its essence, we are searching for what amounts to the faded remains of two lost villages (one of them Thoreau's):

> The height of the adventure is the height
> Of country where two village cultures faded
> Into each other. Both of them are lost.

But from the first Frost has sought to lose *us* too, to make *us* castaways (". . . if you'll let a guide direct you/Who only has at heart your getting lost . . ."). So, after all, who is lost? And lost to what? "Lost enough to find yourself," he concludes. Thoreau had remarked:

> not till we are completely lost . . . do we appreciate the vastness and strangeness of nature. . . . Not till we are lost, in other words not till we have lost the world, do we begin to find ourselves, and realize where we are and the infinite extent of our relations.[10]

To Frost, also, being lost is prelude to discovery; once we are lost we can make ourselves at home. The water privileges are before us. And we proceed now in childlike innocence, for the "Grail" is a child's plaything.

But this must not mislead us.[11] Every child plays house, Thoreau reminds us (p. 262); but in children's play at life they "discern its true law and relations more clearly than men." Grownups, he goes on, live their lives meanly because their vision does not "penetrate the surface of things. We think that that *is* which *appears* to be" (p. 308). Children know better; lost before the welter of the world's confusion they quite naturally make snug in their imagination.[12]

A further extension may be made at this point, for Frost's "Directive" suggests conjuration in another, more specialized way. This is the indirection of a poet hinting at his own play. The height of this adventure is also the height of poetry which, as Frost has remarked, is the "attempt to say matter in terms of spirit and spirit in terms of matter."[13] One conjures with the word, ad-ventures into the imagination, and the results are metaphor—the cross of matter and spirit. If obscurities result, they are inevitable—not willful, Thoreau had explained, but inseparable from the "very nature [of my trade]. I would gladly tell all that I know about it, and never paint 'No Admittance' on my gate" (pp. 254–255). Yet ironically this ingenuousness immediately precedes one of *Walden's* most famous obscurities: the hound, the bay horse, and the turtle-dove.

Thus if Frost on the other hand advises us at the height to

> . . . pull in your ladder road behind you
> And put a sign up CLOSED to all but me

he merely recognizes, like Thoreau, an exclusiveness in metaphorical expression. For Thoreau in the concluding chapter of *Walden* rejects the "ridiculous demand which England and America make, that you shall speak so that they can understand you":

> The volatile truth of our words should continually betray the inadequacy of the residual statement. Their truth is instantly *translated*; its literal monument alone remains. The words which express our faith and piety are not definite; yet they are significant and fragrant like frankincense to superior natures.

* *

I do not suppose that I have attained to obscurity, but I should be proud if no more fatal fault were found with my pages on this score than was found with the Walden ice. (pp. 459–460)

Frost's No Admission sign, then, marks "conjuration" ground. There is a spell on the broken goblet (which he had stolen from the children's playhouse) "so the wrong ones can't find it,/So can't get saved, as Saint Mark says they mustn't." The broken goblet becomes a metaphor for poetry, or more narrowly, a metaphor for metaphor: the form and container of the perennial and limitless source.[14] And so the very concluding words of the poem, "Drink and be whole again beyond confusion," points us toward a favorite Frost definition: the poem as a "momentary stay against confusion."[15]

Once such extensive parallels as these become apparent, it seems perfectly proper to insist on a closer kinship of Frost and Thoreau than has usually been noted. Such Frostian themes as his "self-withdrawal," his insistence on freedom and independence, his quest of the present moment, or his stripping of life to its essence—themes rising constantly in his conversation as well as his poetry[16]—may be found as easily in *Walden* as in Emerson's works. But we must remember, finally, that Frost finds *Walden* "near the height of poetry"; and poetry to Frost is, above all, metaphor. Both the particularity of his imagery and its extension into metaphor align Frost with Thoreau rather than with Emerson, just as do his wit, his verbal precision,[17] and his command of the ironic mode—all features of the same technique, the same informing poetic eye.

When, then, Frost directs us back to our sources, by utilizing image and metaphor from the perennial spring of *Walden* he points us back at the same time to one of the great watering places of American literature.

Notes

1. See, for example, R. L. Cook, "Emerson and Frost: A Parallel of Seers," *NEQ*, XXXI, 200–217 (June, 1958).

2. Lawrance Thompson, *Fire and Ice* (New York, 1942), p. 51.

3. All quotations from "Directive" are taken from the *Complete Poems of Robert Frost 1949* (New York, 1949), pp. 520–521.

4. *New York Times Book Review*, June 1, 1947, p. 4.

5. *The Listener*, LII, 319 (Aug. 26, 1954).

6. *Books We Like* (Boston, 1936), pp. 141–142.

7. *The Works of Thoreau*, ed. H. S. Canby (Boston, 1937), pp. 413–414. (All subsequent quotations from *Walden* will be taken from this edition.) Before his winter fire Thoreau was alone but, emphatically, not lonely. Cf. pp. 336, 357–358.

8. P. 418. The image of the spring rumored but unseen is central to Frost's poem "The Mountain," *Complete Poems*, pp. 56–60.

9. P. 309; cf. p. 463. It may be worth noting that Frost's opening line, here quoted, is a near perfect line poetically, expressing in its web of monosyllabic functional words the very complex clutter of ordinary, day-to-day detail we must escape.

10. P. 359. Thoreau goes on here to speak of men "pawing" man with their "dirty institutions." Cf. Frost's guidance of his students: "I'm entitled to nine hours of your time—three in class and two outside for each of those. All right, I present it to you. This is the time you can lose yourselves. You've got to do some losing of yourself to find yourself. . . . I'll keep the institution off your back to that extent." Quoted in Sidney Cox, *A Swinger of Birches* (New York, 1957), p. 49.

11. It seems to have misled Jarrell; see his review cited above.

12. Hence the veiled allusion in "Directive" to the child's romance of Ali Baba (the "eye pairs out of forty firkins") is not simply a playful development of the multiplied eye pairs of the lilac, but an echo of Thoreau's words in the context just cited: "If men would steadily observe realities only, and not allow themselves to be deluded, life, to compare it with such things as we know, would be like a fairy tale and the Arabian Nights' Entertainments" (p. 308).

13. Quoted in Thompson, p. 55.

14. Twice, at least, this has been Frost's own gloss of the Saint Mark reference. In a public reading of his poetry at Dartmouth College on December 6, 1956, he said, "Saint Mark says that these things of Christ are said in parables so the wrong ones won't understand them and then get saved. It seems that people weren't meant to be saved if they didn't understand figures of speech" (reported in *The Dartmouth*, December 7, 1956). See also the transcription of Frost's "Meet the Press" telecast, reprinted in the *Boston Globe*, December 30, 1956.

15. "The Figure a Poem Makes," *Complete Poems*, p. vi. In the same paragraph Frost remarks on the predestined though unforeseen outcome of a poem: "It finds its own name as it goes and discovers the best waiting for it in some final phrase at once wise and sad—the happy-sad blend of the drinking song."

16. R. L. Cook's *The Dimensions of Robert Frost* (New York, 1958) and Sidney Cox's *A Swinger of Birches*, previously noted, offer abundant recorded conversation, almost to the exclusion of the poetry. Both Thompson and Cook, moreover, seem to me to emphasize an Emersonian alignment.

17. Both men, for example, are neologists. It is worth noting that Frost, in "A Record Stride" (*Complete Poems*, p. 381) hyphenates *extra-vagant* into new meaning as did Thoreau in the "Conclusion" of Walden (p. 459). See also Frost's comments on neologism in *The Listener*.

Robert Frost and the Edge
of the Clearing

James M. Cox*

When Robert Frost nears a university campus in this country there is a bustle of interest and activity extending beyond the confining borders of the English department. A curious observer is struck by the realization that Frost's approaching appearance is no mere item on the college calendar but an event which makes its presence felt in the area of public relations. Even the distant administrative machinery can be heard to stir in anticipation of Frost's arrival, and when the hour comes round for Frost himself to take the stage a member of officialdom above and beyond the orbit of mere liberal arts is likely to perform the rites of introduction as the Frost cycle begins over again. It has been a cycle repeated in one place or another for almost thirty years, expanding with the passage of time as Frost has established himself securely in the position which Mark Twain created in the closing years of the last century—the position of American literary man as public entertainer. Frost brings to his rôle the grave face, the regional turn of phrase, the pithy generalization, and the salty experience which Twain before him brought to his listeners. He is the homespun farmer who assures his audiences that he was made in America before the advent of the assembly line, and he presides over his following with what is at once casual ease and lonely austerity.

Because the popularity surrounding Frost the public figure and hovering about his poetry has become the halo under which admirers enshrine his work, to many serious critics bent on assessing the value of the poetry this halo becomes a sinister mist clouding the genuine achievement. Malcolm Cowley, for example, has raised a dissenting voice against the foggy approval; and even Randall Jarrell, who has written some of the most sensitive appraisals of Frost's poetry, inclines to dissociate the real or "other" Frost from the brassy New England character who parades before his audiences as what Jarrell calls "The Only Genuine Robert Frost in Captivity."

Yet Frost's success as a public figure, rather than being a calculated addition to his poetic career, is a natural extension of it, and one way to

*From *The Virginia Quarterly Review* (Winter, 1959). Copyright © 1959 by *The Virginia Quarterly Review*. Reprinted by permission of the review and the author.

approach his poetry is to see that the character who moves in the poems anticipates the one who occupies the platform. They are in all essentials the same character—a dramatization of the farmer poet come out of his New England landscape bringing with him the poems he plays a rôle in. To observe this insistent regional stance is to realize that Frost has done, and is still doing, for American poetry what Faulkner has more recently accomplished in American fiction. They both have made their worlds in the image of their particular regions, and, moving within these self-contained and self-made microcosms, they have given their provincial centers universal significance. But while Faulkner has concerned himself with establishing the legendary Yoknapatawpha county and its mythical components, Frost has, from the very first poem of "A Boy's Will," been engaged in creating the myth of Robert Frost, The Only Genuine Robert Frost in Captivity. It is a myth with a hero and a drama.

The hero is the New England farmer who wears the mask, or better, the anti-mask of the traditional poet. But it is not a literal mask concealing the poet who lurks behind it; rather, it is a mode of being which releases the poetic personality in the person of a character who lives and moves. Whatever duality we may wish to ascribe between mask and man is actually present in the mask itself, for the mask—or character—of Frost is finally more real than any hypothetical Frost we may envision behind the scenes. The very life of the character depends upon his creator's ability to project his whole personality into the image he assumes. Frost is, for his audience, a "character" simply because he represents both in language and outlook a vastly familiar figure to them, a kind of traditional stage Yankee full of gnomic wisdom and prankish humor, carrying his history in his head and venturing cryptic comment upon all experience in a sufficiently provincial manner to remind them of a preconceived caricature.

It is Frost's ability to *be* a farmer poet which distinguishes him most sharply from Wordsworth, with whom he is often compared. Wordsworth played the part of the Poet concerned with common man, but Frost has persistently cast himself in the rôle of the common man concerned with poetry. Such a strategy, while it cuts him off from the philosophically autobiographical poetry which Wordsworth built toward, opens up avenues of irony, wit, comedy, and dramatic narrative largely closed to Wordsworth. For the poetic ego, held in objectivity by the anti-mask which both releases and contains it, is exposed to a control and ironic self-awareness foreign to the serious and subjective Wordsworth, who, although he felt keenly the joy of experience, rarely descended to humor.

Thus, instead of direct revelation through autobiography and confession, Frost has from the start pursued the more indirect but equally effective mode of dramatizing and characterizing himself. Even the lyrics of "A Boy's Will" lean toward narrative and monologue, and the peculiar Frost idiom, so integral a part of the Frost character who eventually emerges, is evident in remarkable maturity in such early poems as "Into

My Own," "Mowing," "A Tuft of Flowers," and "In Hardwood Groves."
The dramatic monologues and dialogues of "North of Boston," which
have impressed many critics as a wide departure from Frost's lyric vein,
constitute a full discovery and perfection of that idiom. Moreover, Frost
himself emerges prominently as a member of the volume's *dramatis personae*, playing an important rôle in nine of the sixteen poems. As a matter
of fact, "Mending Wall," the first poem in the volume, marks the full-
dress entrance of the farmer poet. Possessed of all the characteristics by
which we have come to know him, this figure is full of sly observations as
he assumes a slightly comic poise with eye asquint—already poetry is "his
kind of fooling." He goes to great length to disarm his audience with colloquial familiarity and whimsical parentheses. Then, after an agile imaginative leap in the grand style, he returns to earth as if he feared being
caught off guard.

This cautious refusal to declaim too far or too soon, while it may
leave too much unsaid or enclose the issue in a blurred dual vision which
accepts both sides, is often one of Frost's most effective modes of self
awareness. Thus, when Yvor Winters, in his discussion of "The Road Not
Taken," holds Frost responsible for refusing to make clear the kind of
choice represented by the two roads which "diverged in a yellow wood,"
he misses the comic criticism the speaker is directing against himself. As
Professor Ben W. Griffith has rightly observed, Frost is indulging in a
bemused self-portrayal. When he made the choice, he made it not profoundly but tentatively and uncertainly; he was even incapable of
distinguishing which road *was* the least traveled—"And both that morning equally lay/In leaves no step had trodden black"—but he envisions the
day when he shall sighingly, and rather heavily, tell of his decision to take
the road "less traveled by," the road that has made "all the difference."
The poem, in addition to demolishing the cliché of life's crossroads, is a vision of as well as a warning against the wise old farmer poet whose
retrospective summary of his past may attribute a wisdom to former actions which was never there.

Beyond this playfully ironic self portrayal so characteristic of Frost,
there is also the tragic self-awareness which enabled him to create the
great dramatic monologues. In such poems as "The Fear," "Home
Burial," and "A Servant to Servants," for example, sensitive wives are so
caught between the lonely natural world and the rigid proverbs of their
husbands that, locked in an unutterable loneliness, they disintegrate into
hysteria or slump into depression. Those husbands bear enough similarity
to the figure of the farmer poet to indicate how much Frost realizes, for
all his willingness to exploit the poetic possibilities of aphorism—how
blind and hard a proverb quoter can be.

If Frost needs self-awareness to protect himself from the Yankee
wisdom in which he specializes, he also needs it to confront the world he
moves in, that lonely and desolate world where the Frost drama is staged.

Despite his literal realism, Frost has never been a mere reflector of his chosen New England locale; rather, he has managed to create the illusion of making the world he describes, and in his hands the region north of Boston becomes a self-sustaining yet surprisingly inclusive microcosm with the character of Frost himself at its center. Even the eccentricities of crabbed New England speech and attitude have poetic validity because, more than being details to characterize and individuate a geographical province, they belong to the central character and constitute his authentic signature upon the world he makes and owns. The entire region beneath his vision becomes his property, an extension of himself, and Frost's ability to project his character into his provincial world has given his poetry the double thrust it so often possesses—a thrust outward into the wild nature in which he persistently finds himself, and a thrust inward to the darker regions of the self.

Like his great New England antecedents, Emerson and Thoreau, he casts his own shadow upon the landscape he surveys. Skeptical in his cast of mind, Frost inclines away from their tendency to abstract doctrine, but he retains much of the method and many of the attitudes they left behind them, nor is it surprising that "Walden" is one of his favorite books. Thoreau's strategy was to move round and round the pond, keeping his eye alertly upon that self-contained body of water until, in the final chapter of his microcosmic odyssey, he had possessed it. His progress was parabolic in the mathematical sense, for his walking arc was midway between the pond, the focus, and the set of principles which formed the directrix of his journey. The more Thoreau discovered about the pond, the more he plotted a central index to life, since the pond was both mirror for man and eye of God in which the traveler could take a final measure of himself. In sounding it he sounded himself, and Thoreau fulfilled his dual rôle of explorer and surveyor by at once discovering and charting a course to sustain him through all modes of existence.

Frost has also been intent on possessing his world, but he started with no given center, no sure assumptions, and no assurance that there would be assumptions. His work has been no experiment to test himself, but the venture of a lifetime. His first poem in "A Boy's Will," significantly entitled "Into My Own," expressed a wish that the deep woods confronting him, instead of being a mere mask of darkness, stretched endlessly out toward the edge of doom. Doubling his subjunctive, Frost wished that he could lose himself in the infinite depths of such a forest, but extended a subdued invitation to those who loved him to follow his footsteps into the trackless wood. Although Frost's title of this first volume of poetry came from Longfellow's memorable refrain, "A boy's will is the wind's will," he was already advancing into the areas where Longfellow had refused to go. For in "My Lost Youth," Longfellow, after quite brilliantly returning into the Portland of his memory toward the secret regions of his boyhood, had paused at the threshold of Deering's Woods as if confronting a secret terror and, content to excuse himself with a pious admonition—"There are things of which I may not speak"—, he retreated back into nostalgia. Taking and retaining the boy's will to explore, Frost has forced a clearing in the woods which Longfellow declined to enter, and his career has been in many ways a realization of his earliest wish.

The clearing he has wrought is his own, and he works constantly at its edge, laying claim to the marginal world between the wild and the tame. The figure of the clearing, while it obviously does not appear in every poem, suggests the quality of experience which Frost has been intent upon possessing, and in "The Last Mowing," one of his most delicate lyrics, the dimensions as well as the drama of his world appear in sharp focus:

> There's a place called Far-away Meadow
> We never shall mow in again,
> Or such is the talk at the farmhouse:
> The meadow is finished with men.
> Then now is the chance for flowers
> That can't stand mowers and plowers.
> It must be now, though, in season
> Before the not mowing brings trees on,
> Before trees, seeing the opening,
> March into a shadowy claim.
> The trees are all I'm afraid of,
> That flowers can't bloom in the shade of;
> It's no more men I'm afraid of;
> The meadow is done with the tame.
> The place for the moment is ours
> For you, oh tumultuous flowers,
> To go to waste and go wild in,
> All shapes and colors of flowers,
> I needn't call you by name.

Remaining in the moving margin where resurgent nature returns upon abandoned meadowland, Frost attempts to wrest the moment of beauty elapsing where order dissolves into chaos. He is no more afraid of the threatening woods than at another time he has been afraid of the men who cleared the field, for the wild flowers perish before both forces. In the face of the oncoming woods, Frost discovers a moment of joy in the midst of his tender elegy, since in that forgotten territory he can perform a solitary celebration for the beauty which remains.

Seeing the nature of his task, one can understand why he contended in "The Constant Symbol" that every poem is "an epitome of the great predicament; a figure of the will braving alien entanglements." Indeed, the woods, always ready to encroach upon his tenuous margin, suggest the alien entanglements against which Frost pits his will, and the drama he sees the poet playing recalls Emerson's insistence that a man must be self-reliant, "obeying the Almighty Effort and advancing on Chaos and the dark." But even as he accepts the antagonists of the Emersonian drama, Frost, lacking Emerson's evangelical temperament, recognizes a larger chaos and sees the drama of existence as man's willingness to risk himself before the spell of the dark woods. For him self-reliance becomes self-possession, and the victory lies not in the march forward into the wilderness but in the freedom he feels while patroling the boundary of consciousness. He accepts with almost joy the entanglements because he knows that the material of the unwrought poem inheres in that wilderness. Thus in "Pertinax" he advocates holding on:

> Let Chaos storm!
> Let cloud shapes swarm!
> I wait for form.

And in "The Figure a Poem Makes," he is even more emphatic: "All I would keep for myself is the freedom of my material—the condition of body and mind to summons aptly now and then from the vast chaos I have lived through."

Cryptic though his prose is, it is his own guarded commentary upon his work, offering essential insights into his poetic terrain. When Frost says that chaos lies behind him, he points up the temporal dimension of his world. Unlike Emerson, he is deeply concerned with his past—not the past of organized tradition so much as the disorganized past he himself has strewn behind. The literal facts of his New England world afford a scenic analogy against which the Frost character performs his act, for the woods he works in are no virgin wilderness but second-growth timber come back to claim abandoned human landscape. The black cottage, the belilaced cellar hole "slowly closing like a dent in dough," the overgrown path, the old barn at the bottom of the fogs remain forsakenly within his rural scenes as the surviving witnesses of lost encounters with the forest. In repossessing them, Frost is turning back upon himself to reclaim the fragments of his personal past—fragments which apparently meant nothing when they were current but which come to constitute the primary medium of exchange in the economy of reorganization.

Frugal as Frost's economy is, its aim is no easy security, for his clearing is as hard to hold as it is to win. In addition to the remnants of abandoned farms, there are also the living victims who linger in stunned confusion along the border—the woman in "A Servant to Servants" for example, whose mind is as hemmed in as the lake she gazes out upon; or the old man in "An Old Man's Winter Night," trapped in a house where "all out of doors looked darkly in at him"; or the witch of Coös, who, living with her mentally arrested son, finds her imaginative release in rehearsing for a stranger her half-forged, half-pathetic ghost story. Above all, there is the poet himself, who feels the terror of loneliness. Caught alone in the woods beneath the onset of winter's first snow, he feels the full threat of alien forces, and, although he knows that "all the precedent" is on his side and that spring *will* come again, he stumbles,

> looking up and round,
> As one who overtaken by the end
> Gives up his errand, and lets death descend
> Upon him where he is, with nothing done
> To evil, no important triumph won,
> More than if life had never been begun.

In these moments of terror, the outer threat of nature, with its ominous woods, its appalling snow, its rustling leaves hissing along the ground, gives rise to the deepest inner fears. The entire landscape becomes a haunting reflection of psychic desolation. If Frost can contemplate the infinity of space with a certain equanimity it is not because he feels more secure than Pascal but because, as he says,

> I have it in me so much nearer home
> To scare myself with my own desert places.

Confronting these desert places of his landscape, Frost needs all the restraint at his command, for the dark woods possess a magnetic attraction drawing him spellbound into them. The trees, whose branches reach out toward him and whose leaves insistently whisper an invitation, are, as Frost has written, the "vague dream heads" come out of the ground to beckon him to succumb to the mystery of their depths. Frost finds his power of resistance and control in the measured language of poetry—he even speaks of the poem as a "momentary stay against confusion." And he loves the metered line, choosing to leave free verse to Carl Sandburg on the ground that he, Frost, "would as soon write free verse as play tennis with the net down."

The haunting rhythms of "Stopping by Woods on a Snowy Evening" express the powerful fascination the woods have upon the lonely traveler, who, in the face of a long journey, descending night, and falling snow, pauses in the gathering gloom of the "darkest evening of the year," transfixed by the compelling invitation of the forest:

> Whose woods these are I think I know.
> His house is in the village though;
> He will not see me stopping here
> To watch his woods fill up with snow.
>
> My little horse must think it queer
> To stop without a farmhouse near
> Between the woods and frozen lake
> The darkest evening of the year.
>
> He gives his harness bells a shake
> To ask if there is some mistake.

> The only other sound's the sweep
> Of easy wind and downy flake.
>
> The woods are lovely, dark and deep,
> But I have promises to keep,
> And miles to go before I sleep,
> And miles to go before I sleep.

The poem is *about* the spell of the woods—the traveler's own woods, we want to say, but they are alien enough and belong to someone else enough for him to sense the trespass of his intent gaze into them at the same time he recognizes their sway over him. His heightened awareness projects his concern for himself back to the representatives of civilization, the unseen owner of the woods and the horse in harness. Thus, the indifferent animal becomes, in his master's alerted imagination, the guardian who sounds the alarm which rings above the whispered invitation.

The poem *is* the counter-spell against the invitation, the act by which the traveler regains dominion of his will. The intricately interlocked rhyme scheme (*aaba, bbcb, ccdc, dddd*) and the strict iambic tetrameter, while they imitate and suggest the hypnotic power of the forest, also form the basis of a protective charm against that power. The logic of the rhyme scheme, in which the divergent third line of one stanza becomes the organizing principle of the next, is an expression of the growing control and determination described in the syntax. Thus, the first line of the last quatrain finally *names* the nature of the spell and also provides the term which is answered in rhyme by the poet's decision to refuse the invitation.

Seen in this light, the poem reveals what Frost means when he says that "every poem written regular is a symbol small or great of the way the will has to pitch into the commitments deeper and deeper to a rounded conclusion. . . ." He sees the form as both instrument and embodiment of the will braving the alien entanglements of experience—the commitments—for it must organize and at the same time contain its material. The poem in its totality is the image of the will in action, and the poet's spirit and courage convert words into deeds. The words are the given, and "We make them do," he says, and continues: "Form in language is such a disjected lot of old broken pieces it seems almost non-existent as the spirit till the two embrace in the sky." In the completed poem both form and spirit have encountered not "in rivalry but in creation." The creation is not a forging of a new world, but the discovery and grasp of a world at once familiar and strange. The act of writing is, to return to the statement I have quoted earlier, a plunge into the vast chaos the poet has lived through and a bringing into the full range of consciousness as much of that half-known life as possible. That is the meaning of self-possession.

And Frost, like the Paul Bunyan in "Paul's Wife," is a terrible possessor; indeed, the action of that poem recapitulates Frost's own process of creation. In the pith of an unsound saw log abandoned in disgust by the practical sawyer, Paul discovered the material which, after he had delicately carved it out and carefully dipped it in the waters of a mountain lake, emerged into consciousness to become the fabled wife whom he protected from the brute tribute to beauty offered by the curious lumbermen:

> Owning a wife with him meant owning her.
> She wasn't anybody else's business,
> Either to praise her, or so much as name her,
> And he'd thank people not to think of her.
> Murphy's idea was that a man like Paul
> Wouldn't be spoken to about a wife
> In any way the world knew how to speak.

Frost too has gone back into the desolation of a world abandoned to seize his own particular kind of beauty.

Of course, he has shared it with the world, but he clings fiercely to his poems as his private property, and even the titles of his several volumes describe the progress of his endeavor to lay claim to his world. From "A Boy's Will" he went on to define his province, "North of Boston," and in "Mountain Interval," "New Hampshire," and "West Running Brook," he established enough landmarks within the region to open what he calls "A Further Range." In "A Witness Tree," the tree, once a part of the wilder woods, bears the wound he has given it as a witness of his ownership, and Frost himself assumes the rôle of landowner, leading his reader along the boundaries of his property. Finally, in "Steeple Bush," the hardhack flowering at the edge of the clearing stands as the precious item he holds against the ever-returning woods. The property he reclaims from the ruins of time he insistently refuses to relinquish:

> I could give all to Time except—except
> What I myself have held. But why declare
> The things forbidden that while the Customs slept
> I have crossed to safety with? For I am there
> And what I would not part with I have kept.

Frost's long career of returning into his own to enlarge his province has been a continual thrust of both will and memory, and he quite logically defines the initial delight of making a poem as the "surprise of remembering something I didn't know I knew." If there are times when his poetry fails, as in the editorializing poems which have been increasing in ratio until they fairly dot "Steeple Bush," he fails because he is remembering something he knew all the time, and his poetry hardens into provincial cynicism. Although critics have lamented this departure from the earlier lyric and dramatic vein, Frost's penchant for bald statement followed as necessarily from his earlier poem as self-assurance follows self-possession. Moreover, out of this almost brash assurance comes "Directive," surely one of Frost's highest achievements.

Here the poet is not the listener or the narrator, but the confident guide leading his reader back into a "time made simple by the loss of detail," to discover among the ruins of a vacant farm the broken goblet the guide has hidden under a cedar tree against the day of his return. The broken goblet, originally cast aside by the adults as a mere toy for the children's playhouse and again abandoned when everyone departed, becomes the all important detail which the poet has seized to save from the ruins of the past. It is for Frost an image of the charmed grail itself, a talisman not carried like a spear of grass but stored away in a secret niche and displayed only to the right persons who, following the poet along the intricate pathways toward the heart of his property, are lost enough to find themselves. Possessing this charm, they can, by drinking with him from the waters of the brook which once supplied water for the farmhouse, "be whole again beyond confusion."

Yet Frost maintains a sharp comic detachment from the central association he exploits, the allusion to the grail quest. His poem is not a recapitulation or variation of the legend but a masque, a performance staged for his audience's benefit by the knowing god who owns the salvaged grail. His whimsy—he "only has at heart our getting lost" and he has hidden the goblet "so the wrong ones can't find it"—is actually an aspect of his comic delicacy as he leads his followers through the "serial ordeal" of being watched from "forty cellar holes," and on to the "height of adventure" which is the height of ground where two village cultures "faded into each other." The chapel perilous is the field "no bigger than a harness gall" marked by a collapsing cellar hole where once a farmhouse stood, and the grail turns out to be a broken goblet stolen from the children's playhouse.

These are the discrepancies which Frost almost mockingly exploits as he conducts the journey, but they are also the miraculous details which authoritatively affirm the reality of this search as opposed to the legendary quest. The guide's command comes from knowing every detail of his private ground, details which were hard to come by but which are securely his own. Even the resurgent woods receive a brashly tender notice as they pass beneath the guide's vision:

> As for the woods' excitement over you
> That sends light rustle rushes to their leaves,
> Charge that to upstart inexperience.
> Where were they all not twenty years ago?
> They think too much of having shaded out
> A few old pecker-fretted apple trees.

In his way an audacious brag, the guide yet makes good on all his claims—and well he might, for "Directive" rehearses the course Frost has pursued as a poet and is thus a survey of the ground he has possessed. But it also points toward what is to come, toward the masques and beyond to his latest poem, "Kitty Hawk," in which, while commemorating the Wright brothers' famous flight, he seizes the chance to celebrate his own first flight into poetry with his sacred muse—an event which considerably anticipated the first propeller-driven flight.

Finally, "Directive" is a performance by the same "character" who so often commands the central stage as lecturer and whose public performances imitate to a remarkable degree the structure of his poems. For Frost's primal subject is always poetry and the poet—*his* poetry and himself the poet. Beginning in a conversational manner, he utters a summary remark about the state of the world, the nature of woman, or the status of science. This aptly stated phrase constitutes the ostensible subject for the evening, and, although he returns to it periodically, his digressions move in ever widening arcs until the initial theme reveals itself as but an association leading toward what is Frost's most private and most public possession—his poems. Even in this introductory movement, Frost is already retreating from his audience toward himself, and the conversational idiom functions as an invitation, never as an appeal.

When he reaches the poems he is to "say," as he puts it, Frost has gained a presence of remote loneliness. His manner of "saying" them is neither recitative, declamatory, nor bardic; rather he seems to be remembering each poem as he moves through it, and even when he forgets his way he usually chooses to find himself without benefit of text. There is a manifest anticipation both in speaker and audience as the remembering proceeds, a kind of wonder and suspense as the tenuous thread of the poem is pursued; and when the end is grasped there is a distinct sense of discovery *and* relief. The disparaging remarks which may be, and have been, leveled at Frost's mode of delivery—at his flatness of voice, his frequent pauses, and his halting delivery—are dwarfed by the essential victory achieved on every poem. And much of his success as a reader of his poems stems from his ability to convey this sense of achievement and repossession.

To know Frost's poems and then to watch his mind close tenderly about them is to see again that they are his triumphs in form wrought out of the chaos he has lived through. They are for him the living emblems —the charms which must be *said*—that, like the broken goblet, he has reclaimed from his abandoned experience and ours. Thus, when Frost, speaking for himself and his muse in "Kitty Hawk," says

> This we're certain of,
> All we do and try
> All we really love
> Is to signify . . .

he is celebrating in poetic language the labor of a lifetime.

Robert Frost and the Darkness of Nature

Roberts W. French*

Rightly or wrongly, Robert Frost has achieved a reputation as a poet of nature; and it is true that one tends to think of him posed against the landscapes of rural New England. He may in his poems be looking at birches, or stopping by woods on a snowy evening, or picking apples, or listening to the thrush or the oven bird; wherever he is, he seems to be participating in the life of nature, deriving sustenance from it, and finding in it a deeply satisfying source of pleasure.

Certainly Frost's poetry is filled with the imagery of nature; but to think of him as a "nature poet," or as a celebrant of nature, is to distort his poetry by overlooking its darker complexities. While Frost has written poems that express a certain joy in nature—"Mowing," for example, or "Putting in the Seed," or "Two Look at Two"—he is far from being a lover of nature; reading through his works, one finds that a major tone involves feelings of profound uneasiness, even of fear, toward nature. Frost may present himself in a natural landscape, but he is far from comfortable there.

In this regard he is not entirely different from Wordsworth and Thoreau, two writers with whom he is often compared. Wordsworth, after all, discovered at last that nature was man's implacable enemy, and he came to realize that his earlier love for nature was based on illusion and self-deception; the record of his discovery may be found in one of his last great poems, "Elegiac Stanzas," a poem that explicitly renounces his former attitudes and points the way toward a new philosophy that will sustain him in the years to come. Thoreau, too, paid full tribute to the dark side of nature, and his concept of nature was always more ambivalent than is generally recognized. At times he could respond to nature as a loving companion; but he also argued that nature was an obstacle to spiritual development, a weight that dragged people down toward mere savagery. "Nature," he wrote, "is hard to be overcome, but she must be overcome." To rise above nature, to improve upon it, to leave it behind—that was the object.

*From *The English Record*, Winter 1978. Copyright © 1978 by *The English Record*. Reprinted by permission.

Frost shares something of Thoreau's concern for the distance between man and nature. "Birches," for example—one of his best-known and most misunderstood poems—is not a poem about birches, primarily, but about the desirability of escaping from this world, if only temporarily; "I'd like to get away from earth awhile," he writes, "And then come back to it and begin over." Birch trees provide the poet with a useful metaphor, since a properly chosen birch tree will lower a person back to earth if he climbs it high enough; but the poem shows no great feeling for such trees, or for any trees. The dominant mood, rather, is one of confused exhaustion; the poet is "weary of considerations," "And life is too much like a pathless wood. . . ." In a similar mood, the young Wordsworth went to nature for consolation and spiritual renewal, but Frost never does that; nature offers no such blessings for him. His way out, if there is one, is not to go *into* nature, but to go beyond nature. In "Birches," as in some other poems, nature has at best a morally neutral value; if it does not oppress, neither does it comfort.

Elsewhere Frost expresses a darker attitude toward nature; indeed, the word "dark" in its various forms occurs with remarkable frequency in Frost's nature poetry. "An Old Man's Winter Night," for example, begins with this line: "All out-of-doors looked darkly in at him. . . ." The line accurately summarizes the poem: Nature seems to be watching the old man, poised like an enemy, hostile, waiting for a sign of weakness. The old man is only human; he struggles as he can to keep going, but his powers are declining while those of nature remain constant. He is fighting a battle that he cannot win; and in him there is a representation of us all. We may erect our pitiful defenses—friends, a house, a fire—but in time they will all prove inadequate; for nature will insist on death, and nature will have its way.

In "An Old Man's Winter Night" nature is a malevolent voyeur; in "Storm Fear" nature is portrayed as an active, diabolical opponent:

> When the wind works against us in the dark,
> And pelts with snow
> The lower chamber window on the east,
> And whispers with a sort of stifled bark,
> The beast,
> 'Come out! Come out!'—
> It costs no inward struggle not to go,
> Ah, no!. . . .

Nature is bestial, savage, intent on luring man to his destruction; and even worse, nature is portrayed as scheming and deceptive, whispering its cruel invitations to disaster. Faced with such active malevolence, the poet feels a deep sense of human inadequacy. What chance is there against such an opponent? One can only try to survive from day to day, but the uncertainty of the struggle leaves the poet troubled: "And my heart owns a doubt / Whether 'tis in us to arise with day / And save ourselves unaided."

Among the darkest of Frost's works, surely, is the five-poem sequence, "The Hill Wife," in which Frost takes an apparently idyllic situation—a young couple on a remote farm—and turns it into a nightmare of loneliness and fear. Like *Heart of Darkness* and *Lord of the Flies*, "The Hill Wife" is an anti-pastoral of the first order. The wife has all the resources of nature at hand, but she can find no solace or satisfaction in them. "One ought not," she complains to her husband,

> to have to care
> So much as you and I
> Care when the birds come round the house
> To seem to say good-by;
>
> Or care so much when they come back
> With whatever it is they sing. . . .

They *have* to care, she laments; there is no alternative, because there is nothing else. Being secluded in nature, they must turn to nature for their satisfactions; and for the wife, it is clear, this is not enough. She knows that they feel "too sad" when the birds leave and "too glad" when they return, and she resents being made so dependent on them, especially when she realizes that the birds are totally indifferent toward her (they only *seem* to say good-by, because that is what she would have them do; but she recognizes the illusion for what it is). Nature she has, in abundance; but nature will not serve her human needs. What she wants, nature cannot give; as a human, she is distinctly uncomfortable in a natural world.

Nature is not only unsatisfactory, however, as a source of spiritual sustenance; what is worse, nature seems actively hostile, a constant threat, and the wife has learned to fear it:

> She had no saying dark enough
> For the dark pine that kept
> Forever trying the window-latch
> Of the room where they slept.

As in "An Old Man's Winter Night" and "Storm Fear," nature—here represented by the "dark pine"—is just beyond the barriers (a house, a window) that protect humans from nature's force; but the barriers are weak and unreliable, and nature tries ceaselessly to penetrate them. The time may come when the barriers will prove inadequate; and then? Not surprisingly, the Hill Wife has nightmares about the dark pine outside her window:

> It never had been inside the room,
> And only one of the two

> Was afraid in an oft-repeated dream
> Of what the tree might do.

Such desperate fears push the wife to the limits of control, and finally past the limits: on a moment's impulse she runs away, disappearing into the woods, and that is the last we hear of her. She has been tried by nature, and she has been found insufficiently strong; she is one of the failures. Again and again Frost's poetry insists that in this life we must be tough, resourceful, and resilient if we are to endure; lacking these qualities, the Hill Wife goes down to defeat.

In Frost's poetry even such a natural process as the cycle of seasons seems bent on destruction. Conventional thought recognizes a pattern that moves from birth (spring) to maturity (summer) through aging (autumn) to death (winter); the pattern reaches its height with the maturity of summer, then declines into the death of winter. In Frost's poems, however, the downward movement begins almost immediately; it seems as if the earth is hostile to the delicacy and beauty that humans value, so soon do the destructive processes exert their powers. Frost's finely crafted little poem "Nothing Gold Can Stay" provides a clear statement of this theme:

> Nature's first green is gold,
> Her hardest hue to hold.
> Her early leaf's a flower;
> But only so an hour.
> Then leaf subsides to leaf.
> So Eden sank to grief,
> So dawn goes down to day.
> Nothing gold can stay.

Similarly, in "Spring Pools" the delicately lovely "flowery waters" and "watery flowers" are doomed to quick extinction; they will be absorbed by roots that "bring dark foliage on." Here as elsewhere the word "dark" is particularly significant. In nature's processes the pools are transformed into leaves, but Frost makes it clear that he thinks this is a poor exchange. The buds on the trees will, in time, "darken nature and be summer woods," but this is a distinct loss, to trade these beautiful pools for darkness. Nature's process is one that destroys, and the trees are its agents, their function merely "To blot out and drink up and sweep away" the exquisite loveliness of the pools.

With springtime's momentary beauty gone, the rest of the year appears as a time of deficiency: "a diminished thing," as "The Oven Bird" tells us. In this poem, the bird of the title is left to contemplate the ruin that is summer, a time when other birds have ceased to sing, when most flowers have disappeared, when pear and cherry blossoms have fallen to earth, when "the highway dust is over all." There is not much left that is attractive, and the oven bird knows it ("the question that he frames in all but words / Is what to make of a diminished thing"). Unlike the Hill Wife, however, he can take whatever life gives him; he is a realist who sees exactly what is happening and can make the proper adjustments. He knows that the summer is a time of loss, and he refuses to sing, for singing would be inappropriate. With his metallic chatter, however, he will at least make a noise. The sound is not beautiful, but it's something; probably it's better than no sound at all. It's not what we would like, but it's as much as we have any right to expect. The oven bird knows how to adapt to circumstances; he is a survivor. He knows a lesser world when he sees one, and he shows us what to do.

"The Oven Bird" leaves us with a world in disarray; nature is drab and desolate, and it has no message for us, either of grief or consolation. In this regard it stands opposed to those nature writings (like Wordsworth's "Prelude" or Faulkner's "The Bear") that center upon moments of illumination, when nature deigns to speak to man, to make some gesture in his direction. At such times the veil is removed and nature stands revealed; one is permitted an insight into essential truth. If Frost's poetry insists on anything, however, it insists on the impenetrable barrier between man and nature: we live in a world that we cannot know, for it will not reveal itself; and yet we yearn for some sort of communion. The speaker in "The Most Of It," for example, fervently asks for a revelation:

> Some morning from the boulder-broken beach
> He would cry out on life, that what it wants
> Is not its own love back in copy speech,
> But counter-love, original response.

He searches for reassurance that he does not live in a world that ignores him and is totally indifferent toward his welfare; he is looking for a *sign:*

> And nothing ever came of what he cried
> Unless it was the embodiment that crashed
> In the cliff's talus on the other side,
> And then in the far distant water splashed,
> But after a time allowed for it to swim,
> Instead of proving human when it neared
> And someone else additional to him,
> As a great buck it powerfully appeared,
> Pushing the crumpled water up ahead,
> And landed pouring like a waterfall,
> And stumbled through the rocks with horny tread,
> And forced the underbrush—and that was all.

And that was all. Does he get an answer? Is this the sign he wanted? We cannot say, for the poem is deliberately uncertain on this point (Characteristically, a Frost poem deals with questions, not with solutions). If this *is* an answer, however, it is not the answer that was sought. The speaker was asking for "counter love"; but this "embodiment" of a great buck, if it is a sign of anything, is a sign of *power*. It knows nothing of love.

Still, it is only human to seek a revelation. In "For Once, Then, Something" Frost returns to the quest, and the poem teases us with its suggestion of discovery. The poet describes his practice of looking into wells, but all he ever sees is his own reflection, "Me myself in the summer heaven godlike. . . ." He finds no god, no ultimate revelation, nothing that is not himself; his search ends where it began. The poem seems so far to be a fine illustration of Democritus' famous assertion, "Of truth we know nothing, for truth lies at the bottom of a well." There is an instant, however, in which the poet has a glimpse of something at the bottom, or so at least it appears to him:

> *Once*, when trying with chin against a well-curb,
> I discerned, as I thought, beyond the picture,
> Through the picture, a something white, uncertain,
> Something more of the depths—and then I lost it.
> Water came to rebuke the too clear water.
> One drop fell from a fern, and lo, a ripple
> Shook whatever it was lay there at bottom,
> Blurred it, blotted it out. What was that whiteness?
> Truth? A pebble of quartz? For once, then, something.

Frost tips his metaphysical hand by equating the abstract "Truth" with the concrete "pebble of quartz," but whether it was one or the other we cannot know; again, as in "The Most Of It," Frost insists on his ambiguities. His poetry reveals no secrets; with the possible exception of "Two Look at Two," the poems present nature in all its blank inscrutability. Nature has nothing to say to us, no matter how much we pry and ponder; persistent inquiry leads nowhere. In "Neither Out Far Nor In Deep" Frost depicts the futility of the human search for certainty: people line the beach, their backs turned to the land, and stare all day at the sea—

> They cannot look out far.
> They cannot look in deep.
> But when was that ever a bar
> To any watch they keep?

The watch is maintained continuously, as though the people were waiting for an imminent sign; but there is no sign, only the overwhelming indifference of an unresponsive nature.

Faced with rejection, Frost does not yearn for any deep relationship with nature; he is no Shelley, crying out for union with powers beyond him. Like the oven bird, he adjusts to the situation and carries on a separate existence; he sees the way things are, and he knows what must be. When, in "The Need of Being Versed in Country Things," he describes the human tragedy of a house destroyed by fire, he does not lament; for tragedy depends on how you see a thing, and Frost realizes that the human perspective is not the only one possible. For the phoebes that flocked around the ruined house, "there was nothing really sad." They went about their ways as usual; human sorrows were none of their business, and in any case, life is like that: one must go on, one must survive. Perhaps the barest (and most effective) statement of this theme in Frost's poetry is in " 'Out, out—,' " a poem describing the death of a child when a buzz-saw accidentally cuts through his wrist. Dead, he is useless: "No more to build on there." The survivors carry on: "And they, since they / Were not the one dead, turned to their affairs." That is what happens; that is the way it must be.

Once in Frost's poetry there seems to be something of an invitation from nature; and that is in "Come In," when the poet, standing by the edge of the woods, hears the song of the thrush:

> Far in the pillared dark
> Thrush music went—
> Almost like a call to come in
> To the dark and lament

It is almost a call, however, not a call; and even if it were one, it would not be entirely attractive, for it would be a call to come into the *dark* (a word used twice in this stanza and four times in the twenty lines of the poem); furthermore, it would be a call to lament, not to rejoice. Understandably, nature's offerings have little appeal, and the poet chooses to go in another direction:

> But no, I was out for stars:
> I would not come in.
> I meant not even if asked,
> And I hadn't been.

The exclusion from nature is complete; the poet remains outside.

This poem may suggest another, the more famous "Stopping by Woods on a Snowy Evening," a work which summarizes neatly Frost's sense of distance from nature. Again the poet is standing outside the woods, looking in; and again it is dark— "the darkest evening of the year." He feels the attractions of the scene, for "The woods are lovely, dark and deep"; and the darkness appeals to him. He seems to be in a melancholy, pensive mood, one that finds congenial the sombre stillness of the woods; but he cannot stay. Turning away from nature, he chooses the world of humanity:

> But I have promises to keep,
> And miles to go before I sleep,
> And miles to go before I sleep.

Human obligations, human responsibilities, must take precedence; and besides, the attractions of the natural scene promised no revelation, but only stasis, a cessation of activity suggestive of death. In the woods there is darkness; the better journey, the poet decides, is toward the lights of the town.

Robert Frost at Eighty-Eight

William G. O'Donnell*

With the passage of the years reviewing a new collection of poems by Robert Frost has become an increasingly difficult task. For a long time now, Frost's poetry has been hard to separate from Frost the talented reader of his own lines, the remarkably gifted public entertainer, and the striking personality and man of wisdom. After Mr. Frost appeared at the Inauguration of President Kennedy and was seen and heard by a television audience estimated at more than 60,000,000 Americans, the critics' difficulties began to multiply. More recently, Frost's journey to the Soviet Union, climaxed by a much-publicized talk with Premier Khrushchev, has added another dimension to the Frost legend and, by making the writing more famous than ever, has made it at the same time somewhat less accessible.

In the Clearing, Frost's eighth collection in a career that goes back to the early 1890's, was published on the poet's eighty-eighth birthday, March 26, 1962, and six months later was still maintaining a place on best-seller lists throughout the nation. Not for more than thirty years has a collection of poems enjoyed so wide a sale in America. The questions raised by the popularity of the hundred-page, forty-poem volume are obvious enough.

How does *In the Clearing* compare with previous Frost volumes from *A Boy's Will* through *Steeple Bush*? What are its best poems? Does it contain any pages to be added to the list of poems that Frost has safely "lodged"—to use one of his own favorite metaphors—beside the finest achievements in American writing?

Understandably enough, *In the Clearing* was handled with great circumspection by the reviewers who helped introduce the book in the spring of 1962. Twenty-five years earlier, with the publication of *A Further Range*, Frost had been misinterpreted and underestimated by several of the nation's most penetrating critics, and this time everyone seemed determined not to say anything that would betray a hasty or insensitive reading of the poems. Some of the reviewers cautiously skirted the whole issue by

*Review of *In the Clearing*. From *The Massachusetts Review*, Autumn, 1962, pp. 213–18. Copyright © 1962 by The Massachusetts Review, Inc. Reprinted by permission.

163

writing essays on Frost's significance in general rather than his achievement or lack of it in the new volume. Not to be overlooked, furthermore, was the attitude on the part of certain reviewers that critical analysis is inappropriate when one is dealing with a symbol of America as enduring as the Flag or Robert Frost.

The volume's distinctive quality, which must be defined before any evaluation of individual poems can be attempted, is its bardic tone. Even the lyrics of *In the Clearing* are marked by this characterizing voice. The bardic role is nothing new for Frost, of course, since he began assuming it years ago. Until the present volume appeared, however, he had never played it with genuine ease and full conviction; in earlier decades the bardic stance was sometimes marred by a tendency to lapse into the narrowly conservative attitudes of "A Brook in the City" or "To a Thinker" or the prosiness of "Build Soil." The years since *A Further Range* have witnessed a liberalizing of Frost's opinions—he would naturally deny the reality of this shift—and a corresponding refinement and improving of the bardic poetry. With *In the Clearing* the culmination of this aspect of Frost's career is reached. America has had bards in the past, but, except for Walt Whitman, it has never had one who fully appreciated the poetic possibilities of the role.

The best poems of *In the Clearing* include—to mention several in the order of their occurrence within the volume—"A Cabin in the Clearing," "Closed for Good," "Escapist—Never," "Forgive, O Lord," "Auspex," "Questioning Faces," "The Objection to Being Stepped On," "In a Glass of Cider," and "In Winter in the Woods Alone"—more than enough for the core of an excellent collection. The two long poems, "How Hard It Is to Keep from Being King When It's in You and in the Situation" and "Kitty Hawk," are interesting as experiments that illuminate some of the lesser known facets of Frost's mind and personality; but the first is too relaxed and garrulous to rank with Frost's major achievements, and the ambitious, seventeen-page "Kitty Hawk," although full of brilliant passages, does not entirely succeed, perhaps because the barrier in the use of a strange, five-syllabled, three-accented line is not finally surmountable. The dignified Inaugural effort, "For John F. Kennedy," the only "occasional" poem Frost has ever published, sums up the poet's admirable sentiments on the subject of America's revolutionary and anti-colonial origins; like "Kitty Hawk" and other things in the book, it exalts the virtue of courage and finds that a willingness to risk all in a bold venture of the spirit is one of the saving American qualities. Among other substantially constructed poems is "America Is Hard to See," where Frost, in spite of a comic tone, gives a bleaker picture of his native land and its prospects than he does in the patriotism of his tribute to the President's "beginning hour." Finally, the volume has two or three items that are not so much light or comic poems as poetic hoaxes, part of an old poet's bag of tricks, useful for public performances, perhaps, but awkward when printed side by side with perfectly fashioned lyrics.

"A Cabin in the Clearing" and "Escapist—Never" demonstrate once again Frost's continuing mastery of a highly original, constantly evolving blank verse. The rhythmical variety that Frost achieves here in the most traditional verse form in the language is one of the volume's successes. Frost's ability to control the deeper subtleties of blank verse, an ability he shares with the later Elizabethan and the Jacobean dramatists, is unequalled by any British or American writer in the twentieth century:

> He is no fugitive—escaped, escaping.
> No one has seen him stumble looking back.
> His fear is not behind him but beside him
> On either hand to make his course perhaps
> A crooked straightness yet no less a straightness.

Yeats, Wallace Stevens, and Edwin Arlington Robinson struggled with the great form—stumbling block for many a poet since the seventeenth century—but rarely attained the marvellous flexibility of these lines from "Escapist—Never," with their assured freedom inside a strict convention and their curiously shifting accents and added syllables.

Frost's accomplishments in blank verse, in poems ranging from the narratives and dramatic monologues of *North of Boston* through "Two Look at Two" in the 1920's to "Escapist—Never" or "A Cabin in the Clearing" from the new collection have never been given their due. Not since Webster and Ford has there been a blank verse that so thoroughly and effectively exploits the rhythmical and idiomatic resources of the English language; yet the years of Frost's life have seen the growth and virtually universal acceptance of a belief that blank verse has outlived its usefulness. A generation ago Ezra Pound started convincing people that blank verse in the twentieth century was an impediment to making language move in the sequence of the spoken or the musical phrase; as Pound understood the problem, the form belonged to the past, to the theater in the days of Elizabeth and the Stuarts, and had no relevance in modern literature. After the erection of "the Chinese Wall of Milton," said T. S. Eliot in 1919, blank verse began to suffer "not only arrest but retrogression." The Pound-Eliot doctrine, which announced that good blank verse could no longer be written and should therefore not be attempted, confronts Frost's accomplishments in the form, not simply a few lines here and there, but more than a score of poems and hundreds of lines composed over a period of six decades.

In the new volume Frost continues his pursuit of the idiomatic essence of his language, a pursuit that commenced in *North of Boston*. As much as anything else in his writing, it is this unending search for an appropriate colloquial form that gives Frost cogency as a modern rather than an old-

fashioned or traditional writer. His love of the prepositional constructions
that lie at the heart of idiom in English and are not translatable into any
other language is as strong and characterizing a trait as it ever has been:

> Forget the myth.
> There is no one I
> Am put out with
> Or put out by.

The accent is unmistakable here. Frost understands how much the
distinctiveness of his style depends upon idiom and how much idiom, in
turn, depends upon the range of effects possible in the various prepositional and prepositional-adverbial usages. He has never tried to reveal the
secret of his creativity, how a poem first begins in his mind, but one
imagines that a sudden flash of idiom, forming an image-idea, must have
marked the starting point of a great deal of the writing. He seems to go
through life searching for these simple yet profoundly suggestive phrases
to use as building blocks. The total number of strikingly idiomatic lines
may be relatively small in any of these poems since idiom, as a writer's
distinguishing quality, is not so much a matter of frequency of occurrence
as it is of emphatic or climactic position. Part of Frost's genius with idiom
is a matter of correct timing, of knowing exactly when to introduce a colloquial, conversational phrase so as to counterbalance a passage composed in the less idomatic language of standard literary English.

A dominant feature of the collection is the brilliance of a number of
the shorter poems. "Questioning Faces," complete in its six lines, will
come to be accepted as one of Frost's best nature poems, an example of his
unequalled ability to capture a simple natural event in all its beauty and
immediacy and, even while doing so, to draw the characteristic line that
always separates the well-loved, closely-observed outer world from the
world of human beings in these poems:

> The winter owl banked just in time to pass
> And save herself from breaking window glass.
> And her wings straining suddenly aspread
> Caught color from the last of evening red
> In a display of underdown and quill
> To glassed-in children at the window sill.

"In a Glass of Cider" is a masterpiece of playful, comic poetry, a medium
in which Frost's imagination often moves with a greater freedom in
establishing remote but convincing associations than it does in the more
"serious" verse. "In Winter in the Woods Alone," the most recent poem of
all, concludes *In the Clearing* with a moment of characteristic optimism,
Frost's feeling of being unwilling to quit until he is finished.

These short lyrics and bardic or gnomic utterances belong to a genre
that becomes more and more common in the collections since *A Further*

Range—that is, the poem in which every detail, no matter how minute, is an imaginative necessity. Perhaps poems of this type—brief, polished, and wise—can be written only by very old poets, men who have seen much of the world, have learned something from their long experience, and have become deeply skeptical of the value of the grand style and grand words. It would be incorrect, of course, to suggest that the genre has been limited to Frost's last years since a few examples may be found in the earlier period as well. The beautiful "Dust of Snow" appeared in the 1920's, and "In Neglect," which was quoted in the first review of Frost's work in 1913, is typical of one element in *A Boy's Will*. It is true, however, that in Frost, as in Yeats, the poem of the utmost brevity and compression is more characteristic of age than of youth, although in neither writer is this fact indicative of an inability to follow a long effort through to completion.

Frost has tried to escape the boredom that a good many people nowadays object to, no doubt wrongly, in certain parts of the long poems of the past. His aim, like Poe's, has been to create poems in which all lines and phrases are poetic. The American writing that Frost has most often admired—Emerson's poetry and the perfectly formed sentences of Emerson's essays—helped to confirm this aim. A writer who complained of the monotonies of epic novels, especially those in the Russian manner, and read the Greek Anthology and the Roman epigrammatists with intense pleasure was probably bound to find out what, if anything, could be done with the six-line, four-line, and two-line poem.

Like "An Answer" from *A Witness Tree*, "Forgive, O Lord" from the new collection will probably become a classic example of the genre and proof that such a thing is really a possibility:

> Forgive, O Lord, my little jokes on Thee
> And I'll forgive Thy great big one on me.

The meaning of this complicated witticism, which delights Frost's audiences, is something of a mystery. Frost places it in a group to which he gives the title "Cluster of Faith," and since its companion pieces are all expressions of the poet's passionately held belief in purpose and design and his rejection of an accidental evolution as a sufficient explanation of man's origin and destiny, "Forgive, O Lord" is undoubtedly intended as a positive assertion, not a denial. Frost, who is more religious than people think he is, knows that jokes about God can be reverent and devout as well as Voltairean. But there is at least a suggestion that the design revealed here is a negative one, "a design of darkness to appall," to use a phrase from a celebrated sonnet. In this sense the poem embodies, to some extent, a feeling that life is basically absurd and meaningless, a joke at man's expense, but not, however, a joke that demonstrates man's spiritual greatness. Perhaps the poem's secret is that a positive meaning exists in the two lines and predominates in spite of the negative undertones of skepticism and doubt.

Several of the poems are more affirmative than anything Frost has previously written, and some of the lines imply, without any precision of statement, a whole vista of religious and theological suggestion in the background. The collection begins with a "Frontispiece" taken from a lyrical passage in "Kitty Hawk":

> But God's own descent
> Into flesh was meant
> As a demonstration
> That the supreme merit
> Lay in risking spirit
> In substantiation.

Exactly what Frost intends this to mean we are probably not going to discover, just as we are not supposed to press too insistently for meanings in any of the more poetic paragraphs of Emerson's essays. It is sufficiently clear, however, that the passage is a positive assertion. On the other hand, a few poems in *In the Clearing* capture a familiar mood of incertitude:

> And still I doubt if they know where they are.
> And I begin to fear they never will.
> All they maintain the path for is the comfort
> Of visiting with the equally bewildered.
> Nearer in plight their neighbors are than distance.

Here, in the moving, blank verse rhythms of "A Cabin in the Clearing," the poet seems as hesitant about asserting too much as he is willing to assert all in parts of "Kitty Hawk." If there is a fault here—and there probably is one—it may lie in Frost's failure to place the divergent moods, the antagonistic tendencies, within the unified structure of a single poem and thus achieve a rich complexity of utterance rather than an impulsive shifting from one sentiment to another. Frost's greatest poems, "Directive" in particular, have a quality of doubleness in their manner of combining statement and counterstatement, affirmation and denial, assertion and an undercutting irony. At times the new volume takes the easier way out and follows Emerson in trying to be honest to the sentiment of the moment while hoping that in the long run the direction will be "A crooked straightness yet no less a straightness."

In the Clearing places value upon a sense of clarification as well as a sense of direction. The title is a phrase from the poem about the people who have subdued nature and made a human clearing in the wilderness; it is to be read, Frost indicates, in the light of a line from "The Pasture," "And wait to watch the water clear, I may." The search for insight, for understanding, for the moment of clarification after a preliminary stirring up of the spirit, is the main theme established through much of the collection. This time Frost seems to be hoping for insights that will be more than momentary stays against confusion, to use a phrase from "The Figure a Poem Makes," and at least part of his hope is realized. *In the Clearing* may have no supremely accomplished poems, like "Two Look at Two" or "Directive," but when it is added to the *Complete Poems*, it will take an honored place in the Frost canon beside the seven collections that preceded it.

Robert Frost: Some Divisions in a Whole Man

Isadore Traschen*

Robert Frost wrote some of the finest verse of our time. He created his own extraordinarily flat, "unpoetic" variant of the conversational idiom which has become the medium of most modern poetry. He restricted himself to the homeliest diction, to words largely of one or two syllables, a remarkable feat. And he countered this simplicity with a highly sophisticated rhetoric, with the devious twistings of the poem's development, with the irony of simple word and subtle thought. His diction was just right for the rural scene he chose in the face of the intimidating international subjects of Eliot and Pound, and just right, too, for its simple particulars. He was no doubt our master of the realistic particular. Things magnified at his touch; they seemed to live. His themes were familiar to most, and appealed—though in widely varying degrees—to everyone: the exhaustion of living, the sense of imminent danger (large as the ocean, small as a spider), personal isolation, the need for community, etc. Frost is so good, so much pleasure to read that you wonder why he needs to be defended so often. What is it about him that makes even enthusiastic admirers like Randall Jarrell—whose appreciation, "To the Laodiceans," should be read by everyone—begin by acknowledging his limitations? After all, everyone has them. Is there some really critical defect in him, one that might explain why Frost never had the passionate following Eliot had? Why didn't Frost so affect us, so transform us that we had no choice but to be his?

What I want to do is to develop an aspect of Frost's poems which I feel represents such a defect. I am aware of the exceptions to what I have to say: these will be occasionally noted. My principal argument is that Frost never risked his life, his whole being; he was never really lost, like the Eliot of *The Waste Land*. He remained in control, in possession of himself. He did this by keeping himself from the *deepest* experiences, the kind you stake your life on. And this is reflected in various ways, all of which point to a central division in Frost's experience, in himself. He has been represented, by himself as well as by others, as one able to integrate

*From *The Yale Review*, Autumn 1965. Copyright © 1965 by Yale University. Reprinted by permission.

his life. "Drink and be whole against confusion," he advised in "Directive," written during the Second World War; and confused as we were, we were grateful for the recipe. Again, in "Education by Poetry," he says the "Greatest of all attempts to say one thing in terms of another is the philosophical attempt to say matter in terms of spirit, or spirit in terms of matter, to make the final unity . . . it is the height of all poetry, the height of all thinking." But when we read his poetry we encounter division of several kinds.

To begin with, it has been pointed out that though Frost looks at nature closely, and renders it faithfully, he often fails to fuse his idea of it with his feeling. Thus poems like "Tuft of Flowers," "Two Tramps in Mud Time," and "Hyla Brook" divide in two: the things described, the pure existent, free of any abstraction, and the abstract comment, the moral or philosophical lesson in the tradition of Longfellow and Emerson, whom he admired. Take "Hyla Brook," less known than the others:

> By June our brook's run out of song and speed
> Sought for much after that, it will be found
> Either to have gone groping underground
> (And taken with it all the Hyla breed
> That shouted in the mist a month ago,
> Like ghost of sleigh-bells in a ghost of snow)—
> Or flourished and come up in jewel-weed,
> Weak foliage that is blown upon and bent
> Even against the way its waters went.
> Its bed is left a faded paper sheet
> Of dead leaves stuck together by the heat—
> A brook to none but who remember long.
> This as it will be seen is other far
> Than with brooks taken otherwhere in song.
> We love the things we love for what they are.

The poem is a marvel of simple particulars enhanced by homely metaphors and the distinctively Frost idiom, concluding with the abstract comment. In this case the comment is at odds with the spirit of the poem: if we love the things we love for what they are we had better resist setting up a philosophy about them. Often, in this way, Frost does not resolve his identification with particulars and his separation from them by laying on a general meaning. His poetry reveals a division between the imagist and the commentator, between the man who is involved and the man who observes, between the naturalist and the rationalist. In some remarks on Edwin Arlington Robinson, Frost says, "I am not the Platonist Robinson was. By Platonist I mean one who believes what we have here is an imperfect copy of what is in heaven." But the structure of many of his poems, an ascent from matter to idea, is Platonic. I do not mean to imply that Frost thought matter inferior to the idea; he is frequently skeptical about the mind's way of knowing, as in "Bond and Free," where love is superior to thought by virtue of its existential involvement: by "simply staying [it] possesses all." Still, it is fair to say that the structure of his poems often gives the impression that matter, or, more generally, existence is an illustration of an idea.

The dramatic narratives ("The Death of the Hired Man," "A Servant of Servants," etc.) are exceptions to Frost's Platonic structure. Because of the form, probably, the action is sustained all the way; no formulation is tagged on; these poems are memorable in themselves, free of abstract wisdom. Of course this fusion of image and idea happens on occasion in the lyrics, as in "The Silken Tent" and "The Most of It," and with fine effect. Here is the less known "Silken Tent," in which the theme of love and bondage is fused in a one-sentence sonnet with the metaphysical skill of Donne or Marvell.

> She is as in a field a silken tent
> At midday when a sunny summer breeze
> Has dried the dew and all its ropes relent,
> So that in guys it gently sways at ease,
> And its supporting central cedar pole,
> That is its pinnacle to heavenward
> And signifies the sureness of the soul,
> Seems to owe naught to any single cord,
> But strictly held by none, is loosely bound
> By countless silken ties of love and thought
> To everything on earth the compass round,
> And only by one's going slightly taut
> In the capriciousness of summer air
> Is of the slightest bondage made aware.

But this fusion is not characteristic. Generally there is a division between subject matter and idea, and the poem suffers. The abstract ending contracts the poem; it freezes and flattens the feelings set in motion, channeling them into an idea, as though the idea were the really important part of the poem, its telos.

This division in Frost is reflected in the frequent disjunction between his subject matter and his verse rhythms. The meter is varied from poem to poem; the iambic measure has a human voice, a quiet one which secures a tension between the dramatic substance and its own effortlessness. Yet as we read a number of poems at a stretch, another effect emerges, one of monotony—especially, as Yvor Winters points out, in those in blank verse. It is as though Frost brings an *a priori* rhythm to each poem, a further Platonic tendency: the *idea* of a rhythm distinct from the matter it will give form to. You get the same rhythm in a poem of rural manners like "Mending Wall," with its theme of community, as you do in a quasi-tragic piece like "An Old Man's Winter Night," with its theme of isolation. The poems call for different intensities of feeling, but there is little evidence of this in the rhythms. Compare Frost's verse to that of Shakespeare and Donne:

> The expense of spirit in a waste of shame
> Is lust in action.

> Batter my heart, three-person'd God; for, you
> As yet but knocke, breathe, shine, and seeke to mend.

Among other things, what makes the earlier poets unmonotonous in their rhythms is the weight of the stressed syllables; this further breaks the even flow. Frost rarely breaks up, rarely staggers under the burden of his subject; his tone is level even when the theme is disintegration. The effect of his rhythms is generally one of understatement—all to the good in the modern canon. But continual understatement acts as an anodyne, beguiling us into what we like to believe is the quiet voice of wisdom. This may have been all right in more contemplative times; but I would think our age is more authentically expressed through pain, through the pure, simple scream it would have been so *pleasant* to hear at times in Frost's poems. Frost's level tone works well in poems of trance-like surrender, as in "After Apple-Picking" or "Stopping by Woods on a Snowy Evening"; here there is a happy conjunction of rhythm and subject matter. Frost's "monotony" may be connected with his philosophic attitude, an even-tempered skeptical rationalism which has been the dominant tradition in Western culture since Plato and Aristotle. It has little in common with another tradition, that of the great howlers who risked everything: the Old Testament prophets, Job (the triviality of "A Masque of Reason" is revealing in this connection), the Greek tragic playwrights and Shakespeare, or romantics like Blake and Rimbaud.

Frost's incapacity for the tragic howl is of a piece, I believe, with the sentimentality which marks a further division in him, the separation of fact and feeling. A typical instance is "The Road Not Taken," with its elegiac air:

> I shall be telling this with a sigh
> Somewhere ages and ages hence:
> Two roads diverged in a wood, and I—
> I took the one less travelled by,
> And that has made all the difference.—

Frost acknowledges that life has limits ("knowing how way leads on to way"), yet he indulges himself in the sentimental notion that we could be really different from what we have become. He treats this romantic cliché on the level of the cliché; hence the appeal of the poem for many. But after having grown up, who still wants to be that glamorous movie star or ball player of our adolescent daydreams? In "The Jolly Corner" James saw the other road leading to corruption, the fate of those who deny themselves, who suffer a division of the self.

These divisions in Frost may help us see what is unsatisfactory about a finely wrought poem like "The Onset."

> Always the same, when on a fated night
> At last the gathered snow lets down as white
> As may be in dark woods, and with a song
> It shall not make again all winter long
> Of hissing on the yet uncovered ground,
> I almost stumble looking up and round,
> As one who overtaken by the end
> Gives up his errand, and lets death descend
> Upon him where he is, with nothing done
> To evil, no important triumph won,
> More than if life had never been begun.
>
> Yet all the precedent is on my side:
> I know that winter death has never tried
> The earth but it has failed: the snow may heap
> In long storms an undrifted four feet deep
> As measured against maple, birch, and oak,
> It cannot check the peeper's silver croak;
> And I shall see the snow all go down hill
> In water of a slender April rill
> That flashes tail through last year's withered brake
> And dead weeds, like a disappearing snake.
> Nothing will be left white but here a birch,
> And there a clump of houses with a church.

Frost is again divided in his response. He resists winter and welcomes spring; he welcomes life but does not see that death is organic to it. Later, in "West-running Brook," he was to say that "The universal cataract of death" sends up our life. But Frost largely flirted with the dark woods that appear with some frequency in his poems; he was not lost in them so deeply, as Dante was, for them to transform him. Instead, he made a "strategic retreat."

If Frost's resistance to death is unnatural, his sense of spring in "The Onset" is incomplete. It lacks the organic singleness of spring and winter of Dylan Thomas' "The force that through the green fuse drives the flower / Drives my green age; that blasts the roots of trees / Is my destroyer." What is also lacking is the pain of birth, as in Lawrence's "Tortoise Shout." Here is the tortoise

> . . . in the spasm of coition, tupping like a jerking leap, and oh!
> Opening its clenched face from his outstretched neck
> And giving that fragile yell, that scream,
> Super-audible,

> From his pink, cleft, old-man's mouth,
> Giving up the ghost,
> Or screaming in Pentecost, receiving the ghost.

Some of this is prosy, but it has a power which if Frost had exercised it might have shaken many of his admirers. For Frost spring is simply another occasion for his even-tempered reassurance, compounded in the idyllic image of houses and church worthy of Rockwell Kent. Quietly brought in, sparely set down, pretty to contemplate . . . yet effective only if we allow ourselves to be coerced by the idyl of the American village. But after Winesburg and Spoon River and Lardner? The village church is pretty to look at, but too often filled with people divided in their own ways: loving mankind but fearing if not hating Catholics, Jews, and Negroes, not to speak of foreigners. As a matter of fact, in "A Star in a Stone-Boat," in the same *New Hampshire* volume, Frost is ironic about those who "know what they seek in school and church."

Now "The Onset" hints at difficulties, but these are overlooked or forgotten in the interests of the pleasant solution. The speaker says he is like one who "lets death descend / Upon him where he is, with nothing done / To evil, no important triumph won, / More than if life had never been begun." This is a characterization of the Laodicean temper comparable to Yeats' "The best lack all conviction," or Eliot's "We who were living are now dying / With a little patience." But Frost does not draw the conclusions Yeats and Eliot do, or Marlow in *Heart of Darkness*, or Baudelaire, Dante, and St. John. April's slender rill will still return as life-giving as ever, untouched by Laodicean lifelessness; April will not be the cruelest month, bringing a rebirth we do not want and cannot stand. Frost's Chaucerian response to spring is simply no longer possible, even before the fallout, except to one who has seriously isolated himself from our times, a division I will say more about.

We have no right to demand anything of a poet but what he gives us, although we do have an obligation to define what he is giving us. Frost himself invites us to judge him, in the terms I have set forth, in one of his great poems, "The Gift Outright." He says that before we were the land's

> Something we were withholding made us weak
> Until we found out that it was ourselves
> We were withholding from the land of living . . .

You must give yourself, surrender yourself, fully to realize yourself. Curiously, this is the point of the first poem, "Into My Own," in Frost's first volume; by going into the woods he will be "more sure of all I thought was true." But Frost generally separates himself from nature, as when he speaks with an oddly exploitive élan of our increasing "hold on the planet"; unlike Wordsworth, who identifies with nature as his spirit is

"Rolled round in earth's diurnal course, / With rocks, and stones, and trees." Now there is a sense of fully meeting nature in "After Apple-Picking," but usually, as in "Come In" or "Stopping by Woods," the poet only seems to give himself, while actually withdrawing. Robert Penn Warren explains the withdrawal in "Stopping by Woods" as "man defining himself by resisting the pull of nature." No doubt we must *distinguish* ourselves from the rest of nature, but we cut ourselves off from a critical part of our existence if we do this by *resisting*. This may lead, for example, to the kind of alienation Lawrence dramatizes in "Snake." A venomous, golden snake appears and "The voice of my education said to me / He must be killed." He throws a log at it, forcing the kingly animal to retreat, "convulsed in undignified haste." He has despoiled nature, and it weighs on him like an albatross: "I missed my chance with one of the lords / of life. / And I have something to expiate; / A pettiness." Sometimes, as in the beautiful "Oven Bird," Frost seems to identify with nature, but even here he is really personifying the bird, imposing his philosophical mood of the moment: "The question that he [the bird] frames in all but words / Is what to make of a diminished thing."

The difference between Frost and Lawrence and Thomas is critical. Lawrence defines his humanness in a mutual encounter with nature, Frost by resisting it. The tortoise's pain is Lawrence's, as Thomas is bent by the same wintry fever as the crooked rose. Both become more profoundly human by surrendering, or at least immersing themselves in nature. They *grow* out of their relation to it; Frost does not because he is curiously divided from it, observing it to introduce his own ideas. He does not sink to come up new; he cannot lose himself, follow his own advice and surrender himself; he will not let go of himself, allow nature to work on him and change him. As a skeptic, the poet of the middle way, not committing himself to extremes—passional or intellectual—Frost remains separate from the objects he looks at, unchanged. There is no mutual penetration which transforms subject and object. Instead, Frost puts on his armor of ideas to confront nature with; perhaps, strangely, to protect him from it. Two impulses work against each other, the naturalistic and the civilized, and the latter prevails. Despite all the suggestions of disaster in his poetry Frost does not really disturb us. He is all too frequently prepared to reach some reasonable agreement. Problems—yes; but solutions too.

What all this comes to is a detachment which in its cultural context is a poetry of isolationism. This is obviously appealing to an American audience. The title of his first volume, *A Boy's Will*, alludes to the favorite American poet of the nineteenth century, Longfellow, and to the poem which appeals to our nostalgia as well as our Edenic impulse. Succeeding titles—*North of Boston, Mountain Interval, New Hampshire, West-running Brook*—all reassure us of the importance, the validity, the worth not merely of our country, but of that part where we began and where our virtues were seeded and flourished. Nor do the images which trouble the scene—the hired man, the servant of servants, and the others— trouble Frost's audience; on the contrary, the harsh realism validates its nostalgia. Rural America is offered as the theatre of this world, appealing to anyone who would like to forget the world.

Delmore Schwartz once called T. S. Eliot our international hero; Frost is our national, isolationist hero, withdrawn as Americans generally are from the dialogue of ideas which give form to living not only in our time but at least as far back as the Old Testament days. Typical of Frost's attitude are the words of the wife in "In the Home Stretch": "New is a word for fools in towns who think / Style upon style in dress and thought at last / Must get somewhere." Nothing could be more appealing to our traditionalist temper; nothing is more alien to our revolutionary tradition; nothing could be plain sillier. The wife is not aware that whatever ideas *she* has are the new ones of Moses, the Prophets, the Greek philosophers, Christ, St. Paul, St. Thomas, Montaigne, Newton, Marx, and Freud. To ignore the ideas of *our* age means that you use them uncritically, for they get into your bones anyway.

Intellectual heat has tempered most of us; but Frost "is able," as Robert Langbaum says, "to shrug off those conflicts between man and nature, thought and reality, head and heart, science and religion, which since the romantic period have torn other poets apart." As a consequence, many of his poems which seem to bear upon our crises do not really confront them. For example, "Once By the Pacific" warns of "a night of dark intent / . . . and not only a night, an age." But it lacks the specific historical sense of Yeats's "Leda and the Swan," "Two Songs from a Play," and "The Second Coming," and so has only a vague effect. Yeats interprets the historical moments and so involves himself in them as he gives us a way of understanding them. Uninvolved, Frost paralyzes us with merely passive or stunned responses to modern terror, as in "Design," "Bereft," or "Once By the Pacific"; he does not take up the arms of the intellect against our sea of troubles. Failing to be involved, he falls back on eternal commonplaces. In "The Peaceful Shepherd" he points out that the cross, the crown, and the scales of trade all might as well have been the sword; in "November" he deplores "The waste of nations warring"; in "A Question" he asks if life is worth all the suffering. These poems do not pretend to much, but their very simplicity allows us to see more readily the commonplace quality of so much of Frost's thought, owing, I would say, to his separation from the intellectual wars of our time.

Frost's withdrawal from the exhausting scene of the mind, of a piece with his withdrawal from the pain in nature, his moralizing use of nature, and his dreamlike response to it—all this can lead to the cruelty of neglect. (Though being *in* the wars of the mind hardly exempts one from cruelty as such.) The highly praised "The Lesson for Today" is very witty, often brilliant, and absolutely heartless in its trite equation of our epoch with other dark ones, particularly so when we remember it was written in 1941. Swinging on one's philosophic swivel, it may be valid to say "One age is like another for the soul," or that "all ages shine / with equal darkness." But this is much like Gertrude, who used the vulgar argument that death is common to all, and therefore why so particular with Hamlet. Hamlet is a tragic figure because what happened *was* particular to him, just as what has happened *is* particular to us—how else can we take it seriously? It is the particulars that speak to us, that it would be obscene to ignore or forget. The poet who maintains his balance before the ideas and events which are unbalancing the rest of us risks being irrelevant. To equate one age with another is to be outside of both. How different Frost seems when he does render modern particulars, as at the end of "The Bonfire"—not one of his better poems, certainly. Speaking to some children, he asks,

> Haven't you heard, though,
> About the ships where war has found them out
> At sea, about the towns where war has come
> Through opening clouds at night with droning speed
> Further o'erhead than all but stars and angels,—
> And children in the ships and in the towns?
> Haven't you heard what we have lived to learn?
> Nothing so new—something we had forgotten:
> *War is for everyone, for children too.*
> I wasn't going to tell you and I mustn't.
> The best way is to come up hill with me
> And have our fire and laugh and be afraid.

But I do not see how he can say that children are no more affected by war today than in the past.

When Frost confronts our civilization in its totality—the encounter that defines our great moderns, as Stephen Spender has pointed out—he is inadequate; all he can muster is a commonplace. Perhaps he is prone to aphorisms in a poem dealing with the modern scene because he does not see it. He talks about it, but is incapable of creating its personae, like Eliot's carbuncular clerk. Having committed himself to by-road, rural figures not shaped by central modern concerns, he falls into archness or waspishness when dealing with features of our world—and not least, incidentally, its representative literature. In the later, rightly admired "Directive," he advises us to retreat from "all this now too much for us" back to a "time made simple by the loss / of detail." Here once more is the refusal to confront the particulars of our world; after a journey which Frost invites us to compare with that of a Grail knight, yet with only a hint of the Grail trials, we will be saved, "be whole again beyond confusion" by drinking the cup of the past, the simple time. Comforting . . . but after Eliot's fragmented Fisher King? Langbaum comments that

Frost's poetry is the kind "that delivers us from the poignancy of the historical moment to place us in contact with a survival-making eternal folk wisdom. We can live by Frost's poetry as we could not by Yeats's or Pound's." On the contrary. The poetry that disturbs us most strengthens us most, much the way the tragic hero affirms himself by acknowledging the last truth. Eternal wisdom is comic to those conscious of the awful fact of *this* historic moment. Divided from our time, Frost, our wisdom-poet, has so little of the kind of wisdom appropriate to our time, the hellish, existential wisdom of Kafka and Camus, or the biological wisdom of Lawrence.

In his famous speech celebrating Frost's eighty-fifth birthday Lionel Trilling links Frost with the tragic poets. He makes this assertion with an unusual rhetorical violence: "when ever have people been so isolated, so lightning-blasted, so tried down and calcined by life, so reduced, each in his own way, to some last irreducible core of being." Professor Trilling ignores most of Frost's poetry, and most of the criticism, that which praises Frost (for his skeptical rationalism or his "strategic retreat," for example) as well as that which criticizes him. He cites "Design" as an example of Frost's tragic sense. Randall Jarrell has demonstrated the power of the poem. Its argument is that the universe is a "design of darkness." But the tragic sense involves something more. It requires a belief in or a coherent vision of the design of life, traditional as with Eliot or private as with Yeats and Kafka; it requires this together with the feeling that the design is breaking down. It implies more than mere ruin. The tragic sense requires a person highly developed in spirit and mind who, broken by the imminent failure of his sense of things, is moved to probe and question—apocalyptically, or humorously, but always passionately, not with the mild, wry, even-tempered humor of Frost.

The great moderns have thought steadily about our age; from this has come intense commitments taking the form of those consistent visions of modern life which have shaped our imagination. What distinguishes them, as Spender has put it, is their sense of the present "as a fatal knowledge that has overtaken the whole of civilization and has broken the line of tradition with the past." Frost writes in a historical vacuum, with almost nothing to say to us about the modern content of our alienation and fragmentation. His efforts here yield little that has not been more passionately and tragically said by many others. "Departmental" is a fairly good, if too clever, poem on specialization; but "Why Wait for Science" and "Bursting Rapture" are pebbly rather than Vermont granite; the latter even childish when we think of Yeats' treatment of the apocalyptic theme in "The Second Coming" and his other annunciation poems. No one seems to be more solidly planted in the world, yet no one of Frost's stature tells us less about our world.

It is the absence of a modern texture which in one way gives Frost his special appeal to moderns. As a poet of particulars, especially of nature,

Frost has an effect on the city person something like that Wordsworth had for John Stuart Mill. For such a person—especially a bookish one—Frost brings a momentary salvation. He restores the *things* that our organized way of living and our abstract way of seeing have obliterated: "Blueberries as big as the end of your thumb," or an ax-helve "slender as a whipstock, / Free from the least knot, equal to the strain / Of bending like a sword across the knee." And in making us see these things he saturates us with the texture of American life, the life of its beginnings. This too is good for the intellectual who for many reasons (the cant, hypocrisy, and immorality of public life, the spiritual deterioration of private life) often feels like an outsider in his own country. Frost has reminded us of all that cannot be spoiled by the politician or the brassy patriot. For this we are grateful. Blueberries, ax-helves, birches, oven birds—these are stable vantage points, solid stations—but not enough. They are the moving particulars common to any time, not the disturbing particulars of our own. Neither his images nor his scenes are modern; his isolation provides him only with situations out of another era. Our representative heroes are fated in images drawn from the modern world: Joseph K. crucified by the celestial bureaucracy, Meursault by the apparatus of the law, reflecting conventional, middle-class values. Irving Howe says that "Frost writes as a modern poet who shares in the loss of firm assumptions." Perhaps, but this could apply equally to Donne or Montaigne. Yvor Winters' remarks on Frost as a thinker are more pertinent. "Frost's skepticism and uncertainty do not appear to have been so much the result of thought as the result of the impact upon his sensibility of conflicting notions of his own era—they appear to be the result of his having taken the easy way and having drifted with the various currents of his time." Frost is contemporary rather than modern. He lives in our time but at bottom is not affected, disturbed, shaken, transformed by it. Everyone rightly praises "An Old Man's Winter Night," but "Gerontion," drawing on fewer particulars of old age, disturbs us more, for it is a portrait of old age in our age, and so becomes a portrait of our age.

The division in much of Frost's poetry between image and idea, matter and rhythm, the naturalist and the rationalist is reflected in Frost's withholding himself from nature, and this in turn we see is a reflection of the division between his subject matter and that of the age. This was fatal to his full development, preventing the kind of growth and transformations that marked Yeats and Eliot. His simplicity and homeliness probably contributed to this fate. He took these qualities too seriously, as though they were the heart of truth. He became his own imitator, beguiling himself enough to keep himself out of the complexities and contentions of our time, out of the political, moral, religious, and philosophical crises which might have led to a passionate commitment. Even if wrongheaded, this at least would have opened hell to him.

"My Rising Contemptuaries":
Robert Frost Amid His Peers

Philip L. Gerber*

The man in the street, questioned about Robert Frost, will give a ready answer: Frost was a kindly old rural farmer; he was a sensitive man who noticed what others overlooked and got it down on paper; he was a New Englander of stalwart down-east virtue. Kindly? That Frost was, yes, especially in public and in his poems. Sensitive? Surely—at times downright irascible. A New Englander? Through and through, if the will to contend is a conspicuous New England quality. One thing is certain: Frost was far from being the rural genius of perpetual even temper which masses of his readers thought him to be. But only by probing beyond the public façade can one discern the man's mortality. Shelved for the moment must be that attractive myth which canonizes Frost as a simple swain who happened to think in stanzas. If one wishes to apprehend Frost the man, the intricate personality capable of producing *Complete Poems*, there is no better beginning than an examination of his protracted "rivalries" with the poets of his time.

Lest this probing be thought mere gossip or a gratuitous casting of stones at the temple, it is wise to recall that Robert Frost at the time of his debut in 1914 was a mature man with a reputation yet to establish. Time was of the essence. Frost's career, hardly the providential affair it seemed in later years, stemmed from a long, not terribly auspicious, foreground. In 1914 the time was as ripe as it was ever going to be; for Frost it was quite literally a case of now or never. If he was apprehensive, there was a great deal at stake. Having severed his New Hampshire roots in order to achieve a crucial "forward movement," Frost had sailed to England with the sole intent of establishing himself as a Poet. He dared not fail. Upon his return to America at age forty, he was fully shaped as a writer, two books had been compiled from his trunk of accumulated manuscripts, and a substantial backlog of new verses awaited their final expression. The two years from 1912 to 1914 formed the great divide for Frost. In commit-

*From *The Western Humanities Review*, Spring 1966. Copyright © 1966 by *The Western Humanities Review*. Reprinted by permission. This essay has been rewritten and enlarged especially for this volume.

ting himself to poetry, he had awarded his career an essential and decisive priority over all other considerations.

While Robert Frost cannot be credited with inventing the image of himself as an uncomplicated bard well versed in country things, this element "hit" with the public at once, and Frost, sensing it, shrewdly did little to disillusion his growing body of readers. Whatever furthered his career without sacrifice of integrity was quite obviously to be encouraged. As early as 1916 Frost revealed to Louis Untermeyer that he had already passed through "several phases, four to be exact" as a poet and considered himself permanently shaped. Knowing what it was he could do well, he intended making certain that those whose opinion counted knew also. "I have myself all in a strong box where I can unfold as a personality at discretion," he declared matter-of-factly. "I am become my own salesman."[1] But let it be understood that it was quality goods Frost could offer. Entering the market place with such calculation aforethought and under great stress, he considered all other poets sharing the public eye to be salesmen like himself and therefore his natural competitiors. Most definitely his plan for the future did not include gratuitous puffing of "rival" poets whose accomplishments might detract from his own. During those wartime years Frost's potential rivals were four: Vachel Lindsay, Carl Sandburg, Edgar Lee Masters, and Amy Lowell. All were prolific and highly active when Frost disembarked from England, all had published works placing them in the vanguard of "the new poetry," and each happened to be a strong personality, expert in techniques of the "hard sell." These four being already the acknowledged leaders, Frost, if he were to become king of the hill, must one way or another outperform them all.

Vachel Lindsay, the chaotic midwestern troubadour, the neurotic chanter of American songs, was discernibly killing himself with strenuous reading tours and nightmares of the mind long before he swallowed Lysol in 1931. Frost treated him gently. He seems to have been genuinely fond of the impractical dreamer from Illinois, even in the privacy of his personal letters speaking of him with affection. Upon Lindsay's death, Frost expressed himself clearly: "I feel more as if I had lost a child (with all sorts of foolish little ways) than a brother and fellow-artist. It comes near me" (219).

Carl Sandburg seemed a more formidable rival. Frost twitted him for the "set routine" he followed in presenting his tour programs. First came the set of definitions of poetry, then the recitation of favorite verses, finally the twanging on the guitar. By now half of America must have heard the story of Sandburg's reading at the University of Michigan (upon Frost's invitation) and how, when Sandburg proved tardy coming downstairs at the Frosts', someone inquired whether he were in his room preparing his program. No, replied Frost, the Chicago poet was standing by his mirror fixing his hair so that it would look as if a comb had never touched it. Frost may have been gifted with precognition; on the other hand, his own lectures could be occasions for remarkably casual dress, and it has been suggested that he was not above mussing his own white thatch with a deliberate sweep of his broad hand. On the lecture circuit, Sandburg remained Frost's most colorful competitor, as if there were not ample room for both. Although the two men aged together into a pair of unofficial poets laureate, they were never close. The strain of early years when the prize seemed yet to be taken endured to the end. Only now and then did Frost have kind words to say of Sandburg, and while Sandburg was characteristically generous upon the event of Frost's death, it was obvious that each was happier when not compelled to dwell on the other.

II

For Edgar Lee Masters and Amy Lowell, Frost reserved his real pettiness. Masters truly alarmed him. *The Spoon River Anthology* came out in the spring of 1915 almost simultaneously with *North of Boston*, with Frost in apparent terror lest Masters' impressive, extremely popular collection of mordant midwestern portraits overshadow his own work. While the two books could hardly have been more different in plan and technique, a basic similarity was obvious: just as *Spoon River* "lifted the lid" off the downstate Illinois village, *North of Boston* probed the darkness behind upstate New England scenes. Both books were immensely popular, and readers purchased far more copies than any volume of poems seemed entitled to sell. But of the two, *Spoon River* aroused the greater controversy, was more talked up, more highly praised, more widely read. This hurt. Frost described the book as "false-realistic" and commented tartly, "I think *Spoon River* is perfectly all right for them as likes it" (10). As for Masters himself, to Frost he became at once "my hated rival" (29) and Frost dreamed of his demise. "There is a Masters Mountain and right beside it a Frost Hollow hereabouts. What can be done to bring low the mountain and cast up the hollow?" (96) he wanted to know. Of the anthologies then being launched, William Braithwaite's annual volumes were among the more noteworthy. His *Anthology of Magazine Verse for 1915* contained high praise of Frost, but the sweetness of the praise, though appreciated, was soured by Braithwaite's inclination to link Frost's name with that of Masters. "The two great successes of the year . . . have been the American poets Frost and Masters," wrote Braithwaite, touching the match to the fuse. Even his laudatory review of *A Boy's Will* and *North of Boston* was poisoned: "With Mr. Masters Robert Frost has contributed the most valuable additions to American poetry of the year." Hailing *Spoon River*, the anthologist declared, "It came out of the West to meet Mr. Frost's achievement in the East." His emphasis upon the Frost-Masters rivalry must, to the sensitive egos concerned, have seemed to border on the perverse. In all, Braithwaite evaluated Masters above Frost, greeting *Spoon River* as not only the most widely discussed book of poetry for the year, but also the most original literary work produced in America for a considerable time. Such bracketing of the two poets, the critical edge awarded to the westerner, could not help but contribute to Frost's singling out Masters as the rival to be brought down in flames, cost what it might.

In doing so, Frost had help. Braithwaite's succeeding volumes continued to praise Masters above Frost as the "most typical" American poet of the day, but with another anthologist things were different. Louis Untermeyer had introduced himself to Frost directly upon the poet's return from England, and after their first meeting in 1915 they became fast friends, exchanging a regular correspondence until Frost's death. Untermeyer's first collection, *Modern American Poetry*, appeared in 1919; in it Frost was pre-eminent, his range illustrated by eight selections. Only Carl Sandburg was allowed as much space. Amy Lowell and Edwin Arlington Robinson trailed closely with seven entries, but Masters was stripped to four. Frost continued to urge Untermeyer to become the active agent in the leveling of Masters Mountain. "Hit 'im with me!" (50) he urged. In time Masters eroded his own mountain; his work declined steadily after *Spoon River*, leaving him a man less to be reckoned with. But Frost could not rid his mind of that early threat. One brush with potential disaster in open competition was sufficient. More than twenty years after *Spoon River*, at a time when Masters' writing and following had deteriorated so badly that he slipped next door to oblivion, Frost continued to refer to "the megacephalus Masters" (299) and worried that Robert P. Tristram Coffin might be "snuggling up" to him. "I am very sensitive to political shifts like this," he explained. "We are choosing up sides, balancing our powers for the next world war in art" (299).

In that world war, which existed less in substance than in Frost's imagination, a formidable opponent was Amy Lowell, whose "wealth, social position, and the influence she [was] able to purchase and cozen" (106) made Frost's hackles stand erect. Amy was overpowering, one must admit, and her money was a constant affront to men who fought against desperate odds to glean a living from verse. Daniel Smythe in *Robert Frost Speaks* reports the poet complaining that Amy told him and E. A. Robinson they had no right to be poets, not being wealthy enough to afford the luxury. Even so, Amy Lowell was never the authentic threat Frost felt her to be. She was devoted totally to her school of Imagists, and even though she did make an overt attempt to snare Frost into that movement, it is obvious that her interest in Frost's work was genuine. Eager to see him gain the recognition he deserved, she was not at all ambitious to dominate him in the public eye. On the contrary, after encountering Frost's work in England, Amy did her level best to locate an American publisher for him.

What really rankled was Amy Lowell's personality. She was an inveterate limelighter, a scene-stealer. She had her way of playing the empress—it came naturally to her—and of summoning admirers and fellow poets to the throneroom. Sensing that she had to be the whole cheese, Frost balked. He cared even less for Amy's habit of traveling always and everywhere and thus being on the spot wherever publicity was likely to arise, or—worse yet—creating her own splash. Of course, the draw of the illustrious Lowell name put him off. And Amy's notorious cigar-smoking was a stupendous bit of stage magic in retaliation against which mussed hair seemed a feeble gimmick indeed. With burning corona in hand, Amy could "upstage" any rival she had a mind to. At the same time, Amy's kindnesses to Frost are a matter of record. Shortly after his books first appeared in America, she generously and foresightedly included him among six pace-setting American poets in her *Tendencies in Modern American Poetry*. With the exception of E. A. Robinson, Frost was the only poet who appeared in a chapter devoted solely to himself. Amy was unstinting in her praise, and her book, considering its author's prestige and that it was the first extended evaluation of Frost's work, gave an enormous boost to Frost's early career. Yet, despite her generosity, he chose to carp at small errors of fact and judgment allegedly contained in Amy's appraisal. He caviled with her assertion that his poems had been inspired completely and solely by New England (actually Amy's point clearly was that with New England Frost had located his ideal subject matter). Especially was he infuriated with Amy's portrait of Elinor Frost as, in his words, "the conventional helpmeet of genius" (62). Unpardonable he called it in 1917, although after Elinor's death Frost evaluated his wife's aid in much more glowing terms than Amy had.

This type of reaction Frost held private, sharing it only with intimates. On the surface he did his utmost to remain friends with Amy Lowell. She was, one had to admit, a most excellent individual to have on one's side in those days, nearly indispensable to an ambitious poet. Frost reserved his snide remarks for private letters, while publicly he placated Amy, allowing her reputation to cast whatever glow it might upon his own. If her poetry became the topic of an open conversation, Frost donned what he admitted was a "light mask" of hypocrisy. When closeted with close friends, however, he ridiculed her efforts unmercifully. "I don't believe she is anything but a fake" (106), he confided to his friend, anthologist Untermeyer. Hopefully he dreamed of a coming time when he might afford to expose Amy "for a fool as well as fraud" (107). Wouldn't it, he mused, be more honest if he were simply and flatly to refuse to allow his poems to be bound between the same covers with those of such a charlatan! Needless to say, such twinges of conscience were transitory. Their poems continued to appear side by side in the anthologies.

Robert Frost's capacity for pettiness in dealing with his "rising contemptuaries" (255) never manifested itself more clearly than when, in deference to Amy Lowell's acknowledged reputation and "power" in the literary world, he invited her to read at the University of Michigan while he was on campus as Poet in Residence. Amy came. The audience clamored for a glimpse of her engaged in smoking her cigar. She pooh-poohed the notion. The audience's fervor of interest only increased. It was infuriating to Frost, her coming as a guest and shamelessly stealing his thunder on home territory. At the speaker's podium, Amy joggled a pitcher of water and a lamp. Both upset. It took ten minutes to disentangle the lamp cord and mop up. Gleefully Frost wrote Untermeyer, "I never heard such spontaneous shouts of laughter" (148–149). But Amy Lowell proved as poised a showman as any. Throughout this comedy of errors she quipped with her audience, winning them securely, forcing Frost to admit grudgingly, "As a show she was more or less success-ful" (148).

At the time of Amy Lowell's death, Frost played at persuading himself that an eerie causal link existed between her inherent sense of the theatrical and her dying at the precise instant when his debt to her was most and his reciprocation least. Could she have planned it this way? He was led to speculate upon his own death, which ever since childhood he had pictured somewhat romantically as arriving at the perfect moment to cap his career with enormous effect. The request of *The Christian Science Monitor* for a statement was one which Frost would have preferred to avoid. In it, he maintained his public ambiguity regarding Amy and her poetry, while with Untermeyer he remained privately obdurate: "I refuse to weaken abjectly" (174). Two years after her death, Frost admitted that a mean streak of "Indian vindictiveness" corrupted his heart. "Really I am awful," he told John Bartlett; "I am worse than you know. I can never seem to forgive people who scare me within an inch of my life."[2]

III

Following the first critical decade of his career, Robert Frost apparently felt more secure of his position as king of the hill—as well he might. His contemporary "rivals" no longer posed a definable threat. Sandburg turned to history and his monumental work on Lincoln. Masters suffered through his steady, agonizing decline. Lindsay committed suicide in a fit of despondency. Amy Lowell died suddenly, in 1925, of a stroke. The momentum of the poetic renaissance, so hectic in 1914, slowed considerably, dissipating the need to bring down Masters Mountain and raise Frost Hollow in its place. Nevertheless, Robert Frost found it difficult to change his tune. The rivalry, the competition, the threat, whether real or imaginary, could not be shrugged off overnight. By now it was ingrained. "It is hard for me not to be jealous of latecomers in my field" (225), Frost confessed, echoing a most natural human emotion. Although he was not incapable of lending a helping hand to young aspirants, those who appeared to be establishing themselves as leaders were, by force of long habit, looked at askance. Even the mighty could be stung: William Butler Yeats, for one. "Whole pages" of Yeats' work amounted to nothing, Frost pointed out, insisting we must be careful not to grant the Irish Nobel winner more than his due: "He's disposed to crowd the rest of us as it is" (133–134). And of course, close alliance with any of the old rivals might prove fatal to a newcomer: John Gould Fletcher, commonly known to be Amy Lowell's protégé. "Amy's pig-eyed young bear-cat" was the name Frost tagged on him; "Look what [he] done all over the Dial for want of a little historical sense. Amy ought to be ashamed of him. Right through his diapers!" (91–92). And there was Eliot, of course, whom Frost could not understand and to whom he remained frigid. And MacLeish, the "college educated and practiced publicist" (255) whose work proved to Frost only that "a man doesn't have to think to be a poet" (257). And "this bird" Jeffers, whom the mightiest appeared to have fallen for and whose potential Frost recognized: "Jeffers would be my quarry if I were out hunting" (221).

Apparently, neither advancing age nor overweening fame served to diminish Frost's obsession; so say those who knew him in later years. Prior to his own success with *The Big Sky*, A. B. Guthrie, Jr., became acquainted with Frost's egregiousness during attendance at the Bread Loaf Writers' Conference, where it was prearranged to avoid Frost's wrath by seeing to it that his team won a game of baseball. Guthrie was perplexed by the poet's contradictory mixture of greatness and smallness. In *The Blue Hen's Chick* he recalls that Frost "was not always the kindly old sage that English-department heads make him out to be but could be and often was the captive of fierce and aberrant passions." That the novelist and poet got along amicably, Guthrie attributes to the tacit understanding that he posed no threat to Frost's determination to remain "the only bull in the pasture." Lawrance Thompson recounts Frost's rage at discovering in 1937 that Henry Holt and Company planned to publish an anthology of American literary opinion which included no essay devoted to himself. Not even the knowledge that publication of Richard Thornton's *Recognition of Robert Frost*—a book wholly devoted to praise of Frost—was imminent could dissuade him from swearing that he would leave the company if they printed the anthology. The company yielded to the ultimatum by selling the plates of the anthology to another house and made a conciliatory gesture toward its "outraged" editor by absorbing his permission costs. The Frost-Holt relationship was never the same thereafter.[3] Alfred Kazin, who served with Frost on the Amherst campus when Frost was eighty, found the poet to be "a raging battlefield of ambition, competitiveness, guilt . . . with everything in his life unforgotten and unforgiven, he bulked over the smug and discreet like a great bear—whom they had to feed with unexhausted attention and praise lest he fall on them snarling." The universally-honored poet "could not stop talking about *them*, early enemies" who, decades earlier, had posed a threat to his ambition. For his tomb Frost wished the largest and most laudatory biography possible. "And I knew why," says Kazin; "He could not bear the life he had lived."[4]

Fully aware that his country had absorbed him as affectionately as he had absorbed it, Robert Frost shrewdly postponed publication of his more private statements—and his biography—until he was "good and dead." Right or wrong, the mass of citizens continued to think of Frost as a kindly old soul, wise, bucolic, and pastoral, with never a grouchy word to grumble about anything or anybody. What matter that the dark side of Lionel Trilling's "terrifying" poet could be found profusely in *Complete Poems*? Who paid any attention to those parts? Even now, so ingrained is the image of Good Gray Poet which Frost himself in word, dress, and action fostered, that the spectacle of poet as cantankerous old curmudgeon jars. Yet what a relief to know that Frost could bleed!

Notes

1. *The Letters of Robert Frost to Louis Untermeyer*, ed. Louis Untermeyer (New York, 1963), p. 29. Hereafter page references to this work are contained in the text.

2. Margaret Bartlett Anderson, *Robert Frost and John Bartlett* (New York, 1963), p. 145.

3. Lawrance Thompson, *Robert Frost: The Years of Triumph, 1915–1938* (New York, 1970), p. 696.

4. Alfred Kazin, *New York Jew* (New York, 1978), pp. 230, 232.

The Myth and the Quest:
The Stature of Robert Frost

Arthur M. Sampley*

How great is a poet who has no consistent vision of man's place in the universe? What are we to think of one who adopts the tone of a seer and yet is uncertain himself about man's fundamental problems? How seriously are we to take a thinker who seems to avoid the complexities of contemporary life by turning constantly to a faded past? If poets, as Shelley says, are the unacknowledged legislators of the world, what are we to make of one whose frequent attitude toward life is one of apprehension and evasion? Have we not the right to expect from our greatest writers a heroic dream to which we may at least try to conform?

These are some of the questions that critics have asked about Robert Frost. Some of the most incisive criticism is found in George W. Nitchie's *Human Values in Robert Frost.* Frost, according to Nitchie, reduces problems to an ultimate and unrealistic simplicity. His fundamental defect is that he has not made up his mind about the kind of universe he lives in and therefore can offer no guidance as to how man should respond to it. Because "Frost never gives one the clear sense of having mastered, even wrongly, any large-scale aggregation of human phenomena," Nitchie would deny to him the stature of a major poet.[1]

Nor is Nitchie the only critic who finds Frost guilty of being absorbed in the past and of failure to face realistically the problems of modern man. Yvor Winters and Malcolm Cowley have presented similar criticism of Frost, finding him guilty of unwillingness to deal realistically with current problems and of sentimental obscurantism.[2]

There is justice in these criticisms. Frost *is* guilty of trying to see the world in the simplistic terms of a New England farmer. He does show a disturbing trend toward anti-intellectualism. His attitude toward the world of others is often myopic, and his views on social planning reveal a failure to comprehend the realities of contemporary life. These weaknesses do derogate from the greatness of Frost. But when Professor Nitchie goes on to declare that Frost is not a major poet because, unlike Yeats and Eliot, he has not constructed a logical view of interpreting life, I must

*From *The South Atlantic Quarterly*, Summer 1971, pp. 287–98. Copyright © 1971 by *The South Atlantic Quarterly*. Reprinted by permission.

demur. I think Frost has such a system, and if it seems at times a bit ram-
shackle, like God's throne in *A Masque of Reason*, it is nevertheless a
fairly coherent and not unreasonable way of interpreting the meaning of
life.

The system is undoubtedly quizzical. That is to say, there will always
be a reservation about any part of it. Even the fundamental question of
whether reality is mind or matter, of whether the universe is monistic or
dualistic, cannot be finally settled. In "All Revelation" Frost with
characteristic playfulness and indirection probes the question of man's
relation to matter with indeterminate results:

> A head thrusts in as for the view,
> But where it is it thrusts in from
> Or what it is it thrusts into
> By that Cyb'laean avenue,
> Or what can of its coming come,
>
> And whither it will be withdrawn,
> And what take hence or leave behind,
> These things the mind has pondered on
> A moment and still asking gone.
> Strange apparition of the mind!

In the last line of the poem Frost does say, "All revelation has been ours."
But this statement clearly does not mean that the mind is the only reality.
In the light of the rest of the poem what it apparently means is that mind
(whatever it may be) is our only way of experiencing reality.

A similar view of the relation of man's mind to the universe is conveyed in "The Most of It." Here the speaker seeks something in nature that
can answer his own deep need:

> He would cry out on life, that what it wants
> Is not its own love back in copy speech,
> But counter-love, original response.

But what comes back is not an answering human cry but an "embodiment
that crashed/ In the cliff's talus on the other side . . ." and revealed itself
as a great buck plunging into the water. There is an answering something
in nature, the poem seems to say, but its relation to us is remote and a
little uncertain.

This is the system, Frost is telling us, that we have to fit into—one
whose relation to ourselves we can never fully comprehend. It is realistic,
then, to admit our ignorance and to make the best adjustment to uncertainty that we can. The fact that Frost reveals his view indirectly and
symbolically does not invalidate the philosophical position.

But Frost does not believe in a directionless universe. There is within
it a unity of mind, of intelligence. This is the certainty of "I Will Sing You
One-O," in which the stroke of the village clock is the symbol of move-

ment interlocking with the revolution of the earth and of the farthest constellations. In "Accidentally on Purpose" Frost shows that he believes in a
centrality which is more than "balls going round in rings." The universe,
he says,

> . . . must have had the purpose from the first
> To produce purpose as the fitter bred:
> We were just purpose coming to a head.
> Whose purpose was it? His or Hers or Its?
> Let's leave that to the scientific wits.
> Grant me intention, purpose, and design—
> That's near enough for me to the Divine.

There is a God, and He has a purpose for what He has created. It is
not so clear, however, that this God is directly interested in individual
man. In the early poems He does seem to be. In "The Trial by Existence,"
for example, God gives each of the souls who have an opportunity to be
born onto the earth a preview of the life which they will have to endure,
and each soul apparently has a choice about whether it will accept the
ordeal of life. In "A Prayer in Spring" God's love is manifested in the
flowers, the orchard, and "darting bird," which man may thankfully accept and enjoy.

In the later poems, however, it is by no means clear that God is interested in the conduct of the individual. *A Masque of Reason* seems to
show that He is not. God explains to Job that the meaning of the tragedy
enacted in Job's sufferings is to demonstrate that God is not involved in
human choices:

> I have no doubt
> You realize by now the part you played
> To stultify the Deuteronomist
> And change the tenor of religious thought.
> My thanks are to you for releasing me
> From moral bondage to the human race. . . .
>
> I had to prosper good and punish evil.
> You changed all that. You set me free to reign.

Indeed the world at times shows some evidence of being ruled, not by
a beneficent God, but by sinister plan or malign fates. In "Design" we are
presented a microcosm in which a white spider on a white heal-all lures a
moth to destruction. To the moth at least this universe is somewhat worse
than indifferent. In "The Lovely Shall Be Choosers" the fates toy with a
woman whom they have deliberately set out to crush. They grant her
seven wishes which she desires, but each of the choices which she makes
commits her more deeply to isolation and heartbreak.

It does not seem to me that Frost is giving in these two poems a
generalized picture of the world of either the spider or the woman. Each

encounters disastrous chances which do occur in the world. So does the boy whose hand and life are cut off in " 'Out, Out—' ". But these chances are not necessarily typical. If they show anything it is that the universe is not so much inimical as unpredictable.

As a matter of fact there is opposing evidence that the world is, on the whole, friendly rather than hostile to man. If such were not the case, Frost says, "Our hold on the planet wouldn't have so increased." So in "The Broken Drought" a rain comes to confute the prophet of disaster, and in "A Serious Step Lightly Taken" those who settle on a farm may, in the light of experience of the past, look forward to "Enriching soil and increasing stock. . . ."

But though conditions on the earth seem to be on the whole favorable to man and though there is a divine purpose at the center of the universe, it is not clear to Frost whether this purpose is revealed to him. This uncertainty seems to be the central meaning of *A Masque of Mercy*. Jonah has had, as he thinks, a revelation in which he is charged to warn those who fail to follow God's commands that they will be destroyed. Now he finds that God has deceived him and is not following through with the threatened catastrophes. Jonah complains:

> I've lost my faith in God to carry out
> The threats He makes against the city evil.
> I can't trust God to be unmerciful.

Nor is Jonah the only one so afflicted. Paul, who represents the new dispensation of mercy, is also uncertain. He has preached a belief in a God who must in all fairness be merciful to those who because of human frailty fail to keep the exalted ethical standards of the Sermon on the Mount. But Paul, like Jonah, cannot be sure that he knows the will of God:

> Yes, there you have it at the root of things.
> We have to stay afraid deep in our souls
> Our sacrifice—the best we have to offer,
> And not our worst nor second best, our best,
> Our very best, our lives laid down like Jonah's,
> Our lives laid down in war and peace—may not
> Be found acceptable in Heaven's sight.

This theory may not be so comforting as Eliot's belief in surrender to the will of God, yet it is no unreasonable way of interpreting human history, as Eliot himself saw in Section III of "Little Gidding." Men cannot with all the variable factors of the future foresee the results of their actions. Those who act out of what seem to them good motives may produce bad or even catastrophic results. Frost is not being irreverent, but realistic, and I think we must respect him for trying to see the world as it is.

Man, then, inhabits a world presided over by Divine Intelligence, but he has no assurance that this intelligence is interested in rewarding or punishing him personally, nor can he even be sure what this power desires for him to do. How, then, does man respond in this precarious situation? If we take the word of the Frost who has a twinkle in his eye, we should follow the worldly wisdom of "Provide, Provide," which is to try to outguess the opposition:

> Some have relied on what they knew,
> Others on being simply true.
> What worked for them might work for you.

If one is pressed into too tight a spot, one may take cover, as does the speaker in "A Drumlin Woodchuck":

> All we who prefer to live
> Have a little whistle we give,
> And flash, at the least alarm
> We dive down under the farm.

In similar circumstances another Frostian persona toys with the idea of escape to the Arctic to live with Indian Joe.

If these were the only responses we found in Frost to the tragic events of life, we might indeed condemn him for triviality or for frivolity. But there is abundant evidence that men and women in Frost's world know how to endure catastrophe with stoic courage. In "The Self-Seeker," the Broken One, who has lost the use of his feet in a mill accident, has resigned himself better than has his friend Willis to the kind of crippled life that he must lead. It is evident that he is accepting a less favorable settlement than he might have obtained by going through a lawsuit, but it is also clear that he has a tranquillity of spirit which may help him as much as money to adjust to the difficulties ahead. Similarly the woman in "The Lovely Shall Be Choosers" is able to find some consolation to help her endure each of the seven stunning blows that the fates have in store for her. So, too, the wife in "A Servant to Servants" is reconciled to the hardships which she endures, even though they may lead her into madness. A rest might help her, but she will not insist that her husband arrange it for her:

> I'm past such help—
> Unless Len took the notion, which he won't,
> And I won't ask him—it's not sure enough.
> I s'pose I've got to go the road I'm going:
> Other folks have to, and why shouldn't I?

The speaker in "Bereft," who is clearly Frost, had undergone a similar period of despair in which all that he has cherished seems to be taken from him. The courage to endure is one answer to the uncertain universe.

Nitchie has written that Frost shows "an unwillingness or an inability to make that crucial act of choice by means of which anthropocentric man fulfills himself" (p. 184). Although in a poem like "Love and a Question" Frost does seem to avoid a decision, the reason for the state of suspension at the end is partly literary. We know from Thompson's biography that when the poet had to face a similar choice in real life between privacy and compassion, he let the tramp sleep on a pallet in the kitchen.[3] In "Into My Own," "Stopping by Woods on a Snowy Evening," and "Come In," Frost relates playfully what seemed to him important decisions. Certainly the characters in the New England eclogues do not shy away from hard choices. The woman in "The Fear" insists on facing alone the unknown and, as she thinks, dangerous figure in the darkness. In "The Death of the Hired Man" Mary unhesitatingly and Warren after brief persuasion agree to assume responsibility for the dying Silas. The hired man in "The Code" certainly shows no lack of decision in attempting to suffocate a demanding employer. Meserve in "Snow" decides to go into a dangerous midnight snowstorm when the Coles have offered him shelter for the night; he apparently makes this decision as an assertion of his manhood because he knows that Cole in particular has a contemptuous attitude towards his offbrand religious views.

The last incident also brings out the fierce pride of these New England people. It is the one thing for which they will unhesitatingly face death or cause it, as the hired man in "The Code" attempted to do. Pride is the reason why Estelle in "The House-keeper" finally leaves John, with whom she has lived as a common-law wife for fifteen years, and pride sustains her helpless old mother in the collapse of a way of life which seems the only one possible to her. It is also pride which causes the Broken One in "The Self-Server" to refuse to enter a court fight for his legitimate rights. Here as elsewhere an admirable quality may assume a pathological form, as we may feel that it does in "The Lone Striker." In this poem the worker locked out of the mill for arriving late, none other than Robert Frost,[4] leaves his job ostensibly to go for a stroll in the woods but actually to put an end to this kind of affront to his independence.

Frost, then, has created in his poems the kind of man who can survive in an uncertain universe. This individual will attempt to protect himself against the exigencies of fate as the speaker suggests in "Provide, Provide." If he is pushed too hard, he will make a strategic retreat, as the woodchuck does when he dives down under the farm. But if he is cornered and sees no way of escape, he will bear his situation with stoic endurance, fiercely resisting any kind of aid which may be thought of as charitable. In all of these vicissitudes he is partly sustained by a feeling that there is a divine purpose in the universe but mainly by a stubborn belief that he can somehow wrestle with whatever he must encounter.

This is the Frost myth, complete in its way as that of Yeats or Eliot. Quite obviously Frost and Eliot cannot both be right about God's relation to the universe and man's relation to God. But Frost's interpretation of the phenomenal world is a possible one and would probably meet with more agreement than would that of Eliot. Frost's response to the universe he envisages is less heroic than that of Yeats, but not necessarily less productive of good results. There is general testimony that the poems of Frost are tonic for the spirit. "Choose Something Like a Star" gives us somewhat diffuse but generally sound guidance. "The Strong Are Saying Nothing" offers a stoic courage in confronting this life and the possibility (not excluded) of another. "Acquainted with the Night" gives testimony of ability to endure through tragedy.

It can be argued, I think, that Frost's conception of man's relation to an unpredictable universe is one which should especially appeal to men in the twentieth century. At a time when old values are being attacked by the thinking and unthinking alike, when the belief in God as the director of individual man's destiny is being questioned in theological as well as in secular circles, when the future seems filled with ominous perils which statesmen in their candid moments admit that they frequently lack the wisdom to avert, then Frost's myth of the individual dodging, at times retreating, but never cowering has a special appeal for men facing an uncertain and perilous world. Independence and courage such as Frost teaches may indeed have survival value.

The myth has its own Grail quest. And though this quest reveals some of Frost's limitations, it indicates no less surely his corresponding strength. In "Directive," playfully but in loving detail, Frost guides those who find "this now too much for us" back to "a house/ Upon a farm that is no more a farm/ And in a town that is no more a town." The road never traveled any more was once a "road home from work" for two village cultures that now are lost. There is a "children's house of make believe" near a cellar hole "slowly closing like a dent in dough." The water in the spring, however, is cold, and Frost instructs his followers:

> I have kept hidden in the instep arch
> Of an old cedar at the waterside
> A broken drinking goblet like the Grail
> Under a spell so the wrong ones can't find it,
> So can't get saved, as Saint Mark says they mustn't.
> (I stole the goblet from the children's playhouse.)
> Here are your waters and your watering place.
> Drink and be whole again beyond confusion.

For Frost "Directive" is the equivalent of "Sailing to Byzantium" in the work of Yeats. Each poet, feeling not spiritually at home in his own time, set out to reach an earlier and more idyllic age. For Yeats it was Byzantium in the sixth century; for Frost it was village New England in the nineteenth. For each it was an excursus into the past in search of a better life; and for each it was a denial of present values and in a sense a retreat. For Frost, however, the life was less remote and more real than it could have been for Yeats. It was indeed the life into which eleven-year-old Robert Frost had moved when he was acutely sensitive to his environment. It was also a life in which he had spent his boyhood and young manhood. He could hardly have had illusions about this existence, for in it he had known poverty, privation, debt, sickness, and death. It was no book-like idyl that he imagined. It was made up of the fabric of the lives of men and women that he had known.

Frost was as aware as anyone that this kind of life was disappearing. He has many poems which show the New England farmer and villager losing the struggle with poverty. In "The Census Taker" the living have departed, and in the poem "In a Disused Graveyard" the dead have ceased to arrive. In "The Birthplace" all the children have scattered to other regions, and in "The Last Mowing" the land returns to wilderness. Why, then, does Frost so persistently seek an obsolescing civilization?

It is a quest for national origins. The quest is indeed one of Frost's favorite types of poems. It typically takes the form of a journey by two people to a place that recalls a former time and thus by Frost's synecdochic manner the spirit of that time. "Directive" is perhaps the finest example of this kind of poem, but "The Black Cottage," "The Generations of Men," "In the Home Stretch," and "A Fountain, a Bottle, a Donkey's Ears and Some Books" are other poems of the same type. The quest into the past also appears with variations in "Maple" and "The Old Barn at the Bottom of the Fogs." In "The Generations of Men" as in "Directive" the scene is an old cellar hole; a boy and a girl who meet at a rained-out family reunion seem to catch the voices of the past affirming the strength of original family strains. The boy comments:

> What counts is the ideals,
> And those will bear some keeping still about.

So in "The Black Cottage" the speaker and a minister visit the deserted house where once lived a widow who had lost her husband in the Civil War. The minister comments on the beliefs which had sustained her in her loss:

> Her giving somehow touched the principle
> That all men are created free and equal.
> And to hear her quaint phrases—so removed
> From the world's view today of all those things.

In these poems the stress is on a manner of life on which the greater part of what became the United States of America was built in its first three centuries as a civilized community. The virtues of prudence, pride, and independence launched a great nation. Frost continued to assert, against the pressure of a new urbanized civilization, their residual values.

The agricultural village as a way of life is disappearing, and Frost displayed little wisdom in conducting a sniping rear-guard action against inevitable change. "Build Soil" can hardly be taken seriously as a solution of the nation's agrarian problems. Enriching the soil in order to improve the product is a worthy aim for a farmer, a poet, or a nation, but it will not necessarily keep the producer alive between harvest times. What is important is the character which this way of life engendered. The importance of an independent spirit and of human dignity has not declined in the twentieth century. In fact the need of these qualities may have increased, for they may be what is required to make a highly systematized way of life tolerable. The individual is now, as in the past, the base of any society. The kind of strength which one finds in the characters in *North of Boston* cannot be imposed from above. Indeed there is a very real danger that a computerized, regimented state may, however unintentionally, turn men and women into manipulatable robots. We can smile wryly at "Departmental," but we know enough of corporations and bureaucracies to understand that the poem is not altogether irrelevant to us.

The critics of Frost are right in saying that he has a tendency to oversimplify, that he is sometimes anti-intellectual, and that he did not sufficiently comprehend the necessity for social planning, especially to take care of the needy. But Frost is right, too, in asserting the priority of an independent spirit, the importance of pride, and the dignity of the lowly.

Frost's world is not so much malign as precarious. A characteristic poem, "Once by the Pacific," expresses his sense of catastrophe lurking at the center of things. But against this violence in the natural world and against the strokes of fate which end life as in " 'Out, Out—' " or threaten human relationships as in "Home Burial," Frost presents a courageous and independent spirit, able to face the uncertainty of things, striving to avert or escape evil, but able, if necessary, to stand and face it, to endure it till the end. The choices which this individual makes reveal the direction of his destiny. In "The Road Not Taken" the poet, following his instinct, chooses the road less traveled by. In "Stopping by Woods on a Snowy Evening" he resists the attraction of the dark woods. As he matures he can even welcome bitter experiences as a part of the necessary process of living:

> The hurt is not enough:
> I long for weight and strength
> To feel the earth as rough
> To all my length.

The struggle between courage and fear was not for Frost an academic exercise. As we learn more of the details of his biography, we can see that throughout his life he carried on an unending combat with the weaknesses of his own nature. The revelation by Lawrance Thompson of some of the more startling episodes in Frost's life brought from some critics a sharp reaction against the poet. But this judgment misses, I think, what is the central meaning of the life and work of Robert Frost. In spite of many errors and defeats he hammered out in poetry and in life his figure of the lonely, hard-set individual who masters his fears, his weaknesses, even his fate through courage and dogged resolution. The hard-won integrity of this individual is the base of society, and his strength is a part of the fabric of our civilization. The instinct of the American people in seeing Frost as spokesman for their aspirations is not faulty. He will continue to be a test not only of their achievements, but also of their character.[5]

Notes

1. *Human Values in Robert Frost* (Durham, N.C., 1960), p. 219.

2. Yvor Winters, "Robert Frost: or, The Spiritual Drifter as Poet," and Malcolm Cowley, "The Case Against Mr. Frost," in *Robert Frost: A Collection of Critical Essays*, ed. James M. Cox (Englewood Cliffs, 1962), pp. 58–82 and 36–45.

3. Lawrance Thompson, *Robert Frost: The Early Years, 1874–1914* (New York, 1966), pp. 377–78.

4. Ibid., pp. 160–61.

5. Passages from Frost's poems quoted in this article are from *The Poetry of Robert Frost*, edited by Edward Connery Lathem. Copyright 1923, 1930, 1939, 1947, 1969 by Holt, Rinehart and Winston, Inc. Copyright 1936, 1942, 1945, 1951, © 1958, 1960, 1962 by Robert Frost. Copyright © 1964, 1967, 1970 by Lesley Frost Ballantine. Reprinted by permission of Holt, Rinehart and Winston, Inc.

The Achievement of Robert Frost

W. W. Robson*

I

An English critic (A. Alvarez in *The Shaping Spirit*) has this to say about Frost's present reputation in England: "Perhaps the only modern American poet who really is concerned with manners is Robert Frost. . . . I think this is why Frost has been so readily accepted in England; he is peculiarly congenial; we are easy with the tradition of country poetry, simple language and simple wisdom. American cosmopolitanism, even Eliot's, has always seemed a suspicious virtue, whereas Frost seems assured, he does not have to strive; he has New England behind him. . . ." Alvarez, perhaps unwittingly, gives the impression (which I do not share) that Frost's poetry is widely read in England. But otherwise this implicit placing of Frost ("country poetry, simple language and simple wisdom") in a familiar minor niche, does, I think, convey a true account of Frost's actual standing here. His reputation is based, it would seem, on a handful of well-known anthology pieces. "Everyone" knows "Stopping by Woods on a Snowy Evening," just as "everyone" knows Masefield's "Cargoes," but that is not enough to put either poet in a context of active discussion. My own impression, for what it is worth, is that if Frost is mentioned at all, it is as a worthy but dull poet of about the rank of Masefield. And if this patronizing attitude is accompanied by a more sympathetic note, that may derive from the memory of America's unofficial poet laureate as a white-haired old man pathetically inaudible at Kennedy's inauguration.

For those English readers who see more in Frost than Alvarez apparently does, this is a pity—especially since it was English readers in the first place who could very largely take the credit for discovering him. True, the first intelligent critique of his verse was written by an American, Ezra Pound. But the review of *North of Boston* in 1914 by the English poet Edward Thomas, though less well-known, gives an equally incisive account of what must on any view be a large part of Frost's permanent claim to a

*From *The Southern Review*, October 1966. Copyright © 1966 by *The Southern Review*. Reprinted by permission.

place in the history of poetry. In its brevity and its clarity of description Thomas' review, modest as it is, is a model of good criticism, as this extract may suggest:

> This is one of the most revolutionary books of modern times, but one of the quietest and least aggressive. It speaks, and it is poetry. It consists of fifteen poems, from fifty to three hundred lines long, depicting scenes of life, chiefly in the country, in New Hampshire. Two neighbour farmers go along opposite sides of their boundary wall, mending it and speaking of walls and of boundaries. A husband and wife discuss an old vagabond farm servant, who has come home to them, as it falls out, to die. Two travellers sit outside a deserted cottage, talking of those who once lived in it, talking until bees in the wall boards drive them away. A man who has lost his feet in a saw-mill talks to a friend, a child, and the lawyer comes from Boston about compensation. The poet himself described the dreams of his eyes after a long day on a ladder picking apples, and the impression left on him by a neglected wood-pile in the snow on an evening walk. All but these last two are in dialogue mainly: nearly all are in blank verse.
>
> These poems are revolutionary because they lack the exaggeration of rhetoric, and even at first sight appear to lack the poetic intensity of which rhetoric is an imitation. Their language is free from the poetical words and forms that are the chief material of secondary poets. The meter avoids not only the old-fashioned pomp and sweetness, but the later fashion also of discord and fuss. In fact, the medium is common speech and common decasyllables, and Frost is at no pains to exclude blank verse lines resembling those employed, I think, by Andrew Lang in a leading article printed as prose. Yet almost all these poems are beautiful. They depend not at all on objects commonly admitted to be beautiful; neither have they merely homely beauty, but are often grand, sometimes magical. Many, if not most, of the separate lines and separate sentences are plain and, in themselves, nothing. But they are bound together and made elements of beauty by a calm eagerness of emotion.

Thomas puts the stress where it should be put, in beginning his discussion of Frost: on Frost's technical innovation. Of course what Thomas, himself, as a poet, owed to Frost was more than technical. That community of spirit between poets which makes it out of place to speak of "imitation" of one by another is evident in passages like these I quote from Thomas; the similarity of accent to Frost's is obvious, but no informed admirer of Frost would suppose these passages to have been written by him:

> . . . Not till night had half its stars
> And never a cloud, was I aware of silence
> Stained with all that hour's songs, a silence
> Saying that Spring returns, perhaps to-morrow.

> And yet I still am half in love with pain,
> With what is imperfect, with both tears and mirth,
> With things that have an end, with life and earth,
> And this moon that leaves me dark within the door.

For I at most accept
Your love, regretting
That is all: I have kept
Only a fretting

That I could not return
All that you gave
And could not ever burn
With the love you have,

Till sometimes it did seem
Better it were
Never to see you more
Than linger here
With only gratitude
Instead of love—
A pine in solitude
Cradling a dove.

The last example reminds us of a note of longing in Frost which sounds at the same time both stronger and sweeter than Thomas:

Love at the lips was touch
As sweet as I could bear;
And once that seemed too much;
I lived on air

That crossed me from sweet things
The flow of—was it musk
From hidden grapevine springs
Down hill at dusk?

I had the swirl and ache
From sprays of honeysuckle
That when they're gathered shake
Dew on the knuckle.

I craved strong sweets, but those
Seemed strong when I was young;
The petal of the rose
It was that stung.

With that passage (from "To Earthward") we have left the characteristic work in *North of Boston*, and the special qualities which Thomas in his review was concerned to bring to the attention of English readers. But displaying the likeness and difference between the sensibilities of the two friends in their most personal work may remove the suspicion that all Thomas learned from Frost was a trick of craftsmanship, a dodge for handling everyday material in those anecdotal/dialogue poems which are as characteristic of his work as of Frost's. What Thomas learned from Frost's work, whether in the lyrical or the "dramatic" mode, was something that belonged to its essence.

But in his review Thomas *is* chiefly concerned with Frost's blank verse, and it is useful to note, in trying to decide what Frost's achievement meant to the English poet, just how Thomas counters the obvious objection to this blank verse, that it is no more than versified prose. He remarks that Frost "would lose far less than most modern writers by being printed as prose." But he continues: "If his work were so printed, it would have little in common with the kind of prose that runs to blank verse: in fact, it would turn out to be closer knit and more intimate than the finest prose is except in its finest passages. *It is poetry because it is better than prose.*" (Italics mine.)

We have here a hint of the kind of influence Frost had on Thomas, the personal and technical impact that made him a poet—though his late flowering was tragically brief, covering only the years of the first world war (he was killed on the Western Front in 1918). What made possible his self-discovery as a poet was this: he had been shown the way out of the late Victorian literariness he had practiced in his previous writings. By being encouraged to admit the prosaic, he was enabled to deal at first hand with genuine experience and feeling; to resist the temptation to adapt them to a manner which seems to prescribe beforehand how one *should* deal with them: so that it is easy to go on to mistake (as conventional poets so often do) what one knows one is supposed to feel, for what one actually does feel—if anything. And this release from late Victorian poetic diction inevitably demanded—what was just as important—a release from conventional rhythm. One of the chief problems for poets at the end of the nineteenth century was how to emancipate themselves from the coarse measures, the emphatic movement, so prevalent in Victorian poetry. *Vers libre* was one seemingly unavoidable consequence of the reaction against the often overemphatic meters of Tennyson or Swinburne or Meredith. But *vers libre*, in the hands of its inferior practitioners, became an excuse for carelessness, or exposed them as lacking the conviction that poetry is an art. Such an attitude was unthinkable in a poetic craftsman like Frost. His solution to the technical problem was to retain meter, but to incorporate into it the cadences of speech. It is the speech of New England speakers; its staple, the talk of an educated man at the point just before it crystallizes into formal prose. We do not speak prose; Moliere's M. Jourdain was wrong; we evolve it from the movement and syntax and cadence of educated speech. The artistic achievement of Frost was to evolve verse from these. Locutions like "admittedly," "to do that to," "of course," he brought into impassioned poems. Yet he did so in a manner which does not disturb our sense that we are reading poetry, something with its origins in song. His versification can always go back to the *cantabile*, yet it includes little that does not belong to modern (if sometimes a little old-fashioned) educated speech. The contrast with an English poet like Edmund Blunden is significant. Blunden can write even in his best poems lines like "The pole-tops steeple to the thrones/ Of stars, sound gulfs of wonder," in which the rhythm imposed by the meaning seems not to fit the metrical pattern. This clumsiness, or constant slight artificiality, is what Frost banished from his poetry.

Frost's colloquialism is famous. It is also notorious, for in his anecdotal poems he can sometimes sink to an unparalleled flatness. But critics have sometimes misrepresented this quality of his work by overstatement, seeing in it the whole of his innovation. This does not do him justice. The most casual reader sees that Frost is colloquial; reading which is more than casual brings out how much of the "archaic" and "literary" language of traditional poetry he has retained. Thus no one familiar with Frost's work will find the following poem uncharacteristic; yet to call it "colloquial" misdescribes it. So far from being the anecdotal jotting down of some incident of New England rural life, or a piece of gnarled rustic wisdom or country sentiment, it is a gracefully sustained literary fancy which (one might be inclined to say) could have come from an accomplished traditional poet:

> She is as in a field a silken tent
> At midday when a sunny summer breeze
> Has dried the dew and all its ropes relent,
> So that in guys it gently sways at ease,
> And its supporting central cedar pole,
> That is its pinnacle to heavenward
> And signifies the sureness of the soul,
> Seems to owe naught to any single cord,
> But strictly held by none, is loosely bound
> By countless silken ties of love and thought
> To everything on earth the compass round,
> And only by one's going slightly taut
> In the capriciousness of summer air
> Is of the slightest bondage made aware.

At first this seems to belong with "literary" poetry; in its diction, syntactical organization, and structure—the careful and explicit working out of the central idea—it is obviously a "thing made," not a "happening," like a jewel, not like a pebble or a snowflake, as so many of Frost's typical poems seem to be. But "going slightly taut"—that is one's feeling about the poem: it is the reminder of the poet's formal control which here brings into unusual prominence Frost's usual firm grip on the sensory facts which provide the notation for his graceful compliment and comment; so that this delicate, consciously elaborated sonnet is, after all, of a piece with the most rugged of his poems. Frost's is a manner which can accommodate the literary and the artificial as well as other modes.

The critic I previously quoted, Alvarez, notes this retention by Frost of the literary and traditional, but sees it as a simple incongruity, inconsistent with his character as a realist in verse. "Granted that Frost began to write a very long time ago," he says, "so his archaisms are probably not all deliberate; and granted his singleness of colloquial tone must have needed great practice and hard work to perfect. Nevertheless the literariness is a surprising contrast both to his habitual air of plain wisdom and to the lucidity he reaches in his best work." Alvarez seems to see Frost's "singleness of colloquial tone"—his plain diction—as the distinguishing feature of his poetry. And literariness in a plain diction would be a blemish. But he has overlooked that for Frost tone and cadence of voice are not necessarily associated with conversational diction—or syntax. Edward Thomas once more shows his understanding of Frost's art when he writes to Gordon Bottomley to defend it against the criticisms of the traditionalist poet Sturge Moore: "All he [Frost] insists on is what he believes he finds in all poets—absolute fidelity to the postures which the voice assumes in the most expressive intimate speech. So long as these tones and postures are there he has not the least objection to any vocabulary whatever or any inversion or variation from the customary grammatical forms of talk. In fact I think he would agree that if the tones and postures survive in a complicated or learned vocabulary and structure the result is likely to be better than if they survive in the easiest form, that is, in the very words and structures of common speech." What this perceptive statement brings out is that Frost, at any rate in intention, is a less *specialized* poet than some of his admirers, or detractors, have been prepared to recognize. Just as he was not merely offering, in *North of Boston* and the later work in resonance with it, pleasant material for the connoisseur of folkways or panegyrist of rural life, so his colloquialism was a development of something he thought an essential quality of *all* good poetry—an intrinsic naturalness which there is no reason to suppose he thought peculiar to the reported conversation of farmers. After all, there is no particular virtue in a conversational style as such; it is possible to be emotionally cheap, or tedious, or shallow, in a conversational style as in any other. In aiming to restore a vibration and human interest to poetry which late nineteenth-century poets seemed to have lost—and which had not been regained by Frost's immediate English predecessors, the poets among whom Yeats learned his trade, "companions of the Cheshire Cheese"—Frost did not suppose that he could succeed by the simple expedient of writing as differently as possible from Dante Gabriel Rossetti. That may have been a necessary condition of what he did, but it was certainly not a sufficient one, nor do I see any reason for thinking that Frost himself believed it was.

Properly defined, then, Frost's technical innovation is a notable one, guaranteeing him a place in the history of poetry. A question that naturally arises is how far it was solely *his* innovation; and a related question, whether it should be regarded primarily as an American contribution to the poetry of the common language, or seen more in the terms of English poetic history. It would be ludicrous to deny that Frost's poetry is American poetry, not only in its manifest subject matter, but in more impalpable qualities. But, as often, the definition of "English" as opposed to "American," in literary matters, is not simple. Notwithstanding the debt which American readers may perceive Frost to owe to Edwin Arlington Robinson, it seems clear that the development we note between the bulk of the poems in *A Boy's Will,* and the poems in *North of Boston,* has a vital connection with the work and study in which Frost joined with English poets in England. It was in the course of this association that Frost acquired a knowledge of other poetic experimenting, and a confidence in his own discovered "voice" in poetry, which enabled him in the long run to exert an influence and attain a status denied to the isolated poet of Gardiner, Maine. What seems unquestionable is that Frost, in whatever other ways American critics may want to describe him, cannot be considered altogether apart from the Georgian phase of English literary history. To recognize that may not only be helpful in clarifying the study of his poetry; it may begin to do belated justice to the Georgian phase itself.

"Georgian" was once an honorific description; Wilfred Owen, a poet nowadays much in favor, was proud to be "held peer by the Georgians." But it has now become the reverse, being generally used to stigmatize all the weakness and spuriousness of the writers brought together in *Georgian Poetry* by Edward Marsh. Their work is associated with facile weekend garden sentiment and a false affectation of simplicity. Schoolboys and undergraduates know that they were feeble escapists whom Modern Poetry consigned to the rubbish heap. What is sometimes forgotten, even by more mature students, is that Georgian poetry in its day was modern poetry. At least some of these poets thought of themselves as managing a revolt against established and popular traditionalists like Sir Henry Newbolt and Alfred Noyes. What they thought they were doing is doubtless irrelevant. And there is no need to have a very high opinion, or to weigh seriously the "modernity" or otherwise of that terrain of Georgianism in which Rupert Brooke is the dominant figure and his *Grantchester* the representative poem. The more relevant consideration is that some gifted writers, as well as some less gifted, do seem in retrospect to have enough in common for some characterizing adjective without a contemptuous overtone. The poets with whom Frost worked (Gibson, Abercrombie, Edward Thomas), Frost's own poetry, the short stories of A. E. Coppard, the early work of D. H. Lawrence—the period of English literature which contains these things reveals enough continuity between them and the work of weaker representative writers of the time, to need a historical description; and the word "Georgian," notwithstanding its unfortunate associations, is the only one currently available.

What these writers have in common is a preoccupation, amounting in some cases to a positive obsession, with personal freedom. No reader of Frost will need to be reminded of his obsessive concern with it. This plays a large part, clearly, in that sanctification of whim and impulse for which Yvor Winters, his severest critic, has castigated him; many of the poems quoted for adverse comment by Winters show that this attitude of "let me alone," a stubborn refusal to be pushed around by powers spiritual or temporal, is by no means confined to poems of playful whimsicality; a piece like "The Objection to Being Stepped On" is itself trifling enough, but the protest it epitomizes is the expression of something fundamental in Frost's work. No doubt in Frost it has to be related to the history of New England, and of the United States for that matter, as well as to his personal life and character. But it found a congenial environment, an echo of sympathy, in the Georgianism of "old" England also.

This passion for privacy can be the foundation of a distinguished and strong personal art. But it can also come out in attitudes and mannerisms and tones of voice that have in them something tiresomely complacent and limited. In Frost we see the tiresome side of his cult of freedom in a certain cranky obscurantism in politics and a grumpiness in personal relations (see his letters). In the English Georgians we have something worse (at least from a literary point of view): the attempt to invest with spiritual distinction a self-congratulatory sensitiveness about country walks, garden suburbs, and afternoon tea. That poem by Brooke which begins "Safe in the magic of my woods . . ." is a good example. The individual private responsiveness to nature on which the speaker in this poem congratulates himself, may be called the mysticism of the *rentier;* and mysticism in this context is apt to be the spiritual correlate of a vagueness about the sources of one's income. Certainly in Edward Thomas there is none of this Georgian complacency; the writing which he did for a living meant real hard work, and if it was hackwork it was perfectly decent. But when we read of Thomas' milieu in a book like Eleanor Farjeon's *Edward Thomas: The Last Four Years* we cannot but feel slightly depressed by that ethos of brown bread, knapsacks, "rambles," and living on modest incomes in thatched cottages in the days when the pound was worth a pound. The characteristic note of Thomas' poetry, the note of yearning, recurrent and insistent, makes us feel all this as sad and restricted. It is remarkable how the entry into Eleanor Farjeon's pages of D. H. and Frieda Lawrence brightens things up.

Frost, like Lawrence, seems to have brought refreshment from outside into this somewhat stuffy atmosphere. That there was harshness and bleakness in what he brought was no disadvantage. But these are not the qualities to stress here. The distinction that Frost brought to Georgianism, the moral and emotional stimulus he gave to a poet like Edward Thomas (we think of poems of Thomas such as "Bob's Lane") were due to a positive, attractive quality in his way of writing, a quality that distinguishes him not only from the Georgians but from almost any English poet since Chaucer. For this quality of feeling there is no satisfactory name. If, in default of better, we have to fall back on "democracy," it must be in the full recognition that this word has little descriptive meaning, has become vapid; it belongs to political rhetoric, and—what in the present context is much worse—it suggests a backslapping *faux-bonhomme*, pretending friendliness which is utterly alien to the spirit of Frost's best work. And if we substitute "fellow-feeling," it must again be without any suggestion of the easy gush of egalitarian emotion. There is, it is true, a trace of friendliness in some of Frost's invitations to his reader ("I sha'n't be gone long.—You come too"). But his manner of warm geniality frequently covers something much colder. No one can suppose that the fellow feeling which is the subject of the poet of "Snow" (in *Mountain Interval)* or "The Axe-Helve" (in *New Hampshire*) is a feeling which springs easily into the hearts of the hard, sometimes curmudgeonly, caste conscious people Frost is writing about. No one can doubt that for Frost himself the impulse to "let go" emotionally is not one that is easily yielded to, or that there is much of his own voice in the speaker of "Wild Grapes":

> I had not learned to let go with the hands,
> As still I have not learned to do with the heart,
> And have no wish to with the heart—nor need,
> That I can see. The mind—is not the heart.
> I may yet live, as I know others live,
> To wish in vain to let go with the mind—
> Of cares, at night, to sleep; but nothing tells me
> That I need learn to let go with the heart.

Yet the capacity to express fellow feeling with a deep and complete sincerity seems truly typical of Frost; and to describe it adequately is to give full weight to the importance for criticism of Frost's being an American.

There is, of course, a danger here of oversimplification. We must not sentimentalize away the realities of caste or class consciousness in American life, either in the present or the recent past. The recognition of them is obvious in Frost's poetry itself, and has clearly played an important part in his perception of his subject matter. The situation in "A Hundred Collars," when a professor has to share a room for the night with a traveling salesman, is just as uncomfortable as if they had been Englishmen. But it is uncomfortable in a different way; and to decide just what the difference is, is to bring out something essential in Frost's poetry. The difference is in the poet's attitude. We may imagine the situation treated by a liberal English writer of Frost's generation, like E. M. Forster. The vein might well be lightly ironical; the English writer, in the person of the professor, would have been ashamed of himself, would have known what he ought to feel, and would have done his best to feel it. Frost's attitude also includes an element of irony. But whereas the English writer would know what the professor felt, but would have to guess at what the salesman felt, Frost knows both. That is the difference. The conditions of American society and American life here give the American writer an advantage over his English counterpart.

Such an observation, however, could be made about a novelist or short story writer. In speaking of a poet we should be more closely concerned with technical considerations. What Frost brought home to some English poets in the early twentieth century was the truth in the famous description of a poet as a man speaking to men. The phrase is Wordsworth's; and the point in question may be brought home by suggesting the advantage Frost enjoys over Wordsworth in this capacity. Here are two passages from the earlier poet:

> "Oh saints! what is become of him?
> Perhaps he's climbed into an oak,
> Where he will stay till he is dead;
> Or sadly he has been misled,
> And joined the wandering gipsy-folk."
>   ("The Idiot Boy")

>   . . . Once again I see
> These hedge-rows, hardly hedge-rows, little lines
> Of sportive wood run wild; these pastoral farms
> Green to the very door; and wreaths of smoke
> Sent up, in silence, from among the trees,
> With some uncertain notice, it might seem,
> Of vagrant dwellers in the houseless woods.
>   ("Tintern Abbey")

Wordsworth, it is often said, has two voices, and lovers of his poetry will recognize them in these two passages, and recognize also an underlying harmony between them; but the immediate effect of the comparison is to show how "unnatural" is the voice of the speaker in "The Idiot Boy" passage, how little flavor or savor has been given to the speech of the old woman; in contrast, the "literary" voice of the second passage is the "natural" one. Frost's comparable "two voices" have a much happier affinity:

> Mind you, I waited till Len said the word.
> I didn't want the blame if things went wrong.
> I was glad though, no end, when we moved out,
> And I looked to be happy, and I was,
> As I said, for a while—but I don't know!
> Somehow the change wore out like a prescription.
> And there's more to it than just window-views
> And living by a lake. I'm past such help—
> Unless Len took the notion, which he won't,
> And I won't ask him—it's not sure enough.
> I s'pose I've got to go the road I'm going:
> Other folks have to, and why shouldn't I?
>   ("A Servant to Servants")

> There is a singer everyone has heard,
> Loud, a mid-summer and a mid-wood bird,

Who makes the solid tree trunks sound again. . . .
He says the highway dust is over all.
The bird would cease and be as other birds
But that he knows in singing not to sing.
The question that he frames in all but words
Is what to make of a diminished thing.
                    ("The Oven Bird")

Here both voices, the poet's own, and that of someone very different from himself in education and culture, seem equally "natural." The critical inference from this comparison of Frost and Wordsworth might be generalized in a discussion of their treatment of a common interest, "humble and rustic life." Wordsworth conveys the impression that he found "speaking to men" difficult—speaking to uneducated men belonging to a world and a mode of life that he feels as external to him; and they find it difficult to speak to him: as like as not they call him "Sir." In this respect Wordsworth is typical of English poets belonging to the central literary tradition, over several centuries; it is when they have most sought to avoid the note of "Yonder peasant, who is he?" that they have most fallen into a stiff uneasiness which is the forerunner of insincerity. The New England poet has no such difficulty. But to suppose that this superiority just "came naturally" to him—the unearned advantage of an American poet—is to forget the history of American poetry, and to forget that Frost is above all an artist. It was the artist in Frost, not the common man (whose notion of poetry may be a very banal and "literary" one) which made him recognize that to *express* the common man he must use words and rhythms very differently from Longfellow or Whittier.

II

But when we have granted the value of Frost's technical innovation, have we said anything more than that he achieved a style which (in Auden's words) is "quiet and sensible"? Whether one agrees with Winters' essay or not, it is surely its virtue to insist that criticism—as distinct from "appreciation"—*begins* here. Frost may have developed an all-purpose style which he could go on using for the rest of his life, and which other poets could learn from—English as well as American poets: for if some present-day English poetry (as is often said) has gone back to Georgianism, it is a Georgianism which has learned the lesson of Frost, unpretentiousness, plainness, lightness; that "pinch of salt," not taking everything seriously that is said solemnly, which William James is said to have brought back into philosophy, Frost brought back into poetry. But what is to be *done* with that style? And what did Frost himself do with it?

In considering the last question, an English critic's disadvantages are obvious. He has to consider Frost's New England, Frost's America, purely as a country of the mind. And he has to remember the warning conveyed by the answer a Frenchman gave when Matthew Arnold asked why the French thought Lamartine a great poet: "He is a great poet *for us.*" But there may be one or two compensating advantages. The American critic appraising Frost is in danger of other disturbances of judgment, as examples have shown. He cannot but be concerned with politics in the widest sense of that word. It is his critical duty, for example, to consider whether or not Frost has been rated beyond his merits as a poet because of an idealization of the older, rural America for which his work, and his supposed personal qualities, have been used as a sanction and a symbol. And it is his duty to consider how far Frost's work really does warrant this use. He must consider the issue, mentioned by Alvarez, of "cosmo-politanism" against "rootedness"; he must consider what conclusions for American criticism and American literature should be drawn from the fact—if it is a fact—that, as an American poet, Frost is the antithesis of Pound. Such questions can arouse heat and passion, as a distinguished New York critic found out at the cost of much uproar. An English critic can pass them by.

The question he cannot avoid is whether Frost has ever written a really considerable poem. This is not very different from the question whether he is a great poet; but a critic might be discouraged from asking that question, partly no doubt because of the vagueness of the category, but in the main because of Eliot's authoritative insistence, over the years, on the relative unimportance of surmises about "greatness" in comparison with considerations of "goodness" or "genuineness." Yet it seems a reasonable condition even of the good and genuine poet that he shall have a poem to offer us. The search for it surely takes precedence over the historical inquiry (in itself of some interest) how the "Georgian" poet of 1914 developed into the candidate for the status of American national poet—vacant since Whitman—which was urged for him when it began to be felt that Carl Sandburg somehow would not do. No amount of national appeal, country charm, regional flavor, or anecdotal personality can be a substitute for a poem; it is only in the world of the higher publicity and literary fashions that "poems," "poetry," a general poetical atmosphere, appear to compensate for the absence of a "Sailing to Byzantium," a "Cimetière Marin," a *Four Quartets.*

But it may be objected that Frost is not the kind of poet who invites description in terms of single masterpieces: that his claim to distinction is the impressive level maintained in a large body of work. In that case the question may be put in a different form, while remaining in essence much the same: what has he to say? what is the substance of his poetic achievement? And when we turn our attention to that question the frequent embarrassment of Frost's commentators is ominous. Something has gone wrong when we find an intelligent critic writing like this—his text being the poem "Design," of which he is analyzing the first line ("I found a dimpled spider, fat and white"): "At first we hear the cheerfully observant walker on back-country roads: 'I found a dimpled . . .' The iambic lilt adds a tone of pleasant surprise: 'I found a dimpled darling—' 'Little Miss Muffet sat on a tuffet!' But in 'spider' the voice betrays itself, and in 'fat' and 'white' the dimpled creature appears less charming. On a small scale the first line, like the whole poem, builds up a joke in tone, rhythm, and image that grows into a 'joke' of another sort." Anyone holding an academic post must feel sympathy with this critic. But what is troubling, as we explore their commentaries, is the thinness which he and other writers on Frost seem to sense in their subject matter, and their apparent need to import some density into it by paraphrasing Frost's thought and considering Emerson, Thoreau, and a cultural tradition and habit of sensibility deriving from them. Of course this embarrassment of the commentators may reflect no more than the unsuitability of modern critical techniques, influenced by modern poetic fashions, to get hold of so traditional and unfashionable a poet. The kind of ironies, ambiguities, or "polysemy" to which those techniques are adapted—and which indeed, in some poets of academic provenance, they may have actually inspired—are not there. Nor is Frost the kind of poet congenial to erudite exegetes; he has not constructed an esoteric world system, or a scheme of private allusions; there is no code to be broken. To be an adequate critic, it would seem, all you need is a heart and feelings and a capacity for independent thoughts about your life and your world; ingenuity and tenacious industry are not only not enough, they are irrelevant and distracting. Hence the plight of the commentator. But to take this line is to come dangerously near the position of those admirers who have institutionalized our poet, removed him from the talons of criticism, by insisting (in effect) that the scope of his achievement is no more open to rational discussion than the goodness of maple syrup. This kind of protectiveness really insults him. Frost's work may well require a different critical approach or procedure from that appropriate to discussion of Yeats's, Eliot's, or Valéry's; but the final considerations of value, substance, and interest are as relevant in appraising it as to theirs.

If we do find a certain thinness in Frost's poetry, it is not because he has omitted to bolster it up with anything equivalent to Yeats's *A Vision* or Eliot's arcane allusiveness. Once again a comparison with the earlier poet, Wordsworth, seems in order; but this time the comparison is not to Frost's advantage. Frost has left us no poem of the quality of *Resolution and Independence*, a particular vision of man's life with its natural setting and tragic destiny. To avoid the charge of unfairness, we should at once turn to a poem of Frost which may come to mind as a counter-example, "The Death of the Hired Man." This is one of Frost's best known and finest poems, and no better illustration could be given of the poignancy he can achieve in spare allusive dialogue. Yet something forbids us to call "The Death of the Hired Man" great poetry, and what this is may come out when we place it beside Wordsworth's "Michael." What strikes the reader of Frost's poem in comparison with Wordsworth's is the *absence* of something. There is nothing in it corresponding to the poetic intensity with which Wordsworth invests the Dalesman's feeling about his owner-ship of his bit of land, a man's elementary desire to have something to hand on to his children. This inner lack may be pointed out locally, when we consider those passages of "The Death of the Hired Man" in which we are most aware that we are reading poetry:

> Part of a moon was falling down the west,
> Dragging the whole sky with it to the hills.
> Its light poured softly in her lap. She saw it
> And spread her apron to it. She put out her hand
> Among the harp-like morning-glory strings,
> Taut with the dew from garden bed to eaves,
> As if she played unheard some tenderness
> That wrought on him beside her in the night.
> 'Warren,' she said, 'he has come home to die:
> You needn't be afraid he'll leave you this time.'
>
> 'Home,' he mocked gently.
>   'Yes, what else but home?
> It all depends on what you mean by home.
> Of course he's nothing to us, any more
> Than was the hound that came a stranger to us
> Out of the woods, worn out upon the trail.'
>
> 'Home is the place where, when you have to go there,
> They have to take you in.'
>   'I should have called it
> Something you somehow haven't to deserve.'

This is the emotional center of the poem, what the poem is "about." But, moving and tender as it is, the effect of the "background" passage about the moonlight is curiously extraneous. Indeed, the pathos of what is said in the poem about the life and death of Silas depends largely on the *absence* from the dialogue of anything like this capacity to give a univer-sal representation of human sympathy; Frost's art, that is, is more akin to that of the short story writer than the poet. The passages about the moon seem something added to the story to make it poetry. Wordsworth con-templates the mode of life of the Dalesman with the same poetic vision as he does the mountain landscape:

> Among the rocks
> He went, and still looked up to the sun and cloud,
> And listened to the wind; and, as before,
> Performed all kinds of labour for his sheep,
> And for the land, his small inheritance.

The significant difference between the poems—the difference in spiritual value—lies in the pastoral quality with which Wordsworth invests his simple story. He uses pastoral—normally a mode of irony for Frost—with complete seriousness; and the result is that generalizing effect which we look for in poetry of the highest order. By including this pastoral element Wordsworth has got further away from his characters than Frost; but he has also given a greater universality to his theme.

Similar judgments might emerge from considering other poems in which Frost's art is that of the anecdote, sketch, or dramatic monologue. Pound has praised such work discerningly when he says: "Frost has been honestly fond of the New England people, I dare say with spells of irritation. He has given their life honestly and seriously. He has never turned aside to make fun of it. He has taken their tragedy as tragedy, their stubbornness as stubbornness. I know more of farm life than I did before I had read his poems. That means I know more of 'Life.' " But in the same review (in *Poetry* for December 1914) he is clearly implying a limitation when he says: "Mr. Frost's people are distinctly real. Their speech is real; he has known them. *I don't much want to meet them* (italics mine), but I know that they exist, and what is more, that they exist as he has portrayed them." The point of this observation is not that Frost's characters are sometimes simplified figures, done from the outside, for whom "The Figure in the Doorway," glimpsed from a passing train might serve as an epitome; as Pound suggests, they are often done more inwardly. But even when they are done inwardly, they are not related to anything greater than themselves. Sympathy and understanding are surely not enough for a great poet; there must also be this suggestion of the larger perspective, the wider and finer mind. Frost's art is the antithesis of that practiced by Samuel Johnson in his poem on Levet, the man "obscurely wise and coarsely kind." Johnson, without losing sympathy, speaks with the voice of a highly literate culture on such a man; Frost, in refusing the responsibility of such a judgment, incurs corresponding disadvantages. We sometimes feel that he assumes his task to be complete when he has given a faithful record of particulars; an assumption which admirers of William Carlos Williams may approve, but which is one reason why English readers have found that poet's American reputation inexplicable.

The characteristic difficulty readers have with Frost is not "What does he mean?" but "What is the *point* of it?" Why has he chosen to crystallize *this* perception, rather than countless others? This kind of difficulty, it will be remembered, presented itself strongly—perhaps it still does—to Wordsworth's readers. But Wordsworth's little anecdotes, even if they do not always carry the charge of significance Wordsworth himself found in them, can be better understood in the context of Wordsworth's whole work—in the poems (by far the greater number) in which the poet speaks directly, not dramatically, sets out to communicate explicitly his thought or "message." Now Frost too speaks directly in the greater part of his poetry. And it will hardly be disputed that the quintessence of his work—his rarest and finest achievement—lies in the lyrical-reflective pieces in which he speaks with his own personal voice. But it is in that "personal" work also that we are most conscious, not only of limitations, but of weaknesses.

His principal weakness—the one that makes for the most doubt about his claim to high poetic rank—is monotony. This may be attributed in part to the very nature of his gift. What is represented by *North of Boston,* the achievement praised so warmly by Thomas and Pound, is of a kind that could be represented in comparatively few poems. How much of Frost's whole corpus (we cannot help asking) do we really need? His work calls out for anthologizing, as Wordsworth's, I think, does not. No one will doubt that Wordsworth wrote a great many mediocre poems, or worse, but we have to have *The Prelude,* and much else, before we can form a fair estimate of him. Frost's distinction seems only notably present in a few poems. His average—to speak bluntly—is rather dull. Johnson observes of Dryden that "he that writes much cannot escape a manner"; but "Dryden is always *another and the same.*" This could hardly be said of Frost, at least of the later volumes.

For there are dangerous temptations in a colloquial style, and Frost has often succumbed to them. The chief danger is self-indulgence. So far from making an effort to "escape a manner," he rather cultivates it. Old age can be the extenuation of much of the writing in *Steeple Bush,* where he seems at times to be maundering. But the same tendency can be observed in earlier work; Frost, like Hardy, seems to be a poet who, once he had formed his manner, stuck to it: there is no such technical (or personal) development as we find in a Rilke or an Eliot or a Yeats. This is both his strength and his weakness. He has achieved a continuous literary personality in a sense in which Pound, for example, seems not to have done: on the other hand, he does not appear to have experienced very strongly the need to check himself at the point when the manner becomes mannerism (though, to be fair, it would seem that, considering his long life and not very large output, he did do a good deal of tearing up).

In Frost's least satisfactory work, all that we tend to remember is the manner. "Build Soil," the "political pastoral," is a case in point. No poet deserves to be judged on the basis of his political ideas in a narrow sense. And "Build Soil" itself shows that Frost is well aware of the warning conveyed in the words of Yeats: "We have no gift to set a statesman right." But as he adopts it in this poem the ironical plain-man manner comes to sound like a form of conceit. Frost has no "public" voice; so that when, as is apparently the case, he is recommending unrestricted laissez-faire (in 1932, a singularly inopportune moment one would think) it sounds like an attempt to elevate personal selfishness into a lofty principle. Undoubtedly the basis of this attitude is that passion for personal freedom, that need to feel self-sufficient, which permeates Frost's best work. But the manner of this poem makes it seem unattractive and smug. Less injurious, perhaps, is the playful manner of Frost's excursions into "astrometaphysics," though one understands the irritation of Malcolm Cowley at the "cracker-barrel-in-the-clouds" effect of much of this writing. Frost's "metaphysics," it is true, are saved by the playfulness from sounding quite so hollow as those portentous reverberations, in cadences reminiscent of the later Eliot, which we hear in Wallace Stevens' philosophical poetry. His paraphrasable content is less empty; the poetry is less pretentious. But unless we find Frost's manner so congenial that we are critically disarmed, we must be tempted to ask why, if the poet himself (apparently) cannot take his ideas seriously, anyone else should be expected to do so.

A worse incongruity results when Frost brings the same manner into the field of tragic experience. In things like "A Masque of Reason" he is plainly out of his depth. The manner of that "masque," contriving as it does to be both smart and naïve, would be an affront if we were to bring it seriously into comparison with the tragic poetry of the Book of Job. No doubt in its characteristic weakness, as in the weakness of some of Frost's political poetry, we may see that tendency to blur the edges of Job's terrible problem in an optimistic transcendentalism where "evil tendencies cancel," and the waywardness, uncanniness, and utter incomprehensibility of the universe become somehow tokens of ultimate good. But optimism and reassurance are not qualities of Frost's deepest genius, which rests upon something hard and cold. Although a generalized geniality and a weak whimsicality are unfortunately common in Frost's work, they do not represent its strength. When he is a poet he is not genial: his true power, his peculiar sensitiveness, is closely bound up with those landscapes in which the season is always late autumn or winter, with flurries of snow, and a feeling of loneliness and danger impending; when a stranger is not a potential friend, but an object of suspicion. In his quasi-homiletic poetry Frost seems to be offering some vague theological equivalent of a friendliness and cosmic optimism which are antipathetic to his own creative powers.

III

But it is time now to draw to a conclusion about Frost's real strength, his personal poetry. This is not to be found in the most characteristic part of that poetry: the pithy observations, the wry gnarled apothegms, engaging and quotable as many of them are; but in more elusive poems, where the personality, or persona, of the poet is not strongly felt at all; where what we are given is the aperçu, the glimpse, the perception crystallized, where the poet seems to be beside the reader, sharing his vision, not gesturing in front. In such poems Frost has affinities with Hardy, the Hardy of poems like "The Wound":

> I climbed to the crest,
>   And, fog-festooned,
> The sun lay west
>   Like a crimson wound:
>
> Like that wound of mine
>   Of which none knew,
> For I'd given no sign
>   That it pierced me through.

We may compare Frost's "Dust of Snow":

> The way a crow
>   Shook down on me
> The dust of snow
>   From a hemlock tree
>
> Has given my heart
>   A change of mood
> And saved some part
>   Of a day I had rued.

In the nature of the case such poems are delicate achievements, and it must be a matter of critical controversy whether some of them succeed or fail. "The Lockless Door," for example, seems to me to fail. These are the closing lines:

> Back over the sill
> I bade a 'Come-in'
> To whatever the knock
> At the door may have been.
>
> So at a knock
> I emptied my cage
> To hide in the world
> And alter with age.

The reader is asked to do too much; to keep pondering over a poem so slight and so imperfectly formulated until he has convinced himself of a significance which the poet may or may not have put there. On the other hand, "Gathering Leaves" seems perfect. (Its method may be usefully contrasted with the beautiful earlier poem "The Quest of the Purple-Fringed.") That the tone of voice is utterly unpretentious, the rhythm light, even gay, far from detracting from the essential poignancy, actually increases it.

> I make a great noise,
> Of rustling all day,
> Like rabbit and deer
> Running away.

> But the mountains I raise
> Elude my embrace,
> Flowing over my arms
> And into my face.

The subject of the whole poem is the same as that of Tennyson's "Tears, idle tears," but how much Frost gains from not *saying* anything like "O Death in Life, the days that are no more." Doing without sonority, doing without any play for a full-volumed response, Frost makes us live through (as we imaginatively participate in the simple actions he describes) the paradox of memory, real and unreal, intangible but substantial.

The obvious way of describing "Gathering Leaves" is to say that it is symbolic. But this suggests another observation about Frost's poetic gift. Too many poets seem to imagine that they have made a thing symbolic by saying so—sometimes in so many words. They expect us to read profound meanings into what they have created, without having created anything. Here Frost's strength is apparent. He can make real to us, as freshly felt, objects, places, processes. His snow is truly cold, his hills barren, his woods impenetrably deep. This solidity, due to the poet's power to convince us that his image or fancy is based on a true and strong perception of a real world outside him, is felt even when, in a poem like "Sand Dunes," the explicit topic is the human mind or spirit's independence of nature.

> Sea waves are green and wet,
> But up from where they die,
> Rise others vaster yet,
> And these are brown and dry.
>
> They are the sea made land,
> To come at the fisher town,
> And bury in solid sand
> The men she could not drown.

The reality of these dunes convinces us of their priority to the thought they suggest to the poet, and so seem to give an anticipatory guarantee of its firmness.

A preoccupation of these short poems is human transience, the poet's deep sense of flux and movement, and the brevity of "the span of life." For this immemorial subject of lyrical poetry Frost finds a note that is peculiarly his own. His strength here, as is customary with him, lies not in any very original formulation, or piece of consecutive thought or argument—the metaphysical passages in the title poem of *West-Running Brook* are not particularly convincing—but in the transmission of a sense of transience as a process which is at one and the same time experienced, lived through, and steadily contemplated. The emotional tone of this contemplation, as often in Frost, has to be described by remarking on an element that is missing. There is no wistfulness. Here Frost differs most strikingly from Edward Thomas:

> . . . When I turn away, on its fine stalk
> Twilight has fined to naught, the parsley flower
> Figures, suspended still and ghostly white,
> The past hovering as it revisits the light.

These lines of Thomas touch upon a recurrent preoccupation of Frost, but Frost's touch is different. Poems like "The Sound of the Trees" or "The Road not Taken," beautiful as they are, are untypical; indeed, we are told that the latter poem is a deliberate exercise in Thomas' manner, and is as such a gentle rebuke to his friend's indecisiveness. Frost avoids the note of nostalgia about the past of an individual, as he does about the historic past; nothing strikes an English reader more in his poetry than his bedrock commonsense assumption that each generation starts from scratch, has to *make* its relationship with its environment.

To say that Frost avoids nostalgia is not to say that his poetry lacks the note of longing. But it seems to have more affinity with what we find in Wallace Stevens' poetry. This poet of grey lives and grey landscapes suffers from "the malady of the quotidian," is hungry for color, radiance, everything that is unexpected, brilliant, spectacular.

> 'Oh, that's the Paradise-in-a-bloom,' I said;
> And truly it was fair enough for flowers
> Had we but in us to assume in March
> Such white luxuriance of May for ours.
>
> We stood a moment so in a strange world,
> Myself as one his own pretense deceives . . .
> ("A Boundless Moment")

The Frost of "A Boundless Moment" is solicited by the same longing as the Stevens of "Some Friends from Pascagoula," surely one of Stevens' finest poems:

> Tell me again of the point
> At which the flight began,
>
> Say how his heavy wings,
> Spread on the sun-bronzed air,
> Turned tip and tip away,
> Down to the sand, the glare
>
> Of the pine-trees edging the sand
> Dropping in sovereign rings
> Out of his fiery lair.
> Speak of the dazzling wings.

In "The Middleness of the Road" Frost might seem to be replying to this sort of appeal; but his sober recall to the prose of life is qualified by his characteristic "almost":

But say what Fancy will,

The mineral drops that explode
To drive my ton of car
Are limited to the road.
They deal with near and far,

And have almost nothing to do
With the absolute flight and rest
The universal blue
And local green suggest.

But most typical of Frost's finest work is "Neither Out Far Nor In Deep." This is the whole poem:

The people along the sand
All turn and look one way.
They turn their back on the land.
They look at the sea all day.

As long as it takes to pass
A ship keeps raising its hull;
The wetter ground like glass
Reflects a standing gull.

The land may vary more;
But wherever the truth may be—
The water comes ashore,
And the people look at the sea.

They cannot look out far,
They cannot look in deep.
But when was that ever a bar
To any watch they keep?

The poem represents in metaphorical form men's constant awareness that they must die; and it does this without appealing to pity or horror or any mode of evasion: we are invited to contemplate the fact within the metaphor quite steadily. Yet there is an emotional tone, however hard to describe; the "they" of the poem are "we" and "I"; this fellow feeling prevents the poem from sounding dry or abstract, or gnomic in the manner of Emerson. Poems like these are perhaps marginal in Frost's work; marginal perhaps in comparison with other poets' more ambitious statements. They offer no easy comfort, are never likely to be popular; they are as remote as they could be from the whimsical or crusty persona of the farmer-poet. Yet it seems to me that in their combination of apparent slightness with extraordinary depth Frost achieves something highly distinctive, and indeed unique.

The Indispensable Robert Frost

Donald J. Greiner*

On 6 April 1935, just before the publication of his last book, Edwin Arlington Robinson died. Soon after, Macmillan and Company, Robinson's publisher, asked Robert Frost to write a preface to the forthcoming *King Jasper*. Following several fits and starts, including a draft that was more about himself than Robinson, Frost completed one of his best essays which is known today as the "Introduction" to *King Jasper*. And in that essay, he wrote one of his clearest descriptions of the poet's goal: "The utmost of ambition is to lodge a few poems where they will be hard to get rid of. . . ."[1] Most readers will agree that Robert Frost lodged more than his share.

What is not easy to agree on, however, is *which* of Frost's poems are lodged forever in American literature. Very few lists of the twelve best poems by Robert Frost would be identical. This is as it should be, for personal preferences always affect judgments of art. Just as difficult—and personal—is the task of examining Frost's canon to determine not only what is best but what is essential. The charge might be put this way: Which dozen parts of Frost's entire corpus, including poems, prose, letters, and remarks, are indispensable to the reader who would be conversant with the poet's achievement? In many cases, of course, the best and the essential are one and the same—but not always. This essay is one man's effort to answer the question.

I

Frost's letter to John T. Bartlett, written in Beaconfield, England, on 22 February 1914, three months before the publication of Frost's second book *North of Boston*, is a crucial explanation by Frost himself of what he was trying to accomplish in his poetry.[2] Bartlett was one of Frost's favorite pupils at Pinkerton Academy (New Hampshire), where the poet taught from March 1906 to June 1911.

Although the fact is common knowledge, it may be necessary to re-

*This essay was written especially for this volume and is printed with the permission of the author.

mind some readers that Frost published his first two volumes, *A Boy's Will* (1913) and *North of Boston* (1914), while residing in England from September 1912 through February 1915. Nearly forty years old before he finally succeeded in publishing a book, he was determined to prevent his work from suffering the usual fate of first books of poetry that greet the world all but stillborn. One of his plans was to send individual poems and proofs of his early books to Bartlett, urging his former student to write reviews for American journals and newspapers. Lawrance Thompson calls this tactic Frost's "almost desperate campaign of self-promotion," and it is interesting to note that the poet asked Bartlett "to cook up something to bother the enemies we left behind in Derry (New Hampshire)."[3] The ideal procedure, thought Frost, would be for him to supply the ideas via letter and for Bartlett to recast the material for reviews. Bartlett was not naive, and at the time he was living thousands of miles from New Hampshire in Vancouver, British Columbia. But he did comply with Frost's request at least once, publishing a review of *A Boy's Will* in *The Derry News* for 7 November 1913.[4]

Frost's so-called enemies may or may not have seen Bartlett's comments, but by the time of this letter to Bartlett, the poet was anticipating the publication of *North of Boston*. Aware that the blank verse poems in that collection, such poems as "Home Burial" and "The Death of the Hired Man," could baffle readers accustomed to the metronomic rhythm of traditional blank verse, Frost renewed the campaign to educate his audience via Bartlett. This long letter is one of his earliest and most complete explanations of what he called his theory of "sentence sounds." It is also important to remember that he expressed the ideas in this letter before he returned to the United States and became a public personality eager to explain his thoughts about poetry to anyone who could advance his career.

Bartlett may not have increased Frost's fame, but he did provide the poet with a needed sounding board in America. As Frost says in this letter, he wanted to write down "two or three cardinal principles." These principles later became the heart of his comments in interviews and letters during the teens and twenties when he was consolidating his reputation as a leading figure of what was then called the "new poetry," and the most important of them was his new definition of a sentence: "A sentence is a sound in itself on which other sounds called words may be strung." Although additional "cardinal principles" about metaphor and the importance of the ear in poetry are discussed in this remarkable letter, the explanation of sentence sounds, written prior to the publication of *North of Boston* and thus before Frost became self-conscious in his public discussions of the concept, is essential to an understanding of what he was trying to accomplish by unifying the free-ranging tones of human speech with the regularity of iambic pentameter. Frost's greatest contribution to poetic technique is his non-traditional blank verse. Reading this letter along with "Home Burial" and "A Servant to Servants," one can begin to see why.

II

"Education by Poetry: A Meditative Monologue," first published in the *Amherst Graduates' Quarterly* for February 1931, is Frost's most extended single statement about his art. It is not so well known as other nominations for the title of Frost's best prose, such essays as "The Figure a Poem Makes," "The Constant Symbol," and the "Introduction" to *King Jasper*, but it should be. "Education by Poetry" sets down his analysis of figurative language, the heart of poetry.

The history of this essay suggests Frost's continuing effort to understand the relationship between metaphorical expression and his own work. It all began five years before "Education by Poetry" was published. On 15 January 1926, Frost gave a talk at Bryn Mawr College entitled "Metaphors." This discussion of analogy and belief became the germ for a more thorough exploration of his ideas when he was invited to address the Amherst Alumni Council on the topic of education and poetry. For that talk, given on 15 November 1930, Frost also drew on his experience from teaching a course at Amherst called "Judgments." When he addressed the Alumni Council, a stenographer took down his comments. The poet then revised the stenographic record to create the article that was published in the *Quarterly*. But Frost was not through, for he continued to tinker with the essay. After his death in 1963, a copy of "Education by Poetry," with revisions in his handwriting, was found in his papers. On 3 July 1966, the Frost estate, Edward Connery Lathem, and Dartmouth College published a limited edition of a facsimile of "An Uncompleted Revision of 'Education by Poetry' " as a keepsake for those attending a Robert Frost gathering at Dartmouth.[5] Since the poet did not live to complete the revision, the 1931 version must be accepted as authoritative.

It is fascinating to read. Although Frost expresses his alarm at the shoddy quality of college education in general, he is primarily concerned with the inability of students to handle figurative language: "They don't know when they are being fooled by a metaphor, an analogy, a parable. And metaphor is, of course, what we are talking about. Education by poetry is education by metaphor." The rest of the essay defines his understanding of metaphorical expression. Confidently and wittily expressed, his ideas focus on his insistence that no one can be at ease with figurative language unless he is at ease with poetry. Poetry "provides the one permissable way of saying one thing and meaning another."

Readers intrigued by the metaphorical center of such tightly crafted lyrics as "Stopping by Woods on a Snowy Evening," "The Silken Tent," and "All Revelation" will find this essay important for at least two reasons. First, Frost illustrates what he means by the famous phrase from

"The Figure a Poem Makes," "a momentary stay against confusion," when he discusses how all metaphors will break down if pushed too far. Only momentary insight is possible in a world that constantly denies permanence. Second, Frost extends metaphor toward metaphysics when he argues that the greatest possibilities for figurative language lie in the attempt to "make" the final unity between spirit and matter. He calls this effort the "height of all poetic thinking," a phrase that echoes in the later poem "Directive" as the "height of the adventure." His notion of unity is also a crucial concept to keep in mind when struggling with the ambiguities of "After Apple-Picking," "Birches," and "Kitty Hawk." Poetry was Frost's way of unifying his consistently chaotic world, and "Education by Poetry" is his best explanation in prose of that effort.

III

The "Letter to *The Amherst Student*" was first published in *The Amherst Student* on 25 March 1935. This little-known document is literally a letter that Frost wrote in response to birthday greetings extended by the editors of the Amherst College undergraduate newspaper. The letter may be read as a statement of affirmation in a century of despair, as an indirect acknowledgment of his kinship with the Ralph Waldo Emerson of "Experience," but such a reading should not overlook Frost's unblinking vision of universal disorder.

Although he wrote the letter in Key West and sent it directly to the *Student*, he had a secondary audience in mind. In 1930, Frost published *Collected Poems*, a book that was generally well received and that won a Pulitizer Prize. But some critics, notably Granville Hicks, took Frost to task. Writing "The World of Robert Frost" for the *New Republic* later that year, Hicks argued that Frost's poems were out of touch with the modern era of industrialism, science, and Freudianism. Although Frost claimed not to bother with reviews, he knew about this one. More important, perhaps, he was also aware of the growing negative reaction to his work articulated by those who believed that he refused to address the complicated issues of his age. Thus, when the editors of the *Student* sent him congratulations on his birthday, he took the opportunity to respond to the students directly and to Hicks and other critics indirectly by commenting on his personal age in such a way that he also explained his views of the time in which he lived.[6] This letter, which may more correctly be called a short essay, is indispensable to an understanding of Frost's ideas about the relationship between confusion and form.

In this instance the confusion is the decade and the form is creativity. Despite a world-wide economic depression, fascism in Europe, and the early rumblings of World War II on the horizon, Frost declares his impatience with those who bemoan how bad the age is. But lest readers mistake his opinion as naive optimism, he qualifies it with a statement that echoes through much of his best poetry: "All ages of the world are bad." His point is that the 1930s are no worse than past decades and that this is as it should be. For, as the rest of the letter makes clear, his interest is not in exposing the evils of the age but in urging the creativity of man: "When in doubt there is always form for us to go on with." The conscious creation of form, the "stay," need not result in a poem; "a basket, a letter, a garden, a room, an idea, a picture" will all do. Man may find himself against a background of "hugeness and confusion shading away from where we stand into black and utter chaos," but this terrifying dilemma will not defeat the person who insists on asserting his own handiwork.

This pivotal letter looks both ways in Frost's career: back to 1928 and "West-Running Brook" in which he writes of "The universal cataract of death/That spends to nothingness" and that is unresisted except for the resistance of form, and forward to "The Figure a Poem Makes" (1939) in which he coins his definition of poetry as "a momentary stay against confusion." Not too many readers in the 1930s and, surprisingly, not too many today want to recognize Frost as a poet of fear. The "Letter to *The Amherst Student*" places that fear in perspective.

IV

A Sermon by Robert Frost was first published in a limited edition of 500 copies by the Spiral Press of New York in 1947. Because this scarce pamphlet was printed without Frost's consultation, one may wonder if he would have deleted or expanded some of the remarks had he planned in advance for publication.

The issue of Frost's role in the publication of the sermon is not clear. Most scholars agree that the poet's remarks were recorded without his prior knowledge or consent, but whereas Thompson says in *Selected Letters* that Frost granted permission to publish the transcript,[7] Joan St. C. Crane argues that the poet did not "authorize" the publication.[8] The matter of permission aside, Frost likely did not have an opportunity to examine the transcription of the recording before it was sent to the publisher.

Thus like "Education by Poetry," the pamphlet had its genesis in one of Frost's talks. In October 1946, Rabbi Victor E. Reichert, the poet's neighbor when both were in Ripton, Vermont, invited Frost to spend a day with him in Cincinnati, Ohio, where he was the leader of the Rockdale Avenue Temple. During the course of their evening together, Frost volunteered to deliver a sermon the next day, October 10th, to help Rabbi Reichert and his congregation celebrate Succoth, the Feast of Tabernacles. Not only were the poet's remarks unplanned and thus closer to his informal discussions with students than to a conventional sermon to adults, but the remarks were also recorded verbatim at Rabbi Reichert's insistence. The text of *A Sermon* was prepared from a transcription of the recording.

Although Frost was not consulted about the procedure, he apparently was not angered by the result. Preaching the sermon was the impetus he needed to formalize the ideas necessary to complete the long and complex *A Masque of Mercy* that was published in 1947 as the companion poem to *A Masque of Reason* (1945). Biographical evidence suggests that Rabbi Reichert indirectly helped Frost with both masques. An Old Testament scholar who had published a study of Job, the Rabbi shared many discussions with the poet about this archetypal sufferer who is the central figure in *A Masque of Reason*. More important, however, was the indirect aid given Frost for *A Masque of Mercy*.

Just before Frost delivered his sermon on 10 October 1946, Rabbi Reichert led the congregation in a reading from the *Union Prayer Book* that was based on the fourteenth verse of Psalm 19: "Look with favor, O Lord, upon us, and may our service ever be acceptable unto Thee. Praised be Thou, O God, whom we serve in reverence." Frost made this verse the heart of his unplanned sermon and went on to define the fear of God as the fear that "one's own human wisdom is not quite acceptable in His sight."[9] Only after he had listened to the Rabbi's prayer and made his remarks was he able to complete the climactic speeches by Paul and Keeper that end *A Masque of Mercy*. Of special note are these lines from Paul's speech:

> We have to stay afraid deep in our souls
> Our sacrifice—the best we have to offer,
> And not our worst nor second best, our best, . . .
> 　　　　　　　　　　　. . . may not
> Be found acceptable in Heaven's sight.
> And that they may be is the only prayer
> Worth praying. May my sacrifice
> Be found acceptable in Heaven's sight.

The connections among Rabbi Reichert's prayer, Frost's sermon, and *A Masque of Mercy* are unmistakable. Indeed, the notion of acceptability that Frost heard in the prayer and expanded in the sermon became so important to him that six years later, on 5 November 1953, he wrote to Rabbi Reichert and requested information about the biblical verse that had inspired both his remarks to the congregation and the end of his masque. In his letter he calls the fourteenth verse of Psalm 19 "the heart and center of all religion."[10]

Religion may not have been the heart and center of Frost's canon, but it provided major themes in many of his poems from the early "Stars" (1913) and "A Prayer in Spring" (1913) to the famous poems of his old age, the two *Masques* (1945 and 1947), "Directive" (1947), and "Kitty

Hawk" (1962). In *A Sermon* he defines religion as "a straining of the spirit forward to a wisdom beyond wisdom." Frost had, as he says in "The Lesson for Today" (1942), "a lover's quarrel with the world." Those who read *A Sermon* and know the *Masques* understand that his quarrel was also with God.

V

"Storm Fear" was first published in *A Boy's Will* (1913) with a prose gloss omitted from subsequent editions of the volume: "He is afraid of his own isolation." Many readers would omit the lyrics in *A Boy's Will* altogether when making nominations for the essential Frost. These readers could argue that *A Boy's Will* may have historical importance because it is Frost's first book but that no one poem in it measures up to the brilliance of the rest of the canon. They would have a point. Yet the problem goes beyond this objection.

It is one thing to dismiss *A Boy's Will* outright, but it is another to try to name a poem in the collection as indispensable. Even readers so inclined would probably not consider "Storm Fear." "Mowing," for example, would be a popular choice. Unlike many of the lyrics in *A Boy's Will*, "Mowing" *sounds* like a Frost poem and thus deserves consideration as an early illustration of his major work. The poem is also an early example of his genius with both the sonnet and the five-stress line. Finally, the suggestion that the fact of labor is an end in itself, that no transcendental message is forthcoming to the isolated laborer arranging his field as if it were a poem, is a primary theme in the rest of his verse.

One might also reject a fine poem like "Mowing" to select a poor one like "My Butterfly." It was Frost's first professional poem, published in *The Independent* for 8 November 1894. It was also one of the five poems that Frost had privately printed and bound in 1894 to make the little volume *Twilight*, and thus it links his very earliest efforts with his major poems. Finally, "My Butterfly" was the first poem in which Frost heard the tones of human speech in his own work and thus began his tentative formulations about the relationship between conversation and iambic rhythm that would later become his theory of "sentence sounds."

Either choice is acceptable: the historically important "My Butterfly" or the esthetically important "Mowing." But my choice is "Storm Fear." The biographical information that Frost may have written this lyric following a late winter blizzard that hit his Derry farm in 1902 is insignificant beside the technique and theme of the poem.[11] Frost's picture of the isolated man all but impotent before the overwhelming energy of non-human otherness looks forward to such important poems as "The Most of It," "Bereft," and "Neither Out Far Nor In Deep."

What strikes me about "Storm Fear," however, is the technique. In a collection full of " 'tweres" and "e'ers," conventional line lengths, and traditional rhymes, "Storm Fear" stands out as innovative and impressive. The rhymes fall free of any predictable rhyme scheme, and the spondees in the line "How the cold creeps as the fire dies at length" suggest how useless man's efforts are to stave off implacable otherness. The free use of rhymes foreshadows the technique in the well-known "After Apple-Picking" and "The Rabbit Hunter," and the rejection of Romantic views of man in nature looks toward the rest of Frost's career.

But the most important accomplishment in "Storm Fear" is the way Frost combines technique and theme in the varying line lengths. "Storm Fear" is an early example of his experimentation with iambic pentameter, the kind of experimentation that prompted Ford Madox Heuffer to call some of the lines in "Mending Wall" a "truly bewildering achievement."[12] The suggestion that "Storm Fear" is written in iambic pentameter would also have bewildered Heuffer because the poem looks like free verse. One line is as short as "Ah, no!" But Frost is showing how man's momentary stays against confusion, even such traditionally formidable stays as a poem, give way to fear before a challenge by non-human otherness. "Storm Fear" may be read as a poem of disintegration. As the cold creeps, the fire dies and, more important, the security of the iambic pentameter line—the stay—breaks down. The poet-figure's sense of creation and use of rhetoric are not enough to "save ourselves unaided." "Storm Fear" is indispensable because it is not only a good poem but also the finest of Frost's initial efforts to unite technique with theme. One could even argue that the poem is, finally, about poetry.

VI

"Home Burial" was first published in *North of Boston* (1914). It is the best of the renowned dialogue poems not only because it movingly details a failing marriage but also because of its dazzling combination of sentence sounds and blank verse. Lawrance Thompson reports that Frost recalled writing the poem in 1912 or 1913 and that his inspiration was the marital estrangement between Nathaniel and Leona Harvey following the death of their first-born child in 1895.[13] Mrs. Harvey was Frost's wife's older sister. But as numerous scholars and Thompson himself point out, the composition of "Home Burial" cannot be totally separated from the death of Frost and Elinor's own first-born child, Elliott, in 1900 at age four. Mrs. Frost could not ease her grief following Elliott's death, and Frost later reported that she knew then that the world was evil. Amy in "Home Burial" makes the same observation. Further evidence that the poem may be partly autobiographical is Thompson's recollection of Frost's once telling him that he could never read "Home Burial" in public because it was "too sad." These biographical particulars are relevant when one remembers the American public's misconception of Frost's forty-three year marriage to Elinor as idyllic and serene.

But even if one dismisses biographical significance, one has to admire the technical virtuosity of "Home Burial." Frost himself did. In a letter (27 July 1914) to John Cournos, he explains both his pleasure with the poem and his innovative technique:

> I also think well of those four "don'ts" in Home Burial. They would be good in prose and they gain something from the way they are placed in the verse. Then there is the threatening
>
> "If—you—do!" (Last of Home Burial)
>
> It is that particular kind of imagination that I cultivate rather than the kind that merely sees things, the hearing imagination rather than the seeing imagination though I should not want to be without the latter.
> I am not bothered by the question whether anyone will be able to hear or say those three words ("If—you—do!") as I mean them to be said or heard. I should say that they were sufficiently self expressive.[14]

Frost was correct. These words are "sufficiently self expressive," and they illustrate his theory of sentence sounds as well as his letter to John Bartlett of 22 February 1914 explains it. His decision to combine the irregular rhythms of colloquial diction and normal speech patterns with the regularity of iambic pentameter revolutionized blank verse. The revolution was so total, in fact, that not only did such perspicacious critics as Ford Madox Heuffer feel bewildered but also such less perceptive readers as Jessie B. Rittenhouse, then the secretary of the Poetry Society of America, wondered if Frost would not be better off leaving the complexities of poetry for the relative safety of the short story.[15]

The four "don'ts" are a case in point. Frost positions them on the page so that the regularity of the iambic pentameter rhythm gives way to the irregularity of the husband's declaration and the wife's despairing response:

> "But the child's mound—"
>
> > > "Don't, don't don't,
>
> don't," she cried.

The stresses fall on "child's," "mound," and the first three "don'ts" to make the pentameter line. Frost then leaves incomplete the line of " 'don't,' she cried" to illustrate the shattered communication between husband and wife that is the theme of "Home Burial."

A home is truly buried in this poem. Marital love is so engulfed by the disaster of the baby's death that the husband and wife exchange the effort to discuss their differences for a tense outbreak of accusations. The development of this theme is as important as the innovative technique in making "Home Burial" indispensable. For sexual love—itself a form of communication—also breaks down. Although the sexual allusions are never explicit, they reverberate throughout the poem from the very beginning: Amy cowers under the husband's "mounting," and their bedroom is equated with a graveyard:

> The little graveyard where my people are!
> So small the window frames the whole of it.
> Not so much larger than a bedroom, is it?

In recent years more and more readers have admitted that the difficulties of communication via sex as well as talk were always major considerations in Frost's work. This theme reaches its climax in the disturbing "The Subverted Flower," published in 1942, but it plays a key role in poems as early as "Love and A Question" and "A Prayer in Spring" in *A Boy's Will* (1913). Despite Frost's comments to the contrary, it seems certain that at least part of his personal experiences went into the writing of "Home Burial." Death and the threat of insanity were inextricably mixed with sex and love in his long marriage to Elinor, and his poetic rendering of this baffling mixture is one of the highlights of his career. "Home Burial" is a masterpiece, as modern in theme as it is in technique.

VII

"After Apple-Picking" was first published in *North of Boston* (1914), and it is my nomination for Frost's greatest poem. In the letter to John Cournos (27 July 1914) mentioned above, Frost explains that "After Apple-Picking" is the only poem in his second book that "will intone."[16] Although he does not elaborate, he means that the rest of the poems sound like human speech whereas "After Apple-Picking" is a lyrical meditation on the tension between a job well done and the uncertainties accompanying the end of something significant. Note that the first word in the title is "After." Frost's refusal to specify what has ended, other than apple-picking, is one of the glories of the poem.

The other glories are the examples of technical brilliance. The rhymes alone are worth the reading. Every one of the forty-two lines is rhymed, but Frost eschews the tradition of rhyme scheme altogether. The result is a beautiful, even haunting, rendering of the natural progression of a person's meditation as he uneasily ponders the ambiguities which suddenly well up before him now that his job is done. Similarly, the brilliant use of irregular iambic pentameter, first experimented with in "Storm Fear," to suggest the uncertain balance between the poet figure's need to maintain form in the face of confusion and the threat to his effort cast in the form of truncated lines illustrates the union of technique and theme when Frost is at his best. Although the poem begins with its longest line, the iambic heptameter, "My long two-pointed ladder's sticking through a tree,"[17] and includes a line as short as "For all," the meter invariably returns to the predominant rhythm of iambic pentameter as the meditator struggles to keep his balance in uncertainty as he has kept it on the ladder of his life.

Nuances of aspiration, satisfaction, completion, rest, and death echo throughout "After Apple-Picking" beginning with the title. Like the speaker, the reader never knows how far to pursue the mythical associations between apples and man's expulsion from Eden. If such associations are to be dismissed, then the speaker has safely and satisfactorily completed his task—whatever it literally is—of harvesting the "ten thousand thousand fruit." The phrase "after apple-picking" thus suggests rest. But the genius of the poem is that the speaker is never sure. If the associations between apples and Eden are not to be dismissed, then the poet figure has finished his life's work only to be confronted with an overwhelming uncertainty about what awaits him now. "After Apple-Picking" thus suggests death.

The imagery of hazy speculation is precise. The phrase "toward heaven" indicates the speaker's ultimate aspiration, and the line "Essence of winter sleep is on the night" reverberates with suggestions of termination and the question of rebirth. The point is that the poet figure needs answers to questions he will not pose, and he can only see as through a glass darkly:

> I cannot rub the strangeness from my sight
> I got from looking through a pane of glass
> I skimmed this morning from the drinking trough. . . .

The woodchuck, so unthinkingly confident of rebirth from its winter hibernation, cannot help him. "After Apple-Picking" is a poem of encroaching fear because it is a poem of uncertainty. Although the religious connotations are never obtrusive, this great poem is another of Frost's explorations of what he considered to be man's greatest terror: that our best may not be good enough in Heaven's sight.

VIII

"An Old Man's Winter Night," first published in *Mountain Interval* (1916), was probably begun as early as the winter of 1906–1907. Thompson speculates that at least twelve of the thirty-two poems in *Mountain Interval* were started before the publication of *A Boy's Will* in 1913, and that "An Old Man's Winter Night" may have been inspired by a hermit named Charles Lambert who lived near Frost in Derry.[18] Be that as it may, it is significant that Frost himself named the poem the highlight of *Mountain Interval*. In a letter to Sidney Cox (c. 7 December 1916), for example, he calls "An Old Man's Winter Night" "probably the best thing in the book," and in a letter (c. 7 January 1917) to Harriet Monroe, editor of the influential journal *Poetry*, he wrote that " 'Old Man' is the flower of the lot, isn't it?"[19] This is high praise indeed when one considers that

Mountain Interval also contains such justly renowned poems as "The Road Not Taken," "Hyla Brook," "The Oven Bird," "The Hill Wife," "Out, Out—," and "Birches."

Yet as fine as these poems are, Frost's judgment is correct. "An Old Man's Winter Night" is both a great poem and crucial to an understanding of the poet's view of man's unhappy lot. After reading such poems, one is baffled as to how the general public could have misread Frost for decades as a poet of cheery tone and benevolent imagery, as a holdover from the nineteenth century. "Old Man" is nothing if not a poem of despair, and in this sense it is a companion piece, although free of the obvious religious and mythological allusions, to T. S. Eliot's equally fine "Gerontion." Both poems are a long way from Robert Browning's nineteenth-century sentiment in "Rabbi Ben Ezra," "Grow old along with me!/The best is yet to be,/The last of life, for which the first was made."

Frost's man has grown old with only the worst yet to be. Another blank verse gem, this poem illustrates what Frost called the relationship between "inner and outer weather."[20] Internal terror manifests itself in the threatening landscape that the old man misconstrues as personally directed against him, and the universe—"all out-of-doors"—looms beyond any of his frightened efforts to counter either non-human otherness or his own confusion: "All out-of-doors looked darkly in at him. . . ." Even the house takes on characteristics of the old man's predicament as Frost develops the contrast between inner and outer weather with such suggestions that "his snow upon the roof" is his white hair, "his icicles along the wall" his tears.

The pun in the phrase "the pane in empty rooms" sets the tone. Light, often a symbol of mental activity and creative effort, seems more an emblem of fading consciousness here, for the old man's tilted lamp and lit stove are not sufficient to ward off the stare of the "separate stars" and "broken moon." Memory has given way to the clutches of age, and purpose is now nothing more than a pathetic attempt to scare "the outer night" by stomping through the empty house. As Frost and the reader know, the night does not scare. The familiar sounds of night have a terror all their own—"like the roar/Of trees and crack of branches"—and they echo with suggestions of a coffin being nailed shut. The old man is finally no more than a log that shifts "with a jolt" when he shifts in his sleep. At the end of the poem, Frost reiterates the absolute aloneness of limited man in an ever expanding universe. No one can hold back the night:

> One aged man—one man—can't keep a house,
> A farm, a countryside, or if he can,
> It's thus he does it of a winter night.

"An Old Man's Winter Night" offers evidence for those who still need it that Frost's view of man in nature is not held over from the nineteenth-century Romantic poems of confidence and cheer. This poem of great fear overwhelming the helpless individual is understated and thus more terrifying in the long run than anguished cries of apocalypse and alienation. Frost shows human order breaking down, but the plunge into what he calls "the universal cataract of death" is never quite completed because one bastion of form remains—the poem itself.

IX

"Stopping by Woods on a Snowy Evening" (*New Hampshire*, 1923) was written in late spring 1922 and first published in the *New Republic* (7 March 1923). Yes, I know; the poem is overanthologized and thus overly familiar, but that does not mean that it is overpraised. Its deceptive simplicity, its ambiguity, and its interlocking rhyme scheme have been so lauded that it is now one of the most explicated American poems. But a more important point is that "Stopping by Woods on a Snowy Evening" is *the* poem of dark woods in American literature. Frost himself knew that the poem was memorable; in a letter (2 May 1923) to Louis Untermeyer, he refers to "Stopping by Woods" as "my best bid for remembrance."[21]

The judgment of history may concur. The irony is that the myths that Frost fabricated about the poem have contributed to its reputation. Although Thompson has shown that Frost's stories about the composition of "Stopping by Woods" are false, the poet claimed time and again that he wrote his most famous lyric with one stroke of the pen. The heart of the myth is that, tired from working on the long poem "New Hampshire," he was inspired to write "Stopping by Woods" without a single revision. Such was not the case, of course. For one thing, the Jones Library at Amherst has the rough first draft of the poem. Interested readers may consult Thompson's biography for a complete account of how Frost wove the spell of myth around the composition of "Woods."[22]

For all of Frost's justifiable pride in the intricate rhyme scheme, it is interesting to note that the rhymes of the final stanza gave him the most difficulty. The initial draft of the poem reveals that the first three lines of this famous stanza originally read:

> The woods are lovely dark and deep
> But I have promises to keep
> That bid me give the reins a shake. . . .

If he had continued the *AABA, BBCB, CCDC* rhyme scheme of the other three stanzas, he would have been forced to add a rhyme for "deep/keep," to use "shake" as the predominant rhyming sound in a fifth stanza, and to move on to additional quatrains. Luckily for him—and us—he found a way out of the dilemma. In 1950, twenty-eight years after writing the poem, he explained to Charles Madison, an old friend: "I might confess the trade secret that I wrote the third line of the last stanza of Stopping by

Woods in such a way as to call for another stanza when I didn't want another stanza and didn't have another stanza in me, but with great presence of mind and a sense of what a good boy I was instantly struck the line out and made my exit with a repeat end."[23]

The "repeat end" has intrigued readers for decades. Does it mean that the moods of first casual interest and then momentary fascination in the woods are finally rejected in favor of obligations in the village? Such is the traditionally accepted reading of the poem. The other extreme is more suggestive but perhaps more suspect. In this interpretation the lovely, dark, and endless woods indicate the lure of a final abdication of mundane duties to the extent that the plunge into the darkness and deepness results in death.

Both positions and attendant variations have their advocates, but it seems to me that the poem's greatness is posited on its ambiguity, and its ambiguity results from the speaker's stasis. We do not know which direction he chooses at the end of the poem, woods or village. Chances are that he rejects both. He remains in the clearing, a crucial location in Frost's poetry, not only between the woods and village but also "between the woods and frozen lake." The lure of the woods balances the promises in the town, and the speaker himself is frozen with indecision. To accept one alternative is to give up the other, a predicament, suggests Frost, that is universal. An acceptable way out of the dilemma is not to force a decision but to write a poem about the difficulty of making one.

This is just what Frost does—and a great poem at that. The key to such a reading is not imagery but sound. In his indispensable poems, Frost unites technique and theme so that each illuminates the other. In "Stopping by Woods" the slow, forward progression of the interlocking rhyme scheme reaches a halt in the final stanza where the rhymed words have only one sound. Similarly, the exact repetition in the last two lines emphasizes not reiteration of purpose but inability to get going, a metaphorical spinning in the snow. Finally, the contrast in the third stanza between harsh sounds ("shake" and "mistake") and soothing sounds ("The only other sound's the sweep/Of easy wind and downy . . .") is resolved in the final quatrain in favor of the latter. Frost recalls the hypnotist's trance when he concludes the poem with the interlocking rhymes of "sweep," "deep," "keep," "sleep," "sleep." Not action but reverie is suggested. The traveler remains at the end where he is at the beginning—stopped by the woods on the darkest evening of the year.

One of the highlights of the poem is that its apparent simplicity masks far-reaching complexities at the heart of both man's lot and the creative process. It is not that Frost advocates indecision but that he knows about the difficulties of making a choice. His use of deep woods as the controlling metaphor is fortunate, for the lure of the forest's darkness both beckons throughout the milestones of American literature and threatens the existence of all those who take the plunge—from Carwin to Roderick Usher to Hester and Dimmesdale to Theron Ware to Nick Ad ams to Ike McCaslin to the traveler by the woods to the reader himself.

X

"Design," first published in *American Poetry, 1922, A Miscellany* (1922) before being collected in *A Further Range* (1936), was begun in late 1911 or early 1912. On 15 January 1912, Frost sent a sonnet entitled "In White" to Susan Hayes Ward, one of the editors of the *Independent*, the journal that had first published a Frost poem in 1894. Part of the need to write "In White" came from an argument between Frost and Miss Ward's brother, William Hayes Ward, about the religious qualities of Henri Bergson's *Creative Evolution*. Frost defended Bergson against Ward's charge of athiesm, and he wrote the first drafts of the poem that would become "Design" partly to answer Ward and partly in response to his reading of Bergson and of William James's *Pragmatism*.[24]

Questions about the benevolence of an all-powerful deity may have been in the background when Frost began "Design," but readers familiar with the scope of American literature will note its affinity with Poe's *The Narrative of Gordon Pym* and Melville's chapter in *Moby-Dick* titled "The Whiteness of the Whale." In each case the association between the color white and ambiguity leads to uncertainty or terror. Frost's poem builds from the confidence of "I found" through a series of questions to the crucial word "If."

Yet "Design" is indispensable as much for its form as for its theme. It is one of the most unusual and perfect sonnets by one of the finest son- neteers among major American poets. "Design" is an Italian sonnet with significant variations determined by theme. In the traditional Italian son- net, the fourteen lines are divided into an octave and sestet so that the sestet answers a question or solves a problem posed in the octave. The rhyme scheme may vary, but normally no more than five rhymes are permitted. Such a poem suggests the confidence of order; the sonnet fulfills the reader's expectations of a developing form because both poem and prob- lem are wrapped up at the end.

Not so in "Design." Writing a poem of uncertainty and fear, Frost reverses the traditional division of the Italian sonnet and describes a scene in the octave which he then questions in the sestet. The sestet is composed of three questions and a final line beginning with "If"—hardly the stuff of confidence. Equally important are the rhymes, for Frost limits the rhyme scheme to three rhymes as if he were keeping the tightest possible hold on a baffling scene that could engulf him.

The matter-of-fact beginning—"I found a dimpled spider, fat and white"—dissolves to a vision of evil in the guise of innocence. No allusion to a fat, white, dimpled baby can answer the question of why the blue flower is freakishly white, simultaneously attracting the white moth to it for protection and camouflaging the white spider that will devour the moth. "Design" is a nature poem in which the entire natural scene reeks of unnaturalness. Visions of Melville's albino whale hover behind it, but whereas Melville's whale is associated with both destruction and grandeur, Frost's tableau suggests only the void.

Frost's poet figure tries everything he can to stay his confusion: hints of innocence in such words as "dimpled," "snow-drop," and "flower"; puns on "right" and "appall"; allusions to *Macbeth*. But all of his efforts crumble before the relentless message of possible manipulation in such words as "mixes," "brought," "steered," and "govern." Although he hopes to temper his fear with the word "If" in the final line—"If design govern in a thing so small"—his situation is precarious no matter how he answers the query. If design does govern in such small matters, then what greater terror awaits man, who surely counts for more than a spider and a moth? If design does not govern, then what is man to do in the face of such mindless destruction?

This brilliant sonnet uses an unexpected relationship between octave and sestet and an unusual rhyme scheme to illustrate an unnatural experience. Perverted natural form affects poetic form, and deviation on two levels results. And yet the affirmation of technique counters the pessimism of theme. In the "Letter to *The Amherst Student*" (25 March 1935), Frost writes, "When in doubt there is always form for us to go on with. . . . To me any little form I assert upon it is velvet, as the saying is, and to be considered for how much more it is than nothing."[25] This is the case in "Design." The poet figure may fall to uncertainty, but not the poet. Writing a poem was Frost's way of asserting himself against the void. Faced with a baffling scene and the terrifying prospect of questions forever raised and always unanswered, Frost stays his confusion, if only momentarily, by casting it in the shape of one of the most ordered forms in all poetry, the sonnet.

XI

"The Subverted Flower" was first published in *A Witness Tree* (1942), four years after Elinor's death. Still unresolved is the question of when it was written. Frost told Thompson that a first draft was completed early enough to include the poem in *A Boy's Will* (1913), but that draft has not been located. The time of composition remains unestablished because, as Thompson points out, this unusual poem as we now have it is "obviously written in RF's later manner."[26]

Frost's claim of early composition is intriguing because, if true, it means that he withheld publication for more than thirty years. The primary reason for suppressing "The Subverted Flower" seems to be its close proximity to autobiography. Aware that the poem daringly reveals a sexual crisis in his courtship of Elinor, Frost also knew that his wife would never consent to its publication. Thus he waited until her death in 1938 to include it in his collection of 1942.

Of the poems discussed thus far, "The Subverted Flower" has the most significant references to the poet's biography. The crucial dates in this case are summer 1892 and 19 December 1895. Those familiar with Frost's life know that he and Elinor were graduated from high school together in 1892. Although they were in love, they realized that commitments to college clashed with thoughts of marriage. Staying together as much as possible during the summer of 1892, Frost, says Thompson, was "thwarted and embarrassed" by Elinor's reticent responses to his obvious passion.[27] Later that summer, however, both were convinced by Shelley's argument for rebellious love. Exchanging gold rings, they conducted a private wedding ceremony in a pastoral setting near the Merrimack River. The public celebration of their marriage was not held until 19 December 1895. Thus "The Subverted Flower" recalls those moments of embarrassment in 1892 when Frost believed that Elinor was shaming him by initially refusing to return his desire for sexual love.

For those unaware of the erotic poems in Frost's canon, "The Subverted Flower" is as shocking as it is revealing. It is in every sense an extraordinary accomplishment. On the one hand Frost calls upon youthful passion, frigidity, bestiality, eroticism, and puritanism to depict an unsettling picture of young love. On the other hand he uses the unexpected technique of seventy-three lines of predominantly iambic trimeter, and he consciously rhymes every line but one. That one unrhymed line ends "us"—"If this has come to us"—but love has not come to "us," and thus the absence of a unifying rhyme suggests the shattered affair.

Three points of view are presented, those of the boy, girl, and narrator, but it seems clear that the narrator sides with the young man. The stark contrast begins in the first line—"She drew back; he was calm"—and continues through the poem as the boy's offer of a "tender-headed flower" and all that it may suggest is perverted by the girl into an equation of physical passion with bestiality. Interpreting his smile as a cracking of "his ragged muzzle," she shames him by twisting his presence into that of a brute about to "pounce to end it all/Before her mother came." The introduction of the mother is a key to the poem, for although the narrator all but damns the girl by describing her as possessing a "too meager heart," the source of her frigidity is the parent.

As the girl freezes for fear of provoking "The demon of pursuit/That slumbers in a brute," she hears her mother call from the inside of a garden wall. Suggestions of an ironic Eden hover throughout this consciously perverted pastoral, and the poem ends with a defeat of the natural law as the mother draws her daughter "backward home," thus completing the girl's negative motion begun in the opening line. Frost hints, however, that the degrading accusation of bestiality should be directed not at the boy but at the girl. By the conclusion of the poem, *she* is the one with a bit in her mouth and foam on her chin. The trimeter rhythm indicates the bouncing motion of an animal in flight.

If I had to choose one poem in the more than five-hundred pages of *The Poetry of Robert Frost* to startle the uninformed reader out of his complacent misunderstanding of this great poet as a popular versifier of gentle lyrics, I would select "The Subverted Flower." Frost's instinct to withhold publication may have been correct, for there is no telling the damage to the often shaky foundations of his long marriage had he embarrassed Elinor by offering the poem to the public during her lifetime. But biographical considerations do not finally matter. "The Subverted Flower" is a strange, powerful—indispensable—poem by any standard.

XII

"Directive" (*Steeple Bush,* 1947) was first published in the *Virginia Quarterly Review* for Winter 1946. The poem was probably written between 1944 and 1946; for like two important poems composed during these years, *A Masque of Reason* (1945) and *A Masque of Mercy* (1947), it illustrates Frost's concern at that time with religious matters. Additional evidence that the poem may have been written in the middle 1940s is Theodore Morrison's essay "The Agitated Heart" in which he recalls a conversation between Frost and Hyde Cox during which Cox explained that Christ spoke in parables not because they were easy to understand but because they prevented the wrong listeners from grasping the message.[28] According to Cox, Frost was delighted with this comment. It is indeed probable, then, that the following lines in "Directive" have their genesis in Frost's conversation with Cox:

> A broken drinking goblet like the Grail
> Under a spell so the wrong ones can't find it,
> So can't get saved, as Saint Mark says they mustn't.[29]

Although Frost is reported to have joked once that "Directive" is his "Eliot poem" because it mentions the Holy Grail, the religious trappings are not throw-aways. Allusions to the Crucifixion ("tatters hung on barb and thorn") and to God as the final source ("Too lofty and original to rage") are offered seriously to those readers who would experience the poem as a religious statement. Frost himself pointed to the word "source" as the center of "Directive": "the key lines, if you want to know, are 'Cold as a spring as yet so near its source,/Too lofty and original to rage.' . . . But the key word in the whole poem is source—whatever source it is."[30]

Despite the importance of the religious tone, the poem is indispensable because it nudges the reader to consider sources beyond religion.

Frost hints as much when he comments on "whatever source it is," thus suggesting an extra-religious dimension. Similarly, Morrison quotes Frost as saying, "You can't be saved unless you understand poetry—or you can't be saved unless you have some poetry in you." Yet even if the reader is unaware of Frost's comments about the poem, he should not overlook the crucial hint within it.

"Directive" ends with the word "confusion": "Here are your waters and your watering place./Drink and be whole again beyond confusion." A significant word in the Frost canon, "confusion" is probably best known as part of the memorable phrase in his essay "The Figure a Poem Makes" when he talks about "a momentary stay against confusion." Although the literal meaning of the phrase is that the completed poem stays the confusion which the poet experiences when he first begins to write, the context of the entire essay suggests that any consciously created form, but especially poetry, is a momentary stay against the permanence of confusion. Form stays chaos, but only for a while. Poems must be written again and again.

If this suggestion has merit, then the last great poem of Frost's career is as much about poetry as it is about religion. The source that helps mankind to be "whole again beyond confusion" will be different things to different people, but for Frost himself the source is poetry—it always was. The technique of "Directive" testifies to his artistic prowess in old age; he was seventy three when *Steeple Bush* was published. One can only marvel at the stately blank verse, the sudden opening line of monosyllables, the metaphors of quest and home and child. But "Directive" is a major poem by any standard because it insists on the close relationship between artistic creation and religious faith. Those familiar with the Frost biography know how his commitment to poetry clashed with his commitment to family. Frost was a survivor. He would not be beaten down by anyone's death but his own. When pressure threatened and chaos called, he always had poetry to go on with. Art was his source. To create it was to affirm wholeness.

Affirmation of creativity is the heart of Frost's canon. Even in his darkest verse, those lyrics and dialogue poems that unsettle the reader with glimpses of universal terror and portrayals of domestic fear, the affirmation of technique balances the pessimistic theme. He lodged so many poems in American literature that his best work will be forever necessary to the cultural health of the nation. The phrase "the indispensable Robert Frost" thus cuts two ways: it describes the stature of a major author, and it invites a discussion of those parts of his canon that the reader who would understand his work should know. Frost himself might not have agreed with the choices examined here, but eager to hold the spotlight he would have been pleased that the examination was taking place.

Notes

1. Robert Frost, "Introduction" to Edwin Arlington Robinson, *King Jasper*, in *Selected Prose of Robert Frost*, eds. Hyde Cox and Edward Connery Lathem (New York: Holt, Rinehart and Winston, 1966), p. 63. The original is Edwin Arlington Robinson, *King Jasper* (New York: Macmillan, 1935).

2. The letter is republished in *Selected Letters of Robert Frost*, ed. Lawrance Thompson (New York: Holt, Rinehart and Winston, 1964), pp. 110–114; and in more complete form in Margaret Bartlett Anderson, *Robert Frost and John Bartlett: The Record of a Friendship* (New York: Holt, Rinehart and Winston, 1963), pp. 79–87. (The numbers 1 through 12 in this essay are meant not to rank my choices but to list them.) Unless otherwise noted, Frost's letters will be identified by date and will refer to Thompson's edition.

3. Lawrence Thompson, *Robert Frost: The Early Years, 1874–1915* (New York: Holt, Rinehart and Winston, 1966), p. 417. The other two volumes of the Frost biography are Thompson, *Robert Frost: The Years of Triumph, 1915–1938* (New York: Holt, Rinehart and Winston, 1970); and Thompson and R. H. Winnick, *Robert Frost: The Later Years, 1938–1963* (New York: Holt, Rinehart and Winston, 1976). Further references to these three volumes will be noted by volume and page number. All quotations of Frost's poetry are taken from *The Poetry of Robert Frost*, ed. Edward Connery Lathem (New York: Holt, Rinehart and Winston, 1969).

4. Edward Connery Lathem and Lawrance Thompson note that Bartlett's review was then republished in the school magazine of the New Hampshire State Normal School at Plymouth, *The Prospect*, in November 1913, pp. 24–27. See Thompson, 1, p. 590.

5. The February 1931 version of "Education by Poetry" is included in *Selected Prose of Robert Frost*, pp. 33–46. The essay covers pp. 75–85 in the *Amherst Graduates' Quarterly*.

6. The letter is also reprinted in *Selected Letters of Robert Frost*, pp. 417–419, and in *Selected Prose of Robert Frost*, pp.105–107. Hicks' article is in *New Republic*, 30 December 1930, pp. 77–78.

7. *Selected Letters of Robert Frost*, p. 555.

8. *Robert Frost: A Descriptive Catalogue of Books and Manuscripts in the Clifton Waller Barrett Library, University of Virginia*, compiled by Joan St. C. Crane (Charlottesville, Virginia: University Press of Virginia, 1974), p. 86.

9. Thompson and Winnick, III, p. 140.

10. *Selected Letters of Robert Frost*, pp. 555–556.

11. Thompson, I, p. 280.

12. Ford Madox Heuffer, "Mr. Frost and 'North of Boston,' " *Outlook*, 27 June 1914, pp. 879–880.

13. Thompson, II, pp. 597–598.

14. *Selected Letters of Robert Frost*, p. 130.

15. Jessie B. Rittenhouse, "*North of Boston*: Robert Frost's Poems of New England Farm Life," *New York Times Book Review*, 16 May 1915, p. 189.

16. *Selected Letters of Robert Frost*, pp. 129–130.

17. Accents fall on both "two" and "point. . . ."

18. Thompson, II, p. 540.

19. *Selected Letters of Robert Frost*, pp. 208, 210.

20. See "Tree at My Window" (*West-Running Brook*, 1928).

21. *The Letters of Robert Frost to Louis Untermeyer*, ed. Louis Untermeyer (New York: Holt, Rinehart and Winston, 1963), p. 163.

22. See especially Thompson, I, pp. 596–597; and II, pp. 596–598, 608–609.

23. Thompson, II, pp. 597–598.

24. The sonnet "In White" may be read in Thompson, I, p. 582.

25. *Selected Letters of Robert Frost*, pp. 418–419.

26. Thompson, I, p. 512.

27. Thompson, I, p. 136.

28. Theodore Morrison, "The Agitated Heart," *Atlantic Monthly* (July 1967), 72–79.

29. The biblical allusion is to Mark 4:11–12.

30. Thompson and Winnick, III, p. 406.

INDEX